Literacy in
School and Society

Multidisciplinary Perspectives

TOPICS IN LANGUAGE AND LINGUISTICS

Series Editors
Thomas A. Sebeok and Albert Valdman
Indiana University, Bloomington, Indiana

Literacy in School and Society

Multidisciplinary Perspectives

Edited by
ELISABETTA ZUANELLI SONINO

University of Venice
Venice, Italy

PLENUM PRESS • NEW YORK AND LONDON

LC
3715
L58
1989

Library of Congress Cataloging in Publication Data

Literacy in school and society: multidisciplinary perspectives / edited by Elisabetta
Zuanelli Sonino.
    p.   cm. — (Topics in language and linguistics)
    Bibliography: p.
    Includes index.
    ISBN 0-306-43166-1
    1. Education, Bilingual. 2. Literacy. 3. Language policy. 4. Language and education. 5.
Sociolinguistics. I. Zuanelli Sonino, Elisabetta. II. Series.
LC3715.L58   1989   89-35803
371.97 — dc20   CIP

© 1989 Plenum Press, New York
A Division of Plenum Publishing Corporation
233 Spring Street, New York, N.Y. 10013

Printed in the United States of America

Contributors

Safder Alladina, School of Teaching Studies, The Polytechnic of North London, London NW5 3LB, England

Marcel Danesi, Department of Semiotics, Victoria College, University of Toronto, Toronto M5S 1K7, Ontario, Canada

Márta Dovala, Department of Language and Communication, The Teachers' College, Kaszap utca 6-10, H-6000 Kecskemét, Hungary

Joshua A. Fishman, Ferkauf Graduate School of Psychology, Yeshiva University, Bronx, New York 10461, USA

Gilles Gagné, Faculté des sciences de l'education, Université de Montréal, Montréal H3C 3J7, Québec, Canada

Francisco Gomes de Matos, Universidade Federal de Pernambuco, Recife, Pernambuco, Brazil

Mubanga E. Kashoki, The Copperbelt University (formerly the University of Zambia at Ndola), P.O. Box 21692, Kitwe, Zambia

Sjaak Kroon, Department of Language and Literature, Tilburg University, P.O. Box 90153, 5000 LE Tilburg, The Netherlands

Wallace E. Lambert, Department of Psychology, McGill University, Montreal H3A 1B1, Quebec, Canada

Jeanne Martinet, Ecole Pratique des Hautes Etudes, Section IV, Sorbonne, 75005 Paris, France

Alberto M. Mioni, Department of Linguistics, University of Padua, 35137 Padua, Italy

Luc Ostiguy, Département de français, Université du Québec à Trois-Rivières, Trois-Rivières G9A 5H7, Québec, Canada

Michel Pagé, Department of Psychology, University of Montréal, Montréal H3C 3J7, Québec, Canada

Stephen Parker, School of Education, University of East Anglia, Norwich NR4 7TJ, England

Miguel Siguan, Institut de Ciències de l'Educacion, University of Barcelona, Barcelona 7, Spain

Marc Spoelders, Seminarie en Laboratorium voor Experimentele, Psychologische en Sociale Pedagogiek, Rijksuniversiteit Gent, 9000 Gent, Belgium

Otto Stern, Deutsches Seminar, Abteilung Linguistik, Universität Zürich, Rämistrasse 74, CH-8001 Zürich, Switzerland

Jan Sturm, Dutch Department, Nijmegen University, P.O. Box 9103, 6500 HD Nijmegen, The Netherlands

György Szépe, Research Institute for Linguistics, Hungarian Academy of Sciences, P.O. Box 19, H-1250 Budapest, Hungary

Renzo Titone, Department of Developmental and Social Psychology, University of Rome "La Sapienza," 00185 Rome, Italy

Albert Valdman, CREDLI, Indiana University, Bloomington, Indiana 47405, USA

Lut Van Damme, Seminarie en Laboratorium voor Experimentele, Psychologische en Sociale Pedagogiek, Rijksuniversiteit Gent, 9000 Gent, Belgium

Willie Van Peer, Department of Literary Theory, University of Utrecht, 3512 EV Utrecht, The Netherlands

Elisabetta Zuanelli Sonino, Seminar of Linguistics and Language Teaching, University of Venice, Ca' Garzoni e Moro, San Marco 3417, 30124 Venice, Italy

Preface

The "function" and "notion" of *literacy* may be considered the keystone, a "filigree" principle underlying the educational, social, and cultural organization of the societies of the twentieth century.

It is therefore interesting to try to pinpoint the notion and its implications at the turn of the century by focusing the attention of scholars from various disciplines—sociolinguistics, psychology, psycholinguistics, and pedagogy—on the subject. This is the purpose of this volume, which originated from an interdisciplinary meeting on trends in and problems of research on early literacy through mother tongues and/or second languages, held in Venice under the auspices of the University of Venice, and in particular of the Seminario di Linguistica e di Didattica della Lingue and the Centro Linguistico Interfacoltà, and the Municipality of Venice, together with UNESCO and AILA.

A first far-reaching question touches on the role assigned to or fulfilled by mass "literacy" in modern society. The concept of literacy considered as a social achievement, an essential component in the process of education to be institutionally prompted and controlled, fluctuates between two opposite poles. A polemic-destructive view considers the notion and the educational "practices" connected with it as a potent instrument of social control, a tool for social reproduction and consensus. On the other side, a plurifunctional constructive view considers the acquisition and maintenance of different languages via educational institutions as a concrete possibility for the defense and maintenance of cultural pluralism and identity, be it social, ethnic, or religious.

The relativism of the notion appears paradoxically evident in the confrontation of arguments for debate. In advanced postindustrial societies discussion has raged in recent years over the massifying and passifying action exercised by the media, creating a sort of secondary "literacy" which preludes the possible disappearance of the "written code," the loss of that privileged and highly refined channel and medium of communication that is writing.

The possible risk of a downward slope of the "writing" parabola appears absurd compared with the recent struggles of emergent postcolonial nations, striving for mass literacy through a policy of written standardization of oral languages, to be accomplished by overcoming basic economic conditioning factors such as the lack of books, primers, and teachers.

The list of arguments for research and study within this "broad" perspective is obviously long and discouraging.

To begin with, as we said, the function and scope of literacy in modern societies has to be assessed. The question is "whether" and "how" different languages may be assigned the same or complementary literacy functions in one and all societies. Terminological distinctions implicitly or explicitly reveal the crux of the matter: local, overregional, international languages; major, minor, and minority languages; modern, classical, and "religion" languages; standardized and nonstandardized languages; national, official, and vehicular languages; spoken and written, only spoken and only written languages; autochthonous and immigrant languages; and so on.

Moreover, whether we speak of mono- or of bipluriliteracy, namely, the process of literacy conducted through the learning of one or more than one language, a second and highly debated point concerns the cognitive, cultural, and social relation that takes place between the "mother tongue" of the subject (another crucial notion) and the language/languages used in education. It is not possible to assume the presence of the pupils' mother tongue in education as a commonly accepted and acceptable principle.

In any case, the relation "spoken–written," even in linguistic and functional terms, is not easy to establish. Spoken languages are more or less divergent from the "correspondent" written languages used for education, be they secular or religious. Such a correlation, moreover, varies more or less markedly as a result of the diverse specialization of the written code as well as of the different writing systems, such as ideographic, syllabic, and alphabetic.

Even admitting that the notion of literacy is in itself clear and sufficient, coinciding mainly with learning the reading and writing skills of at least one language, the emergence of cognitive and didactic problems is striking.

What does being able to read and write mean, what is a "literate" person supposed to actually be able to read and write, and what degrees of reading and writing competence are assumed to represent the objective of literacy? If reading means comprehending written texts, it is crucial as well to wonder "if" and "how" the school teaches "reading," with what procedures, objectives, and materials.

Within this perspective, a clarification of linguistic and extralinguistic problems of written comprehension and production is a prerequisite for any possible didactics of reading and writing; questions and answers about factors facilitating the learning of these skills is, therefore, of fundamental relevance for an efficacious educational activity.

These and other matters which cannot be mentioned here for the sake of space are open to discussion and are controversial at the moment.

It is with this awareness that the volume presents different contributions to the debate on literacy, subdividing them roughly into two sections: Sociolinguistic Analyses and Perspectives; and Psycholinguistic, Linguistic, and Educational Issues and Problems.

The first part begins with Kashoki's analysis of the language policy of Zambia, where 7 out of the 25 native languages spoken were recently chosen to become vehicles of education. The main argument is against the indiscriminate adoption of mother tongues in education as a generally agreed upon principle, both for economic reasons and in view of a better fostering in education of the languages chosen; this solution, however, does not satisfy the existing need to protect different ethnic identities represented by other languages.

As against this situation Gomes de Matos stresses the insufficiency of studies concerning bi- and multilingualism of children in Brazil where, besides the national language of Portuguese, 152 native languages as well as the languages of immigrants' groups from European, African, and Asian countries coexist and are in an urgent need of a policy of maintenance and integration.

The quantitative importance and qualitative range of non-English-language ethnic community schools in the USA are pinpointed by Fishman, who stresses this phenomenon as a boundary-maintaining mechanism necessary for distancing from mainstream culture; he also stresses the culturally specific connotation of literacy and its different social and cultural functions.

Linguistic and cultural maintenance and differentiation between language groups as well as the need for social interaction between the groups are at the basis of early immersion second-language programs in Canada. Lambert reminds us, however, of the danger of "subtractive" bilingualism for French-Canadians as well as for minority-language groups. Against the same risk, Danesi values positively the results of heritage language programs in Canada, both on cognitive and social grounds.

The switch to the European situation allows one to deal with partially different and paradigmatic cases.

Kroon and Sturm provide a polemical analysis of the notion of literacy as "oriented to protect vested societal interests," especially in multicultural contexts such as the Dutch one where, however, no minority-language policy exists except for Frisian. This kind of situation is matched by the inadequacy of the language policy in Britain, as regards speakers of languages other than English, in particular, African–French creoles and Asian languages, for which not even basic educational data seem to exist, as pointed out by Alladina.

Problematic results of the institutionalized bilingual Catalan–Castilian programs, depending on socioeconomic and cultural variables not attributable to the educational establishment are analyzed by Siguan. Szépe and Dovala offer a sociolinguistic overview of mother-tongue education both for Hungarian and non-Hungarian speakers, together with an evaluation of educational approaches to early reading in Hungary.

The second part of the volume groups together contributions oriented toward psychopedagogical, linguistic, and methodological matters.

Spoelders and Van Damme describe preliminary research on the correlation between metalinguistic awareness and reading achievement in children. Gagné and Ostiguy present experimental data to confirm metalinguistic awareness of French-Canadian children as regards the use of formal variants, and they propose its classroom exploitation to teach formal registers.

The results of the measurement of comprehension of informative written texts through especially devised tests are analyzed by Pagé, whereas Zuanelli Sonino points out problems of written comprehension and production specifically due to the textual constraints of different types of texts, through the analysis of children's written performances.

Stern presents and discusses the spontaneous acquisition of features of Standard German by Swiss–German dialect-speaking children, a process that is interrupted as they start formal learning of Standard German at school.

Van Peer criticizes the "dysfunctional" and widespread practice of oral reading, while Parker comments on current approaches and materials for teaching reading and writing to children in Great Britain.

The incoherences of the relation between oral and written French as negative factors for the learning of written abilities are discussed by Martinet, as a basis for the experimental "alfonic" method used to teach reading and writing in some French schools. Titone puts forward cognitive and affective arguments to support early biliteracy through appropriate methods and materials; finally Mioni evaluates the possible educational impact of African primers on the basis of linguistic analysis.

The wide array of topics, disciplines, and methodologies that the volume brings together is meaningful in itself: we need to deepen our understanding of problems of theory and practice connected with the notion of literacy both in monolingual and in plurilingual contexts. Theory and practice can be enlighted at the crossroads between different disciplines. Trends and perspectives presented here stand at this crossroads.

Acknowledgments

I wish to thank UNESCO for financial support that helped to make the preparation of a number of the contributions to this volume possible.

I also wish to acknowledge the valuable collaboration of Loretta Incensi in the editing of this volume, and thank Alison Caniato for the English revision of the texts.

Contents

Chapter 3

Non-English-Language Ethnic Community Schools in the USA:
Instruments of More Than Literacy and Less Than Literacy   25

Joshua A. Fishman

Chapter 4

The Development of Bilingual Literacy Skills: Experiences with
Immersion Education   35

Wallace E. Lambert

Chapter 5

Ancestral Language Training and the Development of Bilingual
Literacy: A Canadian Perspective   41

Marcel Danesi

Chapter 6

The Use of Creole as a School Medium and Decreolization in Haiti

Albert Valdman

Chapter 7

Miguel Siguan

Chapter 8

Sjaak Kroon and Jan Sturm

PART II.   Psycholinguistic, Linguistic, and Educational Issues
and Problems

Chapter 11

Psychoeducational Language Awareness Assessment and Early
Reading ·   135
   Marc Spoelders and Lut Van Damme

Chapter 12

Chapter 13

Chapter 14

Chapter 15

Chapter 19

Early Bilingual Reading: Retrospects and Prospects

Renzo Titone

Chapter 20

Problems of Language Growth and the Preparation of Schoolbooks
in Africa

Alberto M. Mioni

PART I

Sociolinguistic Analyses and Perspectives

CHAPTER 1

On the Notion and Implications of the Concept of Mother Tongue in Literacy Education in a Multilingual Context
The Case of Zambia

MUBANGA E. KASHOKI

1. INTRODUCTION

In 1966, in the aftermath of national independence from colonial rule in 1964, the Zambian government enacted, as a temporary phase of a comprehensive Education Act, a policy that prescribed the English inherited from the former British colonial administration as the sole medium of instruction at primary, secondary, and tertiary levels of formal education, thereby breaking away totally from previous practice. Since then the policy has been the subject of sustained informed debate and scholarly research (Africa, 1980; M. M. Chishimba, 1980, 1981, 1984; P. C. Chishimba, 1979; Higgs, 1979, 1980; Kashoki, 1979; McAdam, 1973; Ministry of Higher Education, 1984; Shana, 1980; Sharma, 1973). In the light of this rich proliferation of literature on the implications of imparting early literacy to children by means of a foreign/second language, it is unnecessary to extend the same debate in the present chapter. Instead, it is more profitable to turn our attention to an equally intriguing topic and consider from various vantage points whether the now almost sacrosanct notion of the imperative need to impart literacy skills through the mother tongue does not invite serious second thoughts. In more direct terms, does the concept

MUBANGA E. KASHOKI • The Copperbelt University (formerly the University of Zambia at Ndola), P.O. Box 21692, Kitwe, Zambia.

of the mother tongue as a *sine qua non* in the imparting of literacy skills in both early formal and nonformal (such as adult literacy) education not generate more problems than it solves? Isn't there, therefore, a timely need to reexamine the issue to ascertain its far-reaching implications, especially in the context of multilingual societies?

To answer these and related questions, the present chapter, as its main argument, questions the appropriateness of the continued, firmly established emphasis on the mother tongue as the key to the effective imparting of formalized knowledge in adult literacy programs, using Zambia as a case in point. It also explores the implications of this emphasis from a sociolinguistic, economic, and sociopolitical perspective.

Excluded from what is essentially a preliminary and tentative exploration of a very complex issue is the consideration of whether literacy skills about to be acquired by illiterate adults in a multilingual context are hampered or retarded in a situation where the prevailing official language policy does not enable the target learners to pursue literacy education in their mother tongue or first language. In a sociocultural environment in which systematic studies of the effects of literacy education acquired through non-mother-tongue media of instruction are wholly absent, it is hardly possible to attempt an objective analysis of what the likely consequences are on an individual who has undergone such a type of literacy education. It thus appears more realistic (and certainly more manageable), as reflected in the deliberately limited focus of this chapter, to confine the exercise to an examination of the practical implications of offering literacy education in non-mother-tongue vehicles of instruction. In other words, what is to be dealt with is the question of whether in multilingual contexts the notion of the mother tongue is the one to emphasize when the practical circumstances are such as to virtually preclude the possibility of offering literacy through the medium of the mother tongue.

2. BACKDROP

Adult literacy in Zambia, though with historical origins in the colonial past, was formalized into its present form soon after independence. In August 1965, hardly a year after the attainment of independence (October 1964), the government adopted adult literacy as an essential component of a comprehensive national development policy, placing the Adult Literacy Program administratively in the Department of Community Development. Previously, adult literacy work had been undertaken principally by voluntary agencies, notably by missionaries of different Christian persuasions. Besides missionaries, the mining companies of what is known as the Copperbelt included in their welfare services literacy programs for miners' wives as well as for the illiterate men in the work force.

Two years later, in another cabinet memorandum, the government provided for the use of seven Zambian languages (Bemba, Kaonde, Lozi, Luunda, Luvale, Nyanja, and Tonga) as the only officially recognized media for imparting literacy skills. "By this proviso, no literacy instruction was to be conducted in English nor in any of the Zambian languages not included in the Memorandum" (Ohannessian & Kashoki, 1978, p. 399). For reasons of manageable administration, this arrangement was coupled with the division of the country into language zones, with the stipulation that only the officially prescribed language should be used in the given zone. One consequence of this decision, with immediate relevance to the central argument of this chapter, was to require the local illiterate adult population, whatever their mother tongue, to acquire literacy skills in the language prescribed for the zone in which they were resident.

Only several years afterwards, notably after the introduction during the 1970s of the experimental Functional Literacy Project, was a modest concession made to a limited use of English as a vehicle of literacy instruction. This was after it was recognized that the demand for English was quite high among a fair number of those wishing to learn.

The government's educational reform document of 1977, issued by the Ministry of Education (1977), does not make any mention of the media of instruction officially approved for use in the national adult literacy program. It can only be assumed that the government's decision of 1967 to allow the use of only seven Zambian languages as media of instruction has remained unchanged. This in effect means that the lingua franca (or the language of wider communication), rather than the mother tongue, is the cornerstone of adult literacy education in Zambia.

3. THE LINGUISTIC SETTING

To place what has been stated above in its proper context and perspective, it is first necessary to sketch the language situation observable in Zambia. Zambia, like many other African countries, can be described as a multilingual or plurilingual country in both the number of languages an individual manipulates in his or her daily informal language use and the actual number of languages spoken in the country. As is elaborated more extensively in Chapter 1 of *Language in Zambia* (Ohannessian & Kashoki, 1978), there are approximately 80 "dialects" spoken in the country with varying degrees of lexical correspondence and mutual intelligibility. Using conventional notions, these may be reduced to about 25 "languages." In the context of our discussion, one is here then confronted with either 80 or 25 mother tongues, depending on one's classification of what constitutes a dialect and what constitutes a language.

Another important salient feature of the language situation in Zambia is, as has already been mentioned, the degree of multilingualism, not in the sense of the number of languages found in the country but in that of the number of languages acquired and used by the individual for communication. This phenomenon may best be seen as a survival mechanism devised by the individual as a way of coping with the multiplicity of languages prevailing in his or her social environment.

Detailed sociolinguistic studies concerning the incidence and extent of multilingualism, and in particular how these aspects apply to the individual in Zambia, have yet to be undertaken. Mytton's study (1974), however, provides preliminary tentative evidence that multilingualism in the individual is fairly widespread in Zambia both in rural and urban settings, although, as would be expected, it is more predominant in the latter. On present evidence, taking the country as a whole, the Zambian population speaks an average of 2.2 languages. In the urban sample, Mytton found that urban residents on average claimed competence in 2.8 (or 3) languages. The figure was notably lower for the rural areas where only 1.9 (or approximately 2) languages were claimed by the rural population (cf. also Kashoki, 1982).

One point emerges from this evidence. Monolingual competence is the exception rather than the rule among the Zambian population. To put it differently, Zambian nationals, in their coping strategies in a highly multilingual country, are bi- or multilinguals. This has a direct bearing on our subsequent discussion.

4. IMPLICATIONS OF THE CONCEPT OF MOTHER TONGUE

The implications of the notion of mother tongue as it applies to literacy education in Zambia is discussed under three headings—economic, linguistic–sociolinguistic, and political. The primary aim is to show that while the notion is a most laudable one, being the most democratic if it were practicable, it presents serious practical problems in its application.

4.1. Economic Issues

Two primary factors have to be borne in mind when considering provision of adult literacy education to a country's adult illiterate population. These are the availability of literacy instructors in sufficient numbers and the availability of adequate reading matter. But sufficient numbers of instructors and adequate reading matter cannot be ensured in a literacy program without adequate financial resources. It is in this context that the cost factor becomes most critical and relevant. The cost factor is the common denominator of all educational enterprises that involve the production of teaching materials and the engagement of teaching personnel. This factor is especially aggravated in countries where there is an overall acute shortage of financial resources. It is common knowledge that countries grouped under the label of "Third World" are at present experiencing a prolonged phase of serious financial crisis and that prospects of an early economic recovery are at best doubtful. Even were such recovery possible in the immediate foreseeable future, it is a moot point whether sufficient funds would be on hand to sustain the national economy in all its myriad facets. To complicate the problem, a plethora of development priorities, all making their own claims on the available limited resources, will now and in the future persist in crying out for immediate attention.

It is in the face of these economic realities that one has to pose the question of whether, from a pragmatic perspective, the educational philosophy of setting up the mother tongue as the most appropriate vehicle of instruction in literacy education accords with the imperatives of the real world. Experience has shown that even when only a restricted number of languages are prescribed for use in education, whether formal or nonformal, the expenditure on materials and personnel is considerable. In Zambia, for example, evidence shows that a disproportionate amount of the educational costs (as much as 92% at the primary school level in 1985) is in the form of salaries for teaching and supporting staff. At a more general level, in Zambia the use of seven languages in broadcasting, formal education, and adult literacy represents a significant drain on the national economy. There can be no doubt that if the notion of the mother tongue as fundamental to the imparting of literacy education were strictly adhered to, a considerable proportion of the national resources would have to be diverted to the literacy program from other equally, if not more, important priorities.

One special point needs particular emphasis. In Zambia, as in many African countries, literacy programs are mainly the responsibility of the central government and not that of local communities. This fact puts an undue pressure on the central government to provide almost all the resources necessary to make the literacy program viable. The concept of the mother tongue in this regard is tenable only if the responsibility for mounting literacy programs can be transferred from the central government to local communities. It is the latter that are in a more advantageous position to press the mother tongue in the service of literacy education. But, even less than the central government, the local communities are hardly in a position to provide the resources needed to sustain a viable literacy program.

One recent notable change in policy has made the implementation of the literacy program in Zambia relatively more costly to administer. Prior to 1970, in accordance with the Laubach formula of "each one teach one," a cornerstone of the Zambia Adult Literacy Program was the policy which stipulated that all literacy teaching was to be largely voluntary. This policy was a part of the overall scheme of the Department of Community Development (under whose direct jurisdiction the program fell). This provision reflected and emphasized the basic orientations of the government that individual voluntary participation in the Adult Literacy Program should characterize the contribution of the literate citizen. This, in more direct terms, meant that the literate person who volunteered as an instructor was to receive no remuneration except in instances where the local communities had the means to do so. It was only then that the government would match the payment on a 50-50 basis. This policy was fundamentally changed during the 1970s after it became clear that insufficient numbers of literate citizens were prepared to offer their service free of charge or at the pleasure of the local community. The new policy required the literacy instructor to be paid two Kwacha (K2) per month, which worked out to approximately one fifth of a Kwacha for every class actually taught.

Subsequently, the policy was further modified by a provision that in those literacy classes falling directly under government auspices, only full-time literacy staff would be allowed to teach.

In general terms, paid participation reduces the capacity of the local communities to involve considerable numbers of literate persons in literacy programs. It thus becomes a limiting factor vis-à-vis the expected viability of these programs. Where only a few selected languages are involved, the financial investment to be made is not so great; where, however, mother tongues in their tens are involved, the economic factor becomes more salient and critical.

4.2. Linguistic–Sociolinguistic Issues

The prevalence of the command and use of several languages by an individual in Zambia has already been briefly described. It is the purpose of this section to relate this prevalence to the concept of mother tongue as a basic, guiding principle in literacy education.

The primary importance attached to the notion of mother tongue as fundamental to the imparting of literacy skills is underlain by the assumption that the target learners have a command of only one language, that is, their own mother tongue. The notion, therefore, obscures or ignores the reality that these target learners may in fact be bringing to the literacy class competence in two or more languages. Since this is the predominant reality in most, if not all, multilingual countries, especially where adult learners are concerned, it stands to good reason that attention should be focused elsewhere than the mother tongue when considering what the medium of instruction ought to be.

Even though the correlation between age and multilingualism in the context of Zambia has remained somewhat indeterminate (Kashoki, 1978, p. 43), to some extent it can be asserted that an increasing number of persons above the age of 15 are more likely than those below this age to possess competence in several linguistic codes. In Mytton (1974), as already cited, and as reanalyzed in *Language in Zambia* (Ohannessian & Kashoki, 1978, pp. 43–44), it was shown that persons in the age groups 15–24 and 35–44 claimed to speak an average of 2.2 languages. This increased significantly to an average of 2.3 languages for the age group 25–34. From this evidence, target adult learners, if Zambia is taken to be the reference point, cannot be assumed to be monolinguals.

Besides what has just been said, there is another point, more specifically linguistic, to be considered. A broad survey of the Zambian linguistic scene, as described in considerable detail by Kashoki and Mann (1978a, pp. 47–100), shows that languages indigenous to Zambia exhibit close linguistic affinities, albeit to varying degrees. This affinity is evident not just at one linguistic level but at all levels—phonological, morphological, syntactic, and lexical. For example, at the phonological level, we find that all Zambian languages, which all belong to the Bantu group of languages, have five contrastive vowels, symbolized orthographically as *i e a o u*. While there are variations in the taxonomy of contrastive consonants from language to language, what is more striking is the number of consonants that are common to all the languages. Consequently, even at consonant level, what is characteristic is the close correspondence among all the Zambian languages.

At the suprasegmental level, tone is a characteristic feature of Bantu languages. In the Bantu languages of Zambia, there is only one tonal contrast of high and low, and this is common to all of them. The contrast between short and long vowels is another typical phonological feature of Bantu languages. Among Zambian languages, present evidence shows that only one language, Luvale, does not present a contrast of short and long vowels.

Linguistic affinity among Zambian languages is particularly notable at syllable (or consonant-plus-vowel cluster) level. Thus, syllables in Zambian languages are typically of the following types (where *V* stands for vowel and *C* for consonant): *V; CV; CCV; CCCV*. It is clear from these patterns that syllables in Zambian languages characteristically end with a vowel.

Special account has to be taken of the affinity existing among Zambian languages at the syllable level because, in designing primers and other reading materials in the Zambian Adult Literacy Program, the basic linguistic reference point is the syllable rather than the single (distinctive) sound (or letter). This, coupled with the fact that vowels, consonants, tone, and vowel length are common to Zambian languages, makes it persuasive to argue that learning the skills of reading and writing in a language which is not one's mother tongue makes reasonable sense in circumstances where languages are closely related at practically all levels. In such circumstances the transference of these skills from the nonmother tongue to the mother tongue does not present insurmountable problems, as would be the case if the languages involved were vastly different in linguistic structure.

4.3. Political Issues

The mother tongue as a basic concept in education clearly has political connotations but, for the purpose of the present chapter, only a few of these considerations receive brief attention. In its perhaps more controversial aspect, the concept relates to the fact that insistence on the mother tongue as a fundamental principle in education confers on potential learners an inalienable birthright. Because it is a birthright, the mother tongue is likely to be perceived by those citizens whose mother tongues do not enjoy the privilege of being accorded official recognition in educational programs as a right that must be guaranteed by their governments through its incorporation in the language policies. Failure under these conditions by government to provide such a guarantee is bound to be seen as a denial of a fundamental human right. The persistent pressures on governments, so prevalent in multilingual countries to increase the number of languages prescribed for use in education may be ascribed, at least in part, to these perceptions. One political effect of this is to cause those citizens whose mother tongues have not been accommodated in the prevailing educational policies to question the responsiveness of their governments to legitimate demands. A related effect is the questioning of the whole concept of the mother tongue if it cannot be implemented in a practical way.

There is a cognate point to consider in this respect. Quite frequently what is generally observable in Zambia, and no doubt in other multilingual countries where similar conditions prevail, is that the individual or group of individuals insisting on the inclusion of their mother tongue in the literacy program may be doing so not because they have no knowledge of the language already prescribed for literacy or formal education but because the primary factor at play here is ethnic identity. As Mytton (1978) has observed in respect to the mass media, with particular reference to radio broadcasting when a Cokwe, Mambwe, Tumbuka, or Nkoya listener, for example, makes the legitimate and democratic demand that his or her language should be included among those prescribed for broadcasting on Radio Zambia, the motivation for this may have less to do with the fact that the listener does not possess an adequate knowledge of the languages officially in use on the radio than with the fact that he or she really wants to put forward the more important underlying message of not wishing to see his or her ethnic group subordinated to any other. As Mytton (1978, p. 216) has put it, "One is forced to the conclusion that the majority of these complaints [i.e., regarding certain languages being left out] are not over comprehension but identity." We are here, then, no longer dealing strictly with a concern with language but with factors more immediately related to how people feel about the future of their ethnic group vis-à-vis the groups whose languages already seem to have been accorded official preference.

Therefore, we have to ask the following politically significant question:

when calls for the use of mother tongues in education have to do less strictly with language competence than with asserting ethnic particularity, are there sufficient grounds even for a democratic government to lend a responsive ear to these demands? While they spring from a sound educational principle, they are nonetheless prompted by motivations that bear only a remote resemblance to this principle. May it not be argued, instead, that the principle of the mother tongue in education, as in broadcasting and other official domains, may be adhered to preferably, if not only, in social situations where sociolinguistic evidence shows that nonuse of the mother tongue would indeed greatly disadvantage those citizens compelled by official policy to acquire education in languages in which they are not communicatively competent. May it not also be validly argued that it is not politically prudent to encourage a social perception, which, however pervasive, in essence rests on the underlying assumption that what is important and what is to be emphasized is not so much what languages the citizens actually know and use but the close identity they feel with their ethnic group and the need to preserve this identity. In other words, what is at the core of the problem here is the political stand that a democratic government should take, whether it is that of emphasizing actual language competence and use among the citizens or that of emphasizing ethnic identity as a basis for sound educational policy.

In Zambia there is a corollary to what has just been stated. The widespread primordial association with one's ethnic group rather than with the language or languages one actually speaks intrudes negatively into the educational programs that are devised and implemented in the country. This may be best illustrated by making parallel reference to broadcasting. In broadcasting, it is evident from what seems to be entrenched practice, particularly since the attainment of national independence, that in addition to possessing a native knowledge of the language to be broadcast, a primary qualification for being a good broadcaster is to have an acceptable ethnic name. Thus we find that generally it is the Mubangas, Chandas, Chileshes, and Mwilas (names associated with Bemba ethnicity) that are recruited as competent broadcasters for the Bemba language and the Sililos, Lubasis, Muyanganas, and Mukelebais (typical Lozi names) for the Lozi language. The underlying belief here, as has already been observed, is that it is inconceivable to expect anyone to be a competent broadcaster unless that person combines two essential qualities: (1) a native knowledge of the language to be broadcast, and (2) an authentic name associated with the language permitted officially for use on the radio.

This practice is extended to the classroom, for we find there too that the dominant philosophy in Zambian society is that one is not considered a good teacher of a Zambian language unless one satisfies the dual criteria of being a native speaker of the Zambian language officially prescribed for use in education and of having a name that has a correct ethnic ring to it. The net effect of this predilection robs the nation of a vast reservoir of potentially effective teachers of Zambian languages. Such potential teachers may know and manipulate them competently as second languages or even as first languages, but they may suffer from what the nation appears to see as the inappropriateness and, it may be supposed, disadvantage of carrying the wrong ethnic name. In the second place, this practice perpetuates unnecessarily the erroneous notion that Zambian (and, in more general terms, African) mother tongues can only be taught by mother-tongue speakers. What this practice ignores is that, even at the university level in the education system of Zambia, it is not always the native speaker of French who is assigned to teach French. Nor is it the native speaker of English who is recruited to teach English. Quite the contrary, in the majority of cases it is the person who has acquired and uses it as a second, third, or even fourth language that teaches French or English in Zambia's secondary schools and at the university level. At the primary school level the outstanding feature is that the presence of the native speaker of English in the classroom would be a strange phenomenon indeed. For, at this level, the person who is put in charge of the English class is without exception the Zambian who speaks English as a second language, quite often with a questionable degree of communicative competence. Thus, where perfection or near perfection is required in the teaching of Zambian languages, it appears to be considered unnecessary to insist on the same perfection in the case of English or French. Only adequate knowledge of and acceptable communicative competence in these languages are assumed as necessary. One important consequence of this is that, speaking in relative terms, there is no shortage of trained teachers of European languages, which is not the case when Zambian languages are the focus of concern.

There is a final point worth brief attention. In a world of ever-growing international interdependence, particularly as regards those Third World countries, such as Zambia, which rely for the most part on the contribution of nonnationals (more popularly known as expatriates) to national socioeconomic development, the presence in significant numbers of migrant foreign workers has to be taken into account in educational programs that place a special premium on the concept of mother-tongue education. In Zambia, the 1969 population census clearly indicated the presence in the country of, besides native British speakers of English, sizeable numbers of Europeans and Asians, not to speak of non-Zambian Africans. In this situation it is not misplaced to ask what form and direction the national language policy should take if the mother tongue as a guiding educational principle is to be upheld as universally applicable. For there cannot be any question that, in the context of the now universally accepted sacredness of the place of the mother tongue in education, the expatriate worker too, however transient, has a right to claim his or her own mother tongue as an indispensable foundation for sound education.

Concessions to the foreign worker or foreign diplomat as also having an equal right to claiming his or her own mother tongue as the only basis for a sound education cannot but serve to put an additional burden on the government's responsiveness to demands emanating from the entire population resident in the country. Where it is already difficult enough for the national government to satisfy all the competing claims being made by the nationals only, the situation becomes even more strained when the insistent voices of temporary residents are added to the list.

It is in the light and context of these considerations that the mother tongue in its political dimension becomes a critically salient variable to bear in mind. Reduced to its most basic implications, what is at issue is the ability of a national government, faced with the reality of severely limited resources and options, to respond in appropriate and adequate measure to the seemingly infinite array of challenges that the concept of mother tongue, in its crudest form, seems to pose.

5. CONCLUSION

The preceding discussion has sought to lead to a number of related conclusions. Firstly, the concept of mother tongue as a principle underlying sound educational programs is doubtless a noble ideal, but it presents problems of implementation at the practical level. We have seen that in multilingual countries, such as Zambia, the attempt to accommodate all the mother tongues found in the country would entail considerable cost. Additional burdens on the country's capacity to provide nonfinancial resources would also arise.

Secondly, on linguistic and sociolinguistic grounds, there is a case for supporting in Zambia the present language policies in education, with particular emphasis on literacy programs, whereby only a few selected languages are prescribed as media of instruction. Both because of the close linguistic affinity that exists among Zambian languages and because of widespread multilingualism in the individual, the lingua franca rather than the mother tongue appears a more plausible ideal to uphold in language policies pertaining to education.

Thirdly, the lingua franca rather than the mother tongue is politically a more feasible proposition to translate into practical effect. Where emphasis on the lingua franca gives greater scope to governments to mount educational programs more effectively and at less cost, emphasis on the mother tongue acts to multiply and aggravate problems of implementation.

REFERENCES

Africa, H. P. (1980). *Language in education in a multilingual state: A case study of the role of English in the educational system of Zambia.* Unpublished doctoral dissertation, University of Toronto.

Chishimba, M. M. (1980). Observations on the English medium component of the Zambia primary course. *Zambia Educational Review, 2,* 32–48.

Chishimba, M. M. (1981). Language teaching and literacy: East Africa. *Annual Review of Applied Linguistics, 2,* 67–89.

Chishimba, M. M. (1984). Language policy and education in Zambia. *International Education Journal, 1,* 151–180.

Chishimba, P. C. (1979). *A study of the Zambia primary English course.* Unpublished doctoral dissertation, Teachers' College, Columbia University.

Higgs, P. L. (1979). *Culture and value change in Zambian school literature.* Unpublished doctoral dissertation, University of California, Los Angeles.

Higgs, P. L. (1980). The introduction of English as the medium of instruction in Zambian schools. *Zambia Educational Review, 2,* 21–31.

Kashoki, M. E. (1978a). The language situation in Zambia. In S. Ohannessian & M. E. Kashoki (Eds.). *Language in Zambia* (pp. 9–46). London: International African Institute.

Kashoki, M. E. (1978b). The Zambia Adult Literacy Programme. In S. Ohannessian & M. E. Kashoki (Eds.), *Language in Zambia.* London: International African Institute.

Kashoki, M. E. (1979). English in primary school: By what logic? *The English Teachers Journal, 3,* 4–10.

Kashoki, M. E. (1982). Rural and urban multilingualism in Zambia: Some trends. *International Journal of the Sociology of Language, 34,* 137–166.

Kashoki, M. E. (1983, April). *Production of teaching materials in the seven officially approved Zambian languages in the Zambian curriculum: A brief survey of prospects and problems.* Paper presented at the UNESCO Symposium on "Evolution of content and methods of language teaching in developing countries and the production of materials suited to national needs and bilingual or plurilingual education." Paris, France.

Kashoki, M. E., & Mann, M. (1978). A general sketch of the Bantu languages of Zambia. In S. Ohannessian & M. E. Kashoki (Eds.), *Language in Zambia.* London: International African Institute.

McAdam, B. (1973). *The effectiveness of the new English medium primary school curriculum in Zambia.* Unpublished doctoral dissertation, University of Manchester.

Ministry of Education (Republic of Zambia). (1977). *Educational reform: Proposals and recommendations.* Lusaka: Government Printer.

Ministry of Higher Education (Republic of Zambia). (1984). *First steps in reading: In English or in a Zambian language?* Paper commissioned by the English Curriculum Committee. Lusaka: Curriculum Development Centre.

Mytton, G. (1974). *Listening, looking and learning.* Lusaka: Institute for African Studies, University of Zambia.

Mytton, G. (1978). Language and the media in Zambia. In S. Ohannessian & M. E. Kashoki (Eds.), *Language in Zambia.* London: International African Institute.

Ohannessian, S., & Kashoki, M. E. (Eds.). (1978). *Language in Zambia.* London: International African Institute.

Serpell, R. (1978). Learning to say it better: A challenge for Zambian education. In *Language and Education in Zambia, Communication No. 14,* Institute for African Studies, University of Zambia.

Shana, S. C. B. (1980). Which language?: A brief history of the medium of instruction in Northern Rhodesia. *Zambia Educational Review, 2,* 4–20.

Sharma, R. (1973). *The reading skills of Grade III children.* Unpublished mimeograph, Ministry of Education, Lusaka.

CHAPTER 2

Issues and Trends in Early Bilingual Literacy in Brazil

FRANCISCO GOMES DE MATOS

1. INTRODUCTION

A brief description will be made of literacy materials and programs from 1945 to the present, so as to provide a historical perspective for some of the critical issues and dominant trends in early bilingual and multilingual literacy in Brazil. The history of early literacy in Brazil has been closely linked to that of the design and publication of primers. Some of the very first readers, or primers, were of Portuguese origin, dating from 1820, but Brazilian teachers often created their own materials. From 1945 to the present, hundreds of primers have been used in Brazilian elementary schools. In São Paulo State alone over 30 different primers were used in the mid-1940s.

The appearance of separately printed teachers' books or manuals dates back to the early 1940s. Reading materials followed a variety of approaches: the synthetic, analytical-synthetic, synthetic-analytical, global, storyline, word + sentence, to name some of the most popular pedagogical treatments then prevailing. Some primers reached as many as 300 editions, and they were at first produced mostly in southern Brazil, especially in Rio de Janeiro and São Paulo. Today regional readers and literacy materials can be found, particularly for rural areas. Some of the significant trends have been:

- A transition from single to multiple authorship.
- Greater concern with integrating language, mathematics, biology, and social studies (see *Projeto ALFA*, 1980).

FRANCISCO GOMES DE MATOS • Universidade Federal de Pernambuco, Recife, Pernambuco, Brazil.

Among the problems in early literacy materials design the following stand out:

- Inappropriate sequencing.
- Insufficient background information for teachers.
- Ideological values unrelated to users' rights, needs, and interests.
- Unsystematic treatment of the differences between spoken and written Brazilian Portuguese.
- Exercises and activities that pose very little cognitive challenge to learners.
- Little recognition and use of children's literature.

Elementary school education is still seen as the greatest challenge to the Brazilian Ministry of Education because of the increasing failure and dropout rates. The preschool is now being seen as a tool for partly correcting or remedying the poor learning conditions which still prevail in the elementary school curriculum, particularly in public or government-run schools. From 2 to 7 years of age, Brazilian children are not required to go to school; only from ages 7 to 14 are they required to do so.[1]

2. BILINGUALISM IN BRAZIL: EUROPEAN MINORITIES AND FOREIGN LANGUAGE TEACHING TO CHILDREN

Religious groups have usually expressed an interest in the preservation of the mother tongues used by minorities. According to the Brazilian sociolinguist Vandresen (1983), both Catholic and Protestant groups have favored the maintenance and use of German, Italian, and Polish. The truth of the matter is, however, that very little research has been done in bilingualism in Brazil, and data on child bilingualism is even more scant. Sociolinguistic data collection and analysis is mostly the domain of universities, with a notable exception, the Hans Staden Institute, which is interested in German–Portuguese bilingual studies.

The teaching of Portuguese as a second language in Brazil was, at first, restricted to the pioneering efforts of the Catholic universities of Rio Grande do Sul and Rio de Janeiro, of specialized private language schools, and the American diplomatic and consular posts. Some progress has been made in the teaching of Brazilian Portuguese to adults (see Biazioli & Gomes de Matos,

---

[1] For an introduction to problems in preschool education in Brazil, see the series by P. N. P. de Souza, *A pré-Escola Brasileira, 1984–1989*. São Paulo: Pioneira. For an update and ongoing developments, subscribing to *Boletim Informativo, Educação Pré-Escolar* (Brasilia, Ministério da Educação, Secretaria de Ensino Básico) is especially recommended. The April 1988 issue of that newsletter lists sixteen master's theses and one Ph.D. dissertation on aspects of preschool education in Brazil.

1978), but no commercially published materials are available for children of European origin to learn Portuguese.

In Brazil there is no such thing as a foreign language requirement at the elementary school level. Only in very few specialized language-teaching schools does the learning of English by Brazilian children seem to thrive.

A typical example is that of the Pink and Blue School Network, with branches in most Brazilian state capitals. Its methodology is a composite set of features borrowed or adapted from methodological approaches current in the United States and Great Britain. Very little creative work is being carried out in such schools, as far as a distinctive Brazilian contribution to universal methodology is concerned. A noteworthy exception, however, is that of the Yázigi Institute of Languages (with headquarters in São Paulo City), which designed, produced, field-tested, and made available (for its franchised schools) a six-part *Junior English Program,* an ambitiously conceived, innovative ecological approach to the learning of English by Brazilian preadolescents. Gomes de Matos and Wigdorsky's appraisal, though made in Gomes de Matos and Wigdorsky (1968), still seems to hold: it is hard to assess the seriousness and efficiency of foreign language instruction at the elementary school level in Latin America. However, another statement by those linguists would have to be brought up-to-date and adjusted to contemporary reality: 20 years ago we stated that Latin American elementary school education had more vital problems to solve than that of bilingual education; now we would say that bilingualism is becoming another issue of major concern among Latin American educators, especially the sociolinguistically oriented ones.

3. PIONEERING MEETINGS OF BRAZILIAN LINGUISTS: FOCUS ON BI- AND MULTILINGUALISM

The first meeting of Brazilian linguists to discuss the problem of bi- and multilingualism in Brazil took place in 1976 in an event sponsored by ABRALIN, the Brazilian Linguistics Association. Despite the plea then made that Brazilian linguists should enhance the fact that Brazil is a multicultural and multilingual country, only some advances have been made, particularly within the context of southern universities. The first meeting on bilingualism in southern Brazil took place in Florianópolis, capital of Santa Catarina State, in August 1982, 6 years after the pioneering initiative organized by ABRALIN. At the Florianópolis meeting, 11 papers were given focusing on German, Italian, Slavic languages, and Portuguese. Linguists represented three southern universities: Universidade Federal do Paraná, Universidade Federal de Santa Catarina, and Universidade Federal do Rio Grande do Sul.

A survey is under way in Santa Catarina State to find out what second languages are being learned in official state and municipal schools by children of European or Asian origins. It should be clarified that the legislation enforcing the compulsory use of Portuguese as the language of instruction in Brazil has brought about the adoption of Brazil's national language as the system of communication among children and teenagers in even the smaller cities, such as Blumenau, in Santa Catarina State.

Among the pioneering research efforts on child bilingualism, mention should be made of a study on error analysis done in 1965 by Marchant, from the Catholic University of Rio Grande do Sul. The author made a contrastive analysis of compositions written by fourth-grade children, with a focus on typical spelling, morphological, and syntactical problems faced by bilingual children of German origin living in two communities: (1) a predominantly German-speaking area, and (2) a predominantly Portuguese-speaking area. Ten years later, Bisol (1975) studied aspects of second-language interference on the acquisition of writing skills. The author aimed at providing background data for literacy materials designers, literacy planners, and instructors. Bisol dealt with two sociocultural contexts, one predominantly Italian and the other German. Although Italian immigration in Rio Grande do Sul celebrated its one-hundredth anniversary in 1975, there are very few studies on bilingualism centered on Italian–Portuguese (Levi Mattoso, 1982; Vandresen, 1983).

4. THE DISAPPEARANCE OF MINORITY (EUROPEAN) LANGUAGES IN BRAZIL: AN IMMINENT THREAT

Predictions have been made by Brazilian sociolinguists that unless serious steps are taken to prevent the disappearance of minority languages, in 50 years or so they will no longer be spoken, particularly in smaller cities, such as Crisciuma in Santa Catarina State. Levi Mattoso, a sociolinguist from Rio Grande do Sul, emphasizes the importance of making children from minority groups in Brazil literate in their mother tongue first. She questions the methodology sometimes used for providing literacy for bilinguals and cogently states that what is needed is a carefully planned bilingual education policy for Brazil, based on well-researched educational, linguistic, anthropological, sociological, psychological, and economic issues (Levi Mattoso, 1982).

5. WHAT NEEDS TO BE INVESTIGATED IN BRAZIL?

In the 1982 meeting, questions were raised which require systematic investigation. The following are some of them: Why do many bilingual children who can speak some Portuguese deny being speakers of other languages? (What role does language loyalty seem to play there?) Why don't such children display pride in their ethnic, historical, cultural, and linguistic origins? How should teachers of bilingual children (and the community at large) be sensitized toward respecting them as bicultural citizens? How can mutual respect be fostered or enhanced in schools where monolingual and bilingual children sometimes have to experience the same curricular activities?

The second meeting on Bilingualism and Linguistic Variation in southern Brazil was held at the Federal University of Santa Catarina in 1983. Its goals were to discuss methodological approaches to bilingualism in Brazil, to establish guidelines for an integrated project in bilingualism and language variation, and to train and prepare graduates and students in southern universities to do research in bilingualism and multilingualism.

Among the topics Brazilian linguists have started committing themselves to in the domain of bilingualism is the identification and description of bilingual communities in southern Brazil and, in particular, the study of the sociocultural factors which have enhanced, interfered with, or prevented language contact in the south. Research on bilingualism in Brazil was, until recently, carried out by individual scholars and small groups working independently. Financial support is being given now, either by Brazilian federal agencies (CNPq, CAPES, for example) or by institutions from abroad. An example of the latter is the agreement between the Universities of Santa Catarina and Caxias do Sul and the University of Venice (Italy). The integrated project now under way in southern Brazil also emphasizes the need for interdisciplinary action: areas other then linguistics should also contribute, for example, sociology, psychology, human geography, architecture, economics, methodology of language teaching, and education. In southern Brazil there are minorities speaking eight languages: German, Arabic, Japanese, Polish, Russian, Ukrainian, Dutch, and Italian. Given such a variety of languages, descriptive and comparative studies are still badly needed. The area of Italian settlement ("região de colonização italiana," as it is referred to in Brazilian Portuguese) is of special significance because of the existence therein of bilingualism and multilingualism: many Italo-Brazilians use a specific Italian dialect, a koine, and Portuguese. In Vista Alegre (city of Veranopolis), children of Polish extraction speak Italian and Portuguese, but as a rule, in larger rural communities, children *understand* rather than speak Italian. In rural communities, adults address their children in Portuguese.

6. BILINGUALISM IN BRAZILIAN INDIGENOUS COMMUNITIES

Indigenous bilingual literacy in Brazil was officially introduced through the "Estatuto do Indio," under Law No. 6001, December 19, 1973. According to that legislation, "the literacy of indigenous groups will be carried out in the language of the group to which they belong, as well as in Portuguese, while assuring the maintenance of the mother tongue.'' The goal of indigenous bilingual education is to help the Brazilian Indians to make a gradual transition from their mother tongue to Portuguese. Some of the psychosocial goals inherent in such a policy are self-actualization, self-valuing, and emancipation of the Indians so as to integrate them in the Brazilian educational system. Indigenous bilingualism is another neglected research domain in Brazil. The Brazilian linguist–anthropologist Yonne Leite, from the National Museum in Rio de Janeiro sums up in a personal communication (March 1983) the present situation concerning governmental attention to and scientific academic research on bilingualism among Brazilian Indians. She states that

> there is very little published work on that complex problem; in fact, we lack a systematic survey. It is likely that there are other plurilingual areas besides the Uaupés and Xingu. At the Tapirapé village, where I have been recently, there are some Indians who speak Tapirapé, Karajá, and Portuguese, as a result of Tapirapé men marrying Karajá women.

Leite explains that sometimes men live in the Karajá village and women live in the Tapirapé village, and, as a result, the children of such bilingual marriages understand and sometimes speak Karajá. As a rule, children speak the language of the village in which they live. Generally, men and teenagers speak Portuguese better then women, whereas children speak very little Portuguese, although, as their contacts increase, their comprehension ability may improve.

7. THE BRAZILIAN GOVERNMENT'S PLANS FOR IMPROVING UPON EDUCATION OF INDIGENOUS GROUPS

In 1983 a cooperation agreement was signed between the Brazilian Ministries of Education and of the Interior aimed at rendering educational assistance to Brazilian indigenous communities. It is expected to generate badly needed action both in educational policy and sociolinguistic research, such as the following:

1. Preparation of teaching–learning materials in the indigenous languages.
2. Anthropological orientation for instructors of indigenous groups.
3. Adaptation of curricula to ethnocultural realities of indigenous communities.
4. Expansion of the curriculum in indigenous schools up to the eighth grade (hitherto restricted to the fourth grade).
5. Revising and improving currently used textbooks in Brazilian elemen-

tary schools in relation to the way Brazilian Indians have been presented (How distorted a view is being given? Why?).[2]

6. The offering of job-oriented courses for Indians.

7. The establishment of committees made up of representatives of the Ministry of Education, Ministry of the Interior (FUNAI: National Foundation for the Indian), and State Departments of Education for the purpose of drafting guidelines for the official accreditation of indigenous schools.

As regards the design and publication of materials for bilingual literacy, especially primers and readers, this activity has been supervised to some extent by federal government agencies, but the actual production has been entrusted to an American institution, the Summer Institute of Linguistics, which has its Brazilian headquarters in Brasília. Some of those materials have also been produced with the technical assistance of the National Museum in Rio de Janeiro.

Mention should be made of the "Programa de Educação Bilingüe" for the training of Karajá language instructors, under the sponsorship of MINTER (Ministry of the Interior) and FUNAI (National Foundation for Indian Affairs). The reader on social studies, published in 1982, is the first of its kind (Karajá–Portuguese). It centers on cultural values of the Karajá community, a small group living near Bananal Island in northern Goiás State. Some of the lessons deal with children's topics, for instance, how children study, the family, and Karajá games and dances.

8. WRITTEN PORTUGUESE AND BILINGUAL EDUCATION

The fact that the written form of Portuguese is different from all spoken varieties, functioning as an ideal abstraction (Kindell, 1984, p. 12), seems to aggravate or complicate the acquisition of literacy in Portuguese by speakers of indigenous languages. Among Brazilian indigenous groups, the Karajá face a rather unique problem: in their language, 30% of the words in women's speech are different or slightly modified in relation to men's speech. Kindell draws attention to the fact that "materials used in the Brazilian government bilingual education programme have texts in both styles—men's and women's—on each page, with small, stylized male and female drawings indicating the intended reader."

---

[2] It is significant to note that an interdisciplinary group from the Núcleo de Estudos Indigenistas, Department of Letters, Federal University of Pernambuco, is undertaking a study called "The Brazilian Indian in Textbooks: From Myth to Reality," under the auspices of the Brazilian National Research Council (CNPq).

9. EVALUATION OF MULTILINGUAL MATERIALS: A PLEA FOR AN INTERDISCIPLINARY PERSPECTIVE

The literature on multicultural and multilingual approaches to the education of young children shows that guidelines for evaluating books and other materials are usually centered on one, two, or, at most, three disciplines rather than on half a dozen or more. A typical example of monodisciplinary evaluation is found in Kendall (1983). Her checklist for evaluating "language arts materials" consists of nine items, centered on these key concepts: life-styles, value systems, stereotyping gregariousness (cooperation), adult–child interaction, social roles (played by minorities), lexical realism or authenticity (genuine or fabricated?), ethnocentrism (are Indians presented as savage?), and mutual respect (Kendall, 1983, pp. 59–60). What is needed is an interdisciplinary framework, on the basis of which multicultural and multilingual materials, programs, and curricula can be evaluated. For such a checklist, see Gomes de Matos (1983), and Gomes de Matos and Carvalho (1984).

10. CONCLUDING REMARKS: THE BRAZILIAN SITUATION

1. There are very few studies on the spontaneous acquisition of Portuguese by children of European/Asian/African immigrants or of Brazilian indigenous communities. The acquisition of biligualism in children is still a very unexplored area in Brazilian applied sociolinguistics.
2. There are a few initial projects on the tutored language acquisition of immigrants and their children in Brazil.
3. Most of the research in spontaneous second-language acquisition in Brazil has dealt with the use of Portuguese by immigrants (especially from Europe).
4. Investigations have focused predominantly on the lexicon and on phonology. There is, however, growing attention to syntax and to sociolinguistic variation.
5. Systematic investigation of second-language acquisition of immigrants has only recently become an official line of research in southern Brazilian universities offering M.A. degrees in linguistics. We have very few longitudinal studies of children raised in bilingual environments where no effort has been made to separate the two languages.
6. A major concern of Brazilian sociolinguists and indigenous literacy educators is that of attempting to answer this question: How can we contribute to a relatively well-documented understanding of the kinds of interactions between the Brazilian-Portuguese speaking and the indige-

nous and immigrant communities, that is, between the majority and the minority groups speaking different languages in Brazil?

What seems to be needed in Brazil is a comprehensive, enlightened language policy centered on the use of Portuguese as the official language and the uses of the languages of minority groups as their mother tongues. If development is the set of multidimensional changes (social, economic, political, educational, institutional) that can contribute to the improvement of human condition and organization in specific communities, then, similarly, plurilingual education should be conceived and implemented as an action aimed at the language user's individual linguistic development. In Brazil, unfortunately, such an attitude is not yet being given the recognition it deserves. Except for an incipient Bilingual Education Policy for selected Brazilian tribes, we lack something like a broadly based, experimental bilingual or multilingual policy as suggested, for example, by Bokamba (1984). Ours is essentially a multilingual and pluriethnic country—1 national language and 152 "living" indigenous languages, according to estimates in the SIL-sponsored survey (Summer Institute of Linguistics) organized by Grimes (1984)—but our extremely varied linguistic capital is not being "enhanced and valued," as language planners would put it. Early bilingual (or multilingual) literacy in Brazil is still in its infancy: almost everything is to be done, and therein lies a fascinating challenge to those of us who believe in the assuring of the individual's (particularly the child's) rights to acquiring, using, and maintaining two or more languages.

11. ADDITIONAL REMARKS

A very significant event took place on December 20, 1985: the officially appointed Commission for the Establishment of Guidelines for Improving the Teaching–Learning of Portuguese in Brazil completed its report to the Brazilian President José Sarney. The 32-page document has a section on "Language spoken by minority groups" in which a strong plea is made in favor of a language education policy aimed at the planning and implementation of bilingual education programs (Brazilian Portuguese and the language of the minority, whether indigenous or nonindigenous in origin).

The commission's recommendation to the Ministry of Education emphasizes that Brazilian indigenous groups be assisted so as to enhance their first language or mother-tongue knowledge and use (in written form, too), while learning Portuguese as a second language. As regards nonindigenous minorities (European and Asian immigrants, for example), it was recommended that literacy be promoted optionally in the immigrant's first language or in Brazilian Portuguese.

The fact that Brazil is a pluralistic country from a linguistic viewpoint and that language education policies have to be designed accordingly was highlighted by the members of the national commission, in which the present author took part (during its preparatory phase). In short, the Brazilian linguistic reality, multifaceted and challenging in nature, is gradually being described and assessed (sociolinguistically and politicoeducationally) with a promising outlook for the 1990s.

The new Brazilian Constitution of 1988 has given top priority to literacy and elementary school education, by stating that the child has the right to go to school from an early age and that it is the country's responsibility to provide for such educational experience in specialized schools. Herein lies a great, long-range challenge, being slowly but seriously accepted by the new, creative generation of researchers and teachers committed to overcoming most of the acute problems afflicting early monolingual and bilingual literacy in Brazil. The road to *trans*literacy, to changing and improving the conditions of learners, their teachers, their schools, and their communities, is not easily traveled, but its human significance makes it permanently attractive.

REFERENCES

Biazioli, S., & Gomes de Matos, F. (1978). *Português do Brasil para estrangeiros. Conversação, cultura e criatividade*. São Paulo: Difusão Nacional do Livro.

Bisol, L. (1975). Interferência de segunda lingna, na aquisição da escrita. Porto Alegre: UFRS.

Bokamba, E. (1984). Language and literacy in West Africa. In R. B. Kaplan (Ed.), *Annual review of applied linguistics* (pp. 40–75). Rowley, MA: Newbury House.

Gomes de Matos, F. (1983). *A pluridisciplinary checklist for evaluation of materials used in the teaching of the mother tongue in Brazil*. Paris: UNESCO, Division of Structures, Content, Techniques and Methods of Education.

Gomes de Matos, F., & Carvalho, N. (1984). *Como avaliar um livro didatico-língua portuguesa*. São Paulo: Pioneira.

Gomes de Matos, F., & Wigdorsky, L. (1968). Foreign language teaching in Latin America. In T. L. Sebeok (Ed.), *Trends in Ibero-American and Caribbean linguistics* (pp. 464–533). The Hague: Mouton.

Grimes, B. F. (Ed.). (1984). *Ethnologue. Languages of the world* (10th ed.). Dallas, TX: Wycliffe Bible Translators.

Kendall, F. E. (1983). *Diversity in the classroom*. New York, London: Teachers College Press.

Kindell, G. (1984). Linguistics and literacy. In R. B. Kaplan (Ed.), *Annual review of applied linguistics* (pp. 8–23). Rowley, MA: Newbury House.

Levi Mattoso, M. (Ed.). (1982). *I Encontro sobre Bilinguismo no Sul do Brasil*. Proceedings of the 1st Meeting on Bilingualism in Southern Brazil. Porto Alegre: CLA—Instituto de Letras, Universidade Federal do Rio Grande do Sul.

Projeto ALFA. (1980). São Paulo: Abril.

Vandresen, P. (Ed.). (1983). *II Encontro de Bilinguismo e Variação Linguística*. Proceedings of the 2nd Meeting on Bilingualism in Southern Brazil. Florianópolis, Santa Catarina: Universidade Federal de Santa Catarina.

CHAPTER 3

Non-English-Language Ethnic Community Schools in the USA
Instruments of More Than Literacy and Less Than Literacy

JOSHUA A. FISHMAN

1. INTRODUCTION

The non-English-language ethnic community schools (hereafter, NELECS) in the United States constitute a sidestream phenomenon that, at first glance, may appear somewhat esoteric to the mainstream pursuit of literacy. Actually, however, a careful consideration of the sidestream may enable us to recognize and see in sharper relief certain aspects of literacy, for example, its necessary links to local culture and to concrete, everyday social experience that the mainstream (not only mainstream USA, but modern secularism in general) recognizes insufficiently because it so easily confuses its own emphases with universality and inevitability. A sympathetic and thorough examination of more traditional expressions of literacy may render us more sensitive to literacy as a phenomenon that requires local cultural validity and that may, therefore, take different forms, pursue different goals, be linked to different contextual and institutional supports from one speech community to another and even from one speech network to another. The sidestream, more than the mainstream, may lead us to the comparative study of literacy as a socioculturally regulated activity on the one hand and as a society- and culture-building activity on the other hand. Overly abstract, overly externalized, and overly generalized views of literacy,

JOSHUA A. FISHMAN • Ferkauf Graduate School of Psychology, Yeshiva University, Bronx, New York 10461, USA.

25

Table 1. Ethnic Mother-Tongue Schools by Language and Frequency of Attendance

Language	Daily		Weekday afternoons[a]		Saturday/ Sunday[b]		No data		Total schools
	n	%	n	%	n	%	n	%	
Albanian							1	100.0	1
Amerindian	37	25.7					107	74.3	144
Arabic					2	28.6	5	71.4	7
Aramaic			1	100.0					1
Armenian	12	13.8	3	3.5	43	49.4	29	33.3	87
Bulgarian							2	100.0	2
Byelorussian					3	75.0	1	25.0	4
Cambodian							1	100.0	1
Carpatho-Rusyn					1	50.0	1	50.0	2
Chamorro	6	46.2					7	53.8	13
Chinese	5	2.9	15	8.7	18	10.5	134	77.9	172
Croatian			1	6.7	6	40.0	8	53.3	15
Czech			1	7.7	6	46.1	6	46.1	13
Danish							3	100.0	3
Dutch							1	100.0	1
Estonian					7	43.8	9	56.2	16
Finnish							3	100.0	3
French	23	19.5					95	80.5	118
German	6	3.3	3	1.7	39	21.3	135	73.7	183
Greek	20	4.5	31	7.0	22	5.0	369	83.5	442
Haitian Creole	1	100.0							1
Hebrew	501	19.4	1659	64.1	406	15.7	23	0.8	2,589
Hindi					4	80.0	1	20.0	5
Hawaiian							1	100.0	1
Hungarian	2	2.4	1	1.2	14	16.9	66	79.5	83
Hutterite	61	100.0							61
Italian	2	2.7	4	5.3	7	9.3	62	82.7	75
Japanese	10	5.9	8	4.7	29	17.2	122	72.2	169
Korean					5	4.1	116	95.9	121
Lao							1	100.0	1
Latvian	2	4.0	1	2.0	13	26.0	34	68.0	50
Lithuanian	1	1.1	2	2.4	18	21.2	64	75.3	85
Norwegian							5	100.0	5
Pennsylvania German	584	99.8					1	0.2	585
Persian							1	100.0	1
Pilipino							5	100.0	5
Polish	9	7.1	3	2.4	14	11.1	100	79.4	126
Portuguese	1	2.3	7	15.9	1	2.3	35	79.5	44
Punjabi							1	100.0	1
Romany							2	100.0	2
Rumanian							2	100.0	2
Russian					1	14.0	6	86.0	7
Sanskrit							1	100.0	1
Serbian					1	25.0	3	75.0	4

Table 1 (Continued)

Language	Daily		Weekday afternoons[a]		Saturday/ Sunday[b]		No data		Total schools
	n	%	n	%	n	%	n	%	
Slovak	2	10.0	1	5.0	1	5.0	16	80.0	20
Slovenian					6	50.0	6	50.0	12
Spanish	54	7.4	2	0.3	3	0.4	672	91.9	731
Swedish					2	17.0	10	83.0	12
Thai							5	100.0	5
Tibetan							2	100.0	2
Ukrainian	6	6.8			40	45.5	42	47.7	88
Vietnamese					1	11.0	8	89.0	9
Yiddish	108	25.6	284	67.3	30	7.1			422
Totals	1,453	22.2	2,027	30.9	743	11.3	2,330	35.7	6,553

[a] Includes classes meeting two or more times per week including a Saturday or Sunday.
[b] Includes classes meeting one time per week or less.

based upon exposure only to one or another modern secular setting, may very well represent a professional intellectual bias and, therefore, a fashionable falsification of the reality of literacy and biliteracy in the lives of ordinary adults and children who aspire not so much to international leadership positions as to lives of moderate continuity, controlled change, and respectability at the local level.

2. LOCATING AND EVALUATING NON-ENGLISH-LANGUAGE ETHNIC COMMUNITY SCHOOLS IN THE USA

In order to study sidestream institutions, one must first find them. In order to study a representative sample of such institutions, one must first enumerate the institutional universe. The universe of NELECS in the USA (schools maintained and operated by ethnic communities, usually without any sort of governmental or other "outside" support) is quite large—some 6,500 units at last count (see Table 1; for ample additional detail see Fishman, Gertner, Lowy, & Milan, 1985a,b)—but it is nevertheless one that is almost invisible to the untutored eye. In the USA it has never been fully enumerated by the public authorities (indeed, these authorities often ask *me* for information concerning this universe), and, as a result, I have had to invest 25 years of effort to locate its units in over 50 languages (or 150 languages if Amerindian languages are considered separately). Even so, that task is still far from completed. The absence of national bookkeeping in connection with these schools sadly reveals the extent to which the language resource that they constitute is neither recognized, appreciated, nor fostered. In worldwide perspective, language resources are rarely well documented, certainly not as well as natural resources. To document language resources well, it is necessary to enumerate both *individual resources* (mother tongue and language use) and *institutional resources* (e.g., publications, radio–television broadcasts, ethnic community schools, and local religious units utilizing community languages in some part of their total effort) and then to undertake evaluative research pertaining to language facility in various modes.

While I cannot claim to have done all that is needed in order to fully enumerate or evaluate the language resources of America's NELECS, I have continued to move ahead in that direction, and I am, therefore, now able to present more information than ever before in connection with them.

3. CHARACTERIZING THE UNIVERSE

The lion's share of NELECS, some two-thirds of the total universe of 6,500, are supplementary in nature, that is, they are attended for a few hours per week (modally: 3 hours) by pupils who also attend full-day public schools. For a few hours on weekends or for a few hours during weekday afternoons, when the public schools are not in session, some 300,000 children in the USA study a language (other than English) that is related to their ethnic heritage. An even larger number of children (over 500,000) engage in such study in the remaining one-third of the NELECS, these being all-day schools that are attended *instead* of public schools. These schools fulfill all of the requirements of the public education authorities during part of the school day and use their remaining time (typically, 2 to 3 hours per day) to pursue their ethnic linguistic, religious, and cultural educational goals.

Currently, NELECS are disproportionately maintained by ethnic communities that are neither mainstream Protestant nor mainstream Catholic. Underrepresented (relative to the number of their mother-tongue claimants) with respect to sponsorship of such schools are Spanish, Italian, German, French, and Polish, the "big five" non-English mother tongues in the USA today and throughout this century. Overrepresented are Jews (with schools teaching Hebrew, Hebrew and Yiddish, or, more rarely, Yiddish alone), the Eastern Orthodox (Armenians, Greeks, Ukrainians), and nonparticipationist sects (Amish, Mennonites, Hutterites). Also overrepresented are language groups that are racially separate from the American mainstream (regardless of religion but most frequently non-Christian)—Koreans, Japanese, and Chinese. Both of these factors (nonmainstream religion and nonmainstream race) are indicative of the importance of boundary-maintaining mechanisms (both voluntary and nonvoluntary) in the facilitation of intergenerational language-continuity efforts.

On the whole, recent immigrant groups are underrepresented with respect to the maintenance of their own NELECS. They are either still too few in numbers (or in the numbers of their school-aged children) or too dependent on government-sponsored or on mainstream–church-sponsored schools to have many schools of their own. Given that recent immigrant groups are (thus far) under-represented in this universe, it is understandable that most NELECS serve a third-generation student clientele, mostly of middle-class or lower middle-class compositions. For such children, English is already their dominant language. Neither the ethnic schools nor the ethnic communities of their parents' genera-tion were able to secure oral language maintenance. Thus, NELECS today are generally not involved in mother-tongue education as much as in assuring the intergenerational continuity of *being American in an ethnic way* or *being ethnic in an American way*. By and large they have become second-language acqui-sition schools and are testimony to the continued sociocultural validity of sidestream languages, even after they are no longer mother tongues, and of sidestream cultures, even after substantial Americanization has occurred. Americanization and a degree of ethnic continuity (even re-ethnization) are in-creasingly viewed as commensurable rather than as incommensurable.

Finally, still in a generally descriptive vein, it should be noted that the number of NELECS seems to have doubled from the early 1960s to the early 1980s, and they have done so pretty much across the board (Fishman, Nahirny, Hofman, & Hayden, 1966; Fishman *et al.*, 1985a,b). This increase is not at-tributable to immigration but to the Zeitgeist of the ethnic revival. The same generation that founded thousands of new NELECS also championed various other sidestream causes: protests against the war in Vietnam, rediscovery of fundamentalist religion, and environmental protection against rampant big busi-ness. I am not implying that the same individuals were usually active on all of these fronts but, rather, that the ethnic revival, leading, in part, to startling increases in NELECS, was itself a component of a much more widespread distancing from the mainstream and of much more encompassing efforts to press sidestream claims for legitimacy and public recognition.

4. THE NELECS LITERACY MODE

Most NELECS are maintained by or affiliated with local religious units. Accordingly, they do not stress multifunctional ("general," "modern," "broad scope") literacy in their respective non-English languages but, rather, ritualized literacy or traditional literacy. It should be remembered that all pupils of NELECS are also pursuing "modern" literacy, either under public school aus-pices or under the auspices of the general programs of their NELECS day schools. It would thus be redundant and even counterproductive for non-

English-language literacy to attempt to compete with or parallel the functions
of English literacy. Where biliteracy is a stable, intergenerational fact of life,
each language must have its own distinct literacy goals, whether in connection
with level, genre, or function. Elsewhere in the world, where biliteracy means
the acquisition of English or some other language of wider communication, this
principle of specificity and mutual complementarity is carefully addressed and
worked out. The local language has intragroup functions, and literacy in it is
taught and acquired at a level and in *genres* appropriate to those functions.
Similarly, a different level and different *genres* and functions guide the teaching and motivate the acquisition of the language of wider communication, be
it a regional or international language.

Not only must literacy be culturally specific in order to be culturally meaningful (just as languages are not carbon copies of each other, neither are literacies) but the role of literacy *per se,* in the lives of the bulk of ordinary folk,
must be realistically examined if we are not to fall prey to nineteenth century
idealism in connection with its merits or purported consequences. The role of
reading in modern life is neither entirely obvious (it is *not* something that can
be "intuitively" estimated in the absence of data on specific speech networks)
nor is it necessarily substantial. Even in those Western countries where most
citizens *can* read, they mostly do not read very much more than a popular
newspaper, their mail, and their bills.

The foregoing two paragraphs are needed to arrive at a more dispassionate
view, as well as a more informed interest, vis-à-vis the literacy efforts of the
NELECS in their ethnic tongues. Ritualized, traditional literacy represents a
very clear, reasonable, and meaningful functional goal vis-à-vis third-generation ethnic Americans, a goal whose attainment is culturally motivated and
rewarded, indeed, a goal which provides not only societal rewards but which
promises supernatural ones as well. Such goals serve to remind us that our
intellectual biases, interests, and priorities are not shared by "humanity in general" and that fostering literacy in real (rather than mythical) populations requires us to ask not what type of literacy would gratify *our* sociocultural goals
but, rather, what would gratify *theirs*—what would enlist their literacy motivation, interest, support, and retention. A dose of cultural relativism might do
us some good. We are not gods. We do not have the right, as students of
literacy, to judge cultures, to find them wanting, to restructure them, or to
destroy them. That is exactly what we do when we foist our own literacy goals
upon others.

5. REEXAMINING SOME LITERACY MYTHS

A patient examination of the ritualized, traditional literacy that predominates in American NELECS enables us to reexamine a number of literacy as-

sumptions that are assumed to be universals but that are really components of certain literacy types, genres, and functions other than of literacy *per se*. The widespread assumption that literacy must be built upon prior mastery of the spoken language proves to be inoperative in most American NELECS, in which speaking *per se* is either de-emphasized or totally absent as a socioculturally (and, therefore, as a curricular) goal. The de-emphasis on speaking is well represented in other literacy efforts around the world (e.g., in connection with Koranic Arabic, Coptic Geez, Prayerbook Hebrew, Church Slavonic, Church Greek, Mandarin Classics, Sanscrit Vedas, etc.) and is merely a consequence of the cultural specificity not only of literacy but of languages as a whole. Just as there are many languages in the world that are for speaking but not for reading (indeed, most languages of the world are in this category), so there are some that are for reading but not for speaking (Wagner, 1983). For these languages, methodologies that constitute the literacy specialists' usual stock-in-trade will not do. Our methodological humility should profit from this realization.

Another modern literacy myth that needs to be reexamined in the light of NELECS practice is that reading aloud is either a nonproductive technical skill (i.e., a learning-to-read skill), at best, or a mere relic of the past, a handicap, at worst. In many NELECS it is none of the above but, rather, a socioculturally recognized communication skill that pertains to a variety of personal, familial, communal, and religious communication events (Wagner, 1983). Students who already know how to read are urged to perfect this skill by reading out loud, so that they can enhance their status in the ethnic community.

Finally, even when we deal with literacy efforts that correspond to spoken languages (other than to subvocally or vocally *read* languages), the NELECS serve to remind us that literacy is often pursued in language varieties that are more distant from speech than is usually the case when we compare "school language" with ordinary spoken language. Religious varieties, even when they are varieties of the vernacular, are more conservative (viz., the King James Bible variety of English) and are even less exposed to changes in the vernacular than are most school literacy languages whose functions are primarily secular. Ritual languages do change with time, of course, but their sanctified functions and associations provide them with eternal (and, therefore, by definition, unchangeable) messages clothed in extremely change-resistant grab. Indeed, the language repertoire of many NELECS is a very complex one involving two oral *process languages* (the schoolish versions of spoken English and the spoken ethnic community language), on the one hand, and two written–read *target languages* (the ritualized minority language and schoolish written English), on the other hand. This repertoire is even more complex in NELECS that serve traditionally diglossic ethnic communities (e.g., Jews, Greeks, Chinese, etc.) where more than two process languages and/or more than two target languages are employed. All in all, we must not confuse (bi)literacy with modernization

nor prescribe for it as if it were necessarily a capstone to monolingual modernization. Some of the most traditional cultures have the longest (bi)literate traditions, and even when they come to democratize these traditions (as they generally do in the USA), they never the less often seek to do so within their own
traditional functional framework of values, goals, genres, and functions.

6. HOW SUCCESSFUL ARE AMERICAN NELECS?

Using their own intracommunity standards, we must conclude that the
NELECS are generally successful in attaining their dual primary goal: (1) *eth-
noreligious identity affiliation* (even in the absence of real vernacular competence), and (2) *continuity of ritual language use* at services and at home or at
communal events. Thus, although some groups are realizing for the first time
that ethnicity outlasts mother-tongue facility (at this very moment many Ar-
menian-Americans and Greek-Americans are at this stressfully difficult stage),
they are gratified to find that the sacred texts are still being mastered and used.
The very functional specificity of the NELECS and their languages, limiting
though they be, provides them with a turf all their own and removes them from
a frontal competition with English which they would almost certainly lose.
They exclude English from those very functions (''religion'') where the Anglo
mainstream itself recognizes such exclusion as not only legitimate but desirable, functions that are widely recognized as beyond the meddling intrusions
or regulation of secular society.

7. CONCLUSION

There is always a *marked language* in minority biliteracy, a language that
would not be taught except for special efforts and circumstances. This language
can only be successfully taught by the school if it has socioculturally rewarded
functions and protected, noncompetitive functions vis-à-vis the more powerful,
unmarked language. Accordingly, biliteracy involves more than linguistic considerations, more than pedagogic considerations, and more than psychological
considerations. Biliteracy, particularly minority biliteracy, involves (1) cultural
arrangements providing protected and rewarded functions for the marked language and, therefore, (2) protection and rewards that involve much more than
the school alone and that encompass strong out-of-school institutional contexts
such as home, church, or workplace. The success of monoliteracy depends on
more than schools alone. Without protected and rewarded out-of-school functions, even monoliteracy quickly fades, if it is acquired at all. How much more
so must this be the case for biliteracy in general and for minority biliteracy in

particular. If it is to be more than a passing stage (like so much else that schools teach that is later lost and forgotten), it must have its very definite sociocultural counterparts, institutions, and functions that reward and protect it when school is over and done with. If America's NELECS help us grasp these essential truths, then atypical though they may be in many ways relative to more major and more visible worldwide biliteracy efforts, they will more than repay any attention that may be given to them. Indeed, they clearly exemplify the sociocultural considerations that underlie all successful biliteracy efforts and strikingly emphasize a gap in modern Western thinking: the realization that literacy *per se* is culture specific, first and foremost, in addition to whatever more generalized characteristics it may also possess.

Modern Western efforts that view languages and literacies only from the point of view of their generalizable similarities accomplish little. These efforts, at best, provide jobs for literacy specialists; at worst, they undercut languages and dislocate cultures. They lead to the view that minority languages are superfluous, if not dangerous, as indeed they are if only modern Western national and international functions are considered germane for the school. Biliteracy efforts must not become a new species of internal colonialism, of suppression of the weak by the strong. Complementarity of functions and specificity of goals, genres, and methods is the only responsible solution, albeit a solution that requires the biliteracy specialist to accept cultural self-definitions of literacy rather than make "outsider" judgments in connection with them.

REFERENCES

Fishman, J. A., Nahirny, V. C., Hofman, J. E., & Hayden, R. G. (1966). *Language loyalty in the United States.* The Hague: Mouton.

Fishman, J. A., Gertner, M. H., Lowy, E. G., & Milan, W. G. (1985a). *Ethnicity in action: The institutional language resources of American ethnolinguistic minorities.* Binghamton, NY: Bilingual Press.

Fishman, J. A., Gertner, M. H., Lowy, E. G., & Milan, W. G. (1985b). *The rise and fall of the ethnic revival.* Berlin: Mouton.

Wagner, D. A. (Ed.). (1983). Literacy and ethnicity. *International Journal of the Sociology of Language, 42* (entire issue).

CHAPTER 4

The Development of Bilingual Literacy Skills
Experiences with Immersion Education

WALLACE E. LAMBERT

1. EARLY IMMERSION SCHOOLING

As social psychological researchers interested in language, we tuned in on a state of affairs in Canada some 25 years ago in which relations between English and French Canadians were beginning to become tense and strained. Two extreme solutions to the French Canadian "problem" were coming into vogue: (1) French Canadians should pull up their socks and compete, meaning they should master English and Anglo-American ways, while toning down their French Canadian-ness; (2) French Canadians should pull apart or separate, meaning they should form a new independent nation where they could be masters of their own fate and where the "good old ways" could be protected. Both alternatives worried us because one meant giving up a style of life that was precious, and the other meant closing a society through separation—"closing" in the sense that Karl Popper (1966) uses the term. Instead, we viewed the French Canadian way of life as something precious for Canada as a whole—a nation whose potential and fascination rest in its multicultural, multilingual makeup—whether or not it was appreciated as such by English Canadians. So we became interested in reducing, if possible, the ignorance of French Canadian-ness and in enhancing an appreciation for it among Anglo-Canadian children. This then became the guiding purpose for the Canadian work on "early immersion"

WALLACE E. LAMBERT • Department of Psychology, McGill University, Montreal H3A 1B1, Quebec, Canada.

schooling (Genesee, 1978–1979; Lambert & Tucker, 1972; Swain, 1974), wherein English-speaking children, with no French-language experience in the home or in their communities, entered public school kindergarten or Grade 1 classes that were conducted by a monolingual French-speaking teacher. This early immersion, or "home-to-school language-switch," program, as we call it, is kept exclusively French through Grade 2, and only at Grade 3 is English introduced, in the form of a language arts program, for one period a day. By Grade 4 particular subject matters are taught in English (by an English-speaking teacher) so that by Grades 5 and 6 some 60% of instruction is in English (Lambert, 1979).

What is interesting about this program is that immersion pupils are taken along by monolingual teachers to a level of functional bilingualism that could not be duplicated in any other fashion short of living and being schooled in a foreign setting. Furthermore, pupils arrive at that level of competence without detriment to home-language skill development, without falling behind in the all-important content subjects of education (the immersion experience does not take time from basic educational learning), without any form of mental confusion or loss of normal cognitive growth, and without a loss of identity or appreciation for their own ethnicity. Most important of all in the present context, they also develop a deep appreciation for and a balanced outlook toward French Canadians, whom they have learned about indirectly through their teachers and whose language they have picked up in what appears to them to be an incidental fashion. The details of the research on immersion are available in two recent reviews (Genesee, 1984; Lambert, 1984).

What is exciting about this educational program is the opportunity it gives children (1) to open their minds so that they can make fairer evaluations of an otherwise foreign and possibly threatening outgroup, and (2) to come to the realization that peaceful democratic coexistence among members of distinctive ethnolinguistic groups calls for something more than simply learning one another's languages (Blake, Lambert, Sidoti, & Wolf, 1981; Cziko, Lambert, Sidoti, & Tucker, 1980). Thus, having learned the other language well and having learned to appreciate the other cultural group, children with immersion experience (compared to controls) realize that democratic coexistence calls for more than language competence and cultural knowledge, namely, opportunities for both ethnic groups of young people to interact socially on an equitable basis. This is an insight that monolingual mainstreamers are likely never to have, because they naively assume that learning the other group's language and customs will automatically promote intergroup understanding.

2. DEVELOPING A FUNCTIONALLY BILINGUAL CITIZENRY

Thus a new approach to bilingual education is now available, and since it works as well in other parts of Canada where few if any French Canadians are encountered in social life, this program, or some variation of it, can be expected to work equally well in the USA (Swain, 1974). In fact, there are currently some eight communities in the United States where comparable early immersion programs for mainstream Anglo-Americans are underway (in French, German, and Spanish, so far), and from all available accounts they are working splendidly (Cohen, 1976; Genesee, Holobow, Lambert, Gastright, & Met, 1985; Montgomery County Public Schools, 1976; Samuels & Griffore, 1979). Furthermore, there is strong evidence to show that Anglo-Canadian children can handle easily a "double immersion" program wherein French and Hebrew are used, in separate streams, as the languages of instruction (Genesee & Lambert, 1983). We have then an effective means of developing a functionally bilingual citizenry, but note which segments of the societies we gave the major attention to in these experiments: it was the Anglo-Canadian and the Anglo-American mainstreamers—the segments that are most secure in their ethnic and linguistic identity but most in need of knowledge about and sensitivity toward other ethnic and linguistic groups. To the extent that mainstream children are sensitized to and educated in another language and culture, the better the chances are of developing a fairer, more equitable society. The better too are the chances of improving the self-views of ethnolinguistic minority children, who are heartened and complimented when they realize that mainstream children are making sincere gestures to learn about them, their ways of life, and their language. For Canada and the United States, this means that in time younger generations of ethnic minorities may be able to escape the feelings of inferiority and strangeness that marked their parents and find instead a very likeable and appreciative generation of bilingual young people to associate with.

3. ADDITIVE VERSUS SUBTRACTIVE BILINGUALISM

We have referred to this process of developing bilingual and bicultural skills among English-speaking children in Canada or the United States as an "additive" form of bilingualism, implying that these children, with no fear of ethnic or linguistic erosion, can add one or more foreign languages to their accumulating skills and profit immensely from the experience (Lambert, 1978). Mainstream parents, incidentally, realize these advantages and are generally very anxious to have their children enroll in immersion programs or variants thereof. They want something more for their children than the programs that were offered them in their school days, programs which failed to develop real competence.

We draw a very sharp contrast between the "additive" form of bilingualism described above and the "subtractive" form, which constitutes a totally different ball game, having different potential hazards, and different means-to-ends demands. The hyphenated American or Canadian child, such as the Portuguese-American, Polish-American, Navajo-American, or the French-Canadian or Greek-Canadian, embarks on a subtractive bilingual route as soon as he or she enters a school where a high-prestige, socially powerful, dominant language like English is introduced either as a language of instruction or as a subject matter. Perceptive members of ethnolinguistic minority groups have good grounds for worry and concern about the steamroller effect of a powerful dominant language; it can make foreign home languages and cultures seem "homely" in contrast, ghosts in the closet to be eradicated and suppressed. But, just as French is too precious to be subtracted out of Canadian society, so too are the multitude of "foreign" languages and cultures extant in America too precious to be eradicated from that society. Education's responsibility then becomes one of *transforming* subtractive forms of bilingualism to additive ones for the benefit of the ethnolinguistic minority groups involved.

Community experiments that attempt to implement such transformations, although few in number so far, are now underway (Lambert, 1978). Basically this calls for immersion schooling conducted in the likely-to-be-neglected home language of the ethnolinguistic minority child, starting at kindergarten or Grade 1 and continuing until it is certain that that language is strongly rooted and able to flourish on its own. This might take the first 3 or 4 years of primary education. By then the switch to a bilingual (with separate teachers) or all-English instruction could safely take place. Only then will the society at large profit from the salvaging of minority languages and cultures. But note these two essential ingredients of the plan: (1) it can only work, we believe, if the mainstream child himself or herself is simultaneously developing skills in and an appreciation for at least one of these languages and its associated culture, and (2) if no time is taken from the all-important task of developing competence in the critical content subjects that make up education. The incidental learning of language and learning about another culture need not and should not get in the way of providing a thorough education in science, math, creative language arts, and the like. Nor should educators be distracted by the current confusion about bilingual education, especially in the United States, from their responsibility to produce a curriculum that is really valuable for children, a curriculum that permits both minority and mainstream children to actualize their full potentials.

REFERENCES

Blake, L., Lambert, W. E., Sidoti, N., & Wolf, D. (1981). *Students' views of intergroup tensions in Québec: The effects of language immersion experience. Canadian Journal of Behavioral Science, 13,* 144–160.

Cohen, A. (1976). The case for partial or total immersion education. In A. Simoes, Jr. (Ed.), *The bilingual child* (pp. 65–89). New York: Academic Press.

Cziko, G., Lambert, W. E., Sidoti, N., & Tucker, G. R. (1980). Graduates of early immersion: Retrospective views of grade 11 students and their parents. In R. N. St. Clair & H. Giles (Eds.), *The social and psychological contexts of language* (pp. 131–157). Chicago: Erlbaum.

Genesee, F. (1978–1979). Scholastic effects of French immersion: An overview after ten years. *Interchange, 9,* 20–29.

Genesee, F. (1984). Historical and theoretical foundations of immersion education. In *Studies on immersion education* (pp. 32–57). Sacramento: California State Department of Education.

Genesee, F., & Lambert, W. E. (1983). Trilingual education for majority-language children. *Child Development, 54,* 105–114.

Genesee, F., Holobow, N., Lambert, W. E., Gastright, J., & Met, M. (1985). *An evaluation of partial French immersion in the Cincinnati public schools: The kindergarten year.* Mimeograph, Psychology Department, McGill University.

Lambert, W. E. (1978). Some cognitive and sociocultural consequences of being bilingual. In J. E. Alatis (Ed.), *International dimensions of bilingual education* (pp. 214–229). Washington, DC: Georgetown University Press.

Lambert, W. E. (1979). *A Canadian experiment in the development of bilingual competence: The home-to-school language-switch program.* Mimeograph, Psychology Department, McGill University.

Lambert, W. E. (1984). An overview of issues in immersion education. In *Studies on immersion education* (pp. 8–30). Sacramento: California State Department of Education.

Lambert, W. E., & Tucker, G. R. (1972). *Bilingual education of children: The St. Lambert experiment.* Rowley, MA: Newbury House.

Montgomery County Public Schools (1976). *End of the second year report on the French language immersion program at four corners.* Unpublished report submitted to the Montgomery County Board of Education, Maryland.

Popper, K. R. (1966). *The open society and its enemies* (Vols. 1 and 2). London: Routledge & Kegan Paul.

Samuels, D. D., & Griffore, R. J. (1979). The Plattsburgh French language immersion program: Its influence on intelligence and self-esteem. *Language Learning, 29,* 45–52.

Swain, M. (1974). French immersion programs across Canada. *The Canadian Modern Language Review, 31,* 117–128.

CHAPTER 5

Ancestral Language Training and the Development of Bilingual Literacy
A Canadian Perspective

MARCEL DANESI

1. INTRODUCTION

When the children of immigrant families reach the age at which they enter the school system, their learning needs are clearly different from those of their monolingual schoolmates. Although legislation in several countries requires school systems to provide linguistically diverse children with an education appropriate to their needs, there still seems to be a lingering doubt as to the value of such special educational programs, probably as a result of the fact that it has often proven difficult to implement them in a pedagogically adequate fashion.

One educational program designed to meet some of the needs of immigrant children has been instituted in the last decade in many Canadian urban centers where there are usually large numbers of immigrants. In Canada it is often the case that the languages to which preschool immigrant children are exposed are the language of origin and the culturally dominant language (English or French). In the past, it was all too often the case that when the immigrant child entered the Canadian elementary school system, the use of the ancestral language was often discouraged. Lambert (e.g., 1975) has called the resulting form of bilingualism "subtractive," since the bilingual child's proficiency in the two languages at any point in time is likely to reflect some stage in the subtraction of the ancestral language and its replacement by the dominant

MARCEL DANESI • Department of Semiotics, Victoria College, University of Toronto, Toronto M5S 1K7, Ontario, Canada.

one. In children who entered the school system with some proficiency in the dominant language, few academic problems were seen to emerge; but in those children who started school with little or no knowledge of the dominant language, the academic results tended to be negative, at least initially. This was probably due to the nature of subtractive bilingualism, since the immigrant children had not as yet developed the levels of proficiency in their languages to function properly in an academic environment. (For studies investigating this psychoeducational problem, see, for instance, Cummins, 1976; Cummins & Mulcahy, 1978; Skutnabb-Kangas & Toukomaa, 1976; Tosi, 1984.) Cummins (1976) has referred to this as the "threshold hypothesis," suggesting that there may be levels of linguistic proficiency bilingual children must attain in order to avoid cognitive deficits.

Partially in an attempt to remedy this situation, Canada's decade-old educational experiment, known as the Heritage Language (HL) program, has had the therapeutic effect of counteracting the negative results that might otherwise ensue from the immigrant child's imperfect bilingualism by making it possible for the child to learn the ancestral language formally at school. Despite criticisms occasionally voiced vis-à-vis HL programs—usually traceable to pedagogically induced difficulties—the research findings that have been accumulating, together with the experiences of those directly involved in the programs, have clearly shown the experiment to be a success. In this chapter, I attempt to give an overall psychoeducational assessment of this pilot project on the basis of both the relevant research and the observations of teachers and educators involved in HL programs. An assessment of this project is, I believe, extremely useful at this time, since some misgivings, especially with respect to possible interferences on the learning of the dominant language and its related academic consequences, are still being voiced. In addition, the appropriateness of such programs in an educational context is being questioned, with some educators even suggesting that they may lead to social divisiveness. As Morrison (1980, p. 8) aptly puts it, special language programs are bound to provoke disagreements "because they raise the question of the appropriate place of culture in education." And in the words of Cummins (1980, p. 23), "whereas most educators are willing to accept French–English bilingualism as a worthwhile and attainable educational goal, bilingualism involving languages other than French or English (ancestral languages) is still viewed as a threat to social cohesion and an educational disadvantage."

2. HL EDUCATION: A BRIEF HISTORICAL SKETCH

Before going into a discussion of the relevant psychoeducational research on ancestral language training in an elementary school context, it might prove useful at this point to outline rapidly the history of HL programs in Canada. There are two main reasons for the establishment of HL programs during the last decade or so: the federal government's policy of multiculturalism and the rapid increase in the number of immigrant students in the urban elementary schools.

The intent of the multiculturalism policy, which was approved unanimously by the Canadian Parliament in 1971, is to find ways of helping culturally and linguistically diverse children to realize their educational potential and to help ethnic minorities to preserve, develop, and share their cultural heritage while identifying with other Canadians (see Fleming, 1983). Conscious of the fact that the languages spoken by immigrants constitute the very essence of Canada's multicultural mosaic, and facing pressure from ethnic organizations, most provincial governments—under whose jurisdiction education falls—have set up HL programs within their elementary school systems. In 1971, Alberta became the first province to pass legislation permitting languages other than English or French to be used and taught in the elementary schools. Shortly thereafter, the Ukrainian–English bilingual program in Edmonton became the first HL program in Canada. Following in the footsteps of this successful program, most of the other provinces have established HL programs or courses. In 1977, Ontario—the largest province—legislated an HL program consisting of noncredit courses. In the first 3 years of operation, the program grew from 55,000 to more than 76,000 students. (Overall descriptions of HL programs can be found in Danesi, 1983a,b; Cummins, 1983; Jones, 1984; Laferrière, 1980.)

3. BILINGUAL LITERACY

The educational goal of HL education is the development of bilingual literacy, or biliteracy. In this chapter, the term *biliteracy* is used to designate the state of additive bilingualism that is likely to result from schooling in both of the immigrant child's two languages. Additive bilingualism implies the attainment of high levels of proficiency in both the ancestral and dominant languages. The use of the term biliteracy is somewhat in line with Fishman's (1977) concept of migration-based literacy, according to which immigrant groups add literacy in the dominant language to their earlier literacy. In the case of the immigrant child, the development of biliteracy will, of course, occur best in school. As Fishman (1980, p. 169) has pointed out more recently, schools are crucial literacy-imparting institutions: "If there is ever to be effective ethnic mother-tongue use in most out-of-home-and-community domains, such use will require the school's active assistance to assure ethnic mother-tongue literacy."

The term *heritage* language is essentially an educational concept. It implies the language other than Canada's two majority languages (English and French) that belongs to the child's ethnocultural ancestry or heritage. Thus, for example, Polish is designated an HL when it is taught to a child of Polish background. The study of one's ancestral language at school as a separate subject, while learning all other subjects in the dominant language, is the most common HL educational model throughout Canada. In essence, the child is studying the home language as a school subject. The intention is to help the child perceive his or her language and heritage as worthwhile and valid and not to be rejected in favor of the dominant language and culture. At the same time, the intention is to encourage the child to develop literacy in the ancestral language. It is the research associated primarily with this model of HL education which I discuss shortly. (For a description of the different HL educational models, see Dawson, 1982.)

A heritage language may, of course, be the child's native language or, in the case of later generations, a language which belongs exclusively to his or her ethnocultural ancestry. Thus, the degree of knowledge that the immigrant child brings to the learning task is a function of the degree of acculturation. Perhaps the most typical form of preschool bilingualism is the one exemplified by a child born into an immigrant family who learned the ancestral language first and the dominant language later through exposure to the local media and by playing with other children. The ancestral language is, therefore, used almost exclusively within the family in cross-generational interactions, that is, with parents and older relatives. Understandably, the dominant language is used with other children (siblings included). Thus, the home is the frame of reference for the ancestral language.

The immigrant child, therefore, enters the elementary school system with some knowledge of both the home and the dominant languages. Rather than subtracting the home language from the child's linguistic repertoire, the school offering the opportunity to study the home language formally will go a long way toward the development of additive bilingualism in the child. The model just described is illustrated graphically in Figure 1.

It should be pointed out that HL programs do not prevent children from other ethnic groups from enrolling in the HL course of their choice. As a matter of fact, HL courses have been reported to be more popular among children of different ethnic backgrounds than the dominant language being studied. One survey with which I am familiar (Keyser & Brown, 1981) reveals some remarkable enrollment patterns. Of the more than 10,000 children taking an HL course within the Metropolitan Separate School Board in the city of Toronto in 1981, 26% were studying an HL different from their own. This is indeed a surprising finding, given that these children have no ancestral motivation for studying the HL, and given that the HL is an extra, noncredit subject.

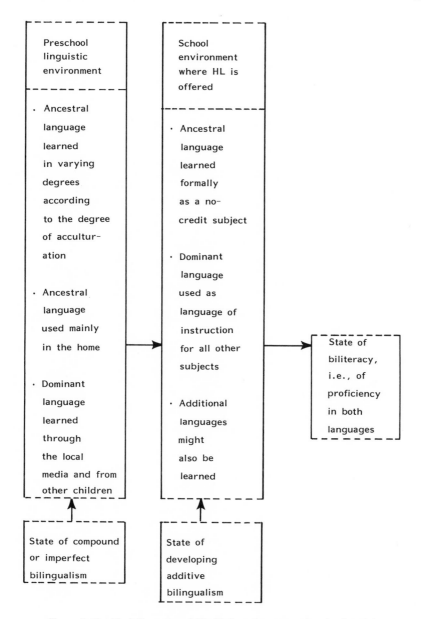

Figure 1. Graphical illustration of The Heritage Language educational model.

4. PSYCHOLINGUISTIC RESEARCH

Perhaps the question most often raised with respect to the learning of the home language at school is the possible delaying effect this might have on the immigrant child's acquisition of the dominant language. The general research findings on early bilingual training should, however, allay such fears (Fishman, 1976; Lambert, 1978; Lambert & Tucker, 1972; Peal & Lambert, 1962; Titone, 1972, 1979, 1983, 1984). Although it is true that speaking two languages does seem to impose some extra burdens—keeping the two systems separate, retrieving the appropriate word from duplicate sets for each meaning, putting incoming messages in their proper pigeonhole, and so on—the empirical evidence that has been accumulating over the past 50 years or so is highly suggestive of an increased mental flexibility resulting from the development of proficiency in two languages. (See Benderly, 1981, for an overall assessment of this line of psychological research.)

The strongest recent evidence that bilingual education works comes, perhaps, from Canada's French immersion programs (see, for example, Carey, 1984; Genesee, 1978–1979; Krashen, 1984; Lapkin, Swain, & Argue, 1983; Stern, 1978, 1984; Swain, 1980; Swain & Cummins, 1979). These programs have, in fact, helped foster a favorable attitude with regard to bilingual education in general. It has been shown quite convincingly that French immersion children:

- Develop a high level of proficiency in French and compare favorably in English-language skills with their English-taught peers in the later grades.
- Perform as well as their English-taught peers in their French-taught subject areas.
- Perform as well, if not better, on standardized IQ tests as their English-taught peers.

In the words of Merrill Swain (1980, p. 6), one of the leading researchers in this field, "the success of French immersion programs in helping our English-speaking students develop high levels of proficiency in the second language, while having no detrimental effect on cognitive development, academic achievement or first language proficiency, has been well documented."

Nevertheless, some contradictory evidence has come forward vis-à-vis the success of early immersion programming as a means of acquiring proficiency in French without detriment to English-language skills (Popp, 1976; Trites, 1976; Trites & Price, 1978–1979). In general, these studies suggest that it takes a rather long period of schooling for the development of an acceptable degree of bilingualism and that the poorest bilingual students will tend to do less well in English-language tasks than the poorest English-only students. The obvious question that comes to mind is how to reconcile the contradictory evidence. Actually, the evidence is not all that ambivalent when viewed comparatively. It is true that early immersion programs tend to produce some delay in acquiring native-language skills, but this is a totally predictable outcome given the nature of the learning task (Doyle, Champagne, & Segalowitz, 1977; Taylor, 1974). However, the evidence also shows that this is normally a temporary delay for most student types (including low achievers). Most immersion children have been found eventually to develop some degree of functional biliteracy. Moreover, some of the observed difficulties might be due to extraneous instructional or curricular variables rather than connected with some intrinsic aspect of the learning process itself (Paulston, 1977). It has also been pointed out (Cummins, 1978a; Swain & Cummins, 1979) that those studies reporting contradictory evidence might be based on inadequate psychometric and methodological criteria, since they normally do not control nonlinguistic background differences, nor do they always take into account the varying nature of bilingualism. In fact, as Francescato (1981) and others have observed, the nature of bilingualism is often misunderstood because it is not a monolithic behavioral phenomenon but is subject to much variation according to psycholinguistic and sociolinguistic parameters (see Baetens Beardsmore, 1982). In the words of Fishman (1971, p. 83), "many of the purported 'disadvantages' of bilingualism have been falsely generalized to the phenomenon at large rather than related to the absence or presence of social patterns which reach substantially beyond bilingualism."

Turning now to the psychoeducational research that has been conducted during the past decade on HL education, it has become abundantly clear that the same kinds of advantages to be derived from immersion schooling are also obtainable from ancestral language training. The work of James Cummins in particular (1978b, 1979, 1980b, 1981a) has established this as a fact. (Cummins gives overall assessments of the relevant research in 1980a, 1981b, 1984a, 1984b.)

Without going into the psychometric and methodological details of the relevant studies, the research on HL training makes it now possible to assert the following. In comparison to their peers, immigrant children enrolled in their HL (usually as a noncredit subject) show:

- An increased ability to analyze language in terms of more general categories, leading to a greater awareness of their linguistic operations.
- A significant improvement in the majority language.
- An increased ability in conceptual and creative thinking.
- A sharpened sensitivity to the communicative needs of their interlocutors.
- A facility in learning additional languages.

The main reason for such positive psycholinguistic outcomes might actually be a very simple one. Immigrant children who become emotionally comfortable with their home language because they are studying it at school will tend to perform better academically than their peers who feel ambivalent about the home language. In the words of Ashworth (1979, p. 81), "a child whose first language and culture have been accorded respect within the school system will have a sense of self-worth which will make him easier to teach." Similar outcomes have, predictably, been noticed wherever ancestral language programs exist (Skutnabb-Kangas, 1984; Skutnabb-Kangas & Toukomaa, 1976; Tedesco, 1980; Tosi, 1980, 1984). From a psycholinguistic perspective, therefore, the HL educational experience has made it emphatically clear that by developing some degree of proficiency in their home language, immigrant children will usually have little difficulty acquiring high levels of proficiency in the dominant language. Understandably, some children with poorly developed intellectual abilities are likely to experience learning difficulties in school. These findings clearly refute the so-called balance effect theory which claims that the time devoted to one of the bilingual's two languages results in a decrease in proficiency in the other.

5. PEDAGOGICAL ASPECTS

As Cummins (1981b, p. 42) states:

> Heritage-language classes which children enjoy and find interesting are extremely valuable in helping children develop L1 proficiency. However, classes which children find boring and unpleasant will not motivate children to take pride in their culture and develop their L1 proficiency.

This statement encapsulates what is perhaps the most commonly expressed concern with regard to HL programs, namely, that a number of HL courses are pedagogically ineffective. Part of the problem is that suitable instructional materials are lacking. Keyser and Brown (1981), in fact, found this to be the HL teacher's major concern. This situation is being gradually remedied but will require more time to resolve completely.

On the basis of my own observations of HL classes in the city of Toronto, it seems to me that potential problems might result if HL teachers:

• Have unreasonable expectations with regard to the child's linguistic abilities.
• Overemphasize the formal, grammatical aspects of the HL to the detriment of its communicative functions.
• Lack an understanding of the child's pedagogical and affective needs.

To compound the pedagogical picture is the fact that the HL spoken by most immigrant children is a dialectal version. Moreover, continual use of the HL in a contact situation with the dominant language has produced a koinè, or a mixed version; that is, the HL demonstrates the presence of many words and constructions borrowed from the dominant language and adapted phonologically and morphologically to native language patterns. My own research on the Italian spoken in Toronto (Danesi, 1982, 1984a, 1985) reveals a typical case in point. Words borrowed from English and restructured phonologically and morphologically have become firmly entrenched in the speech habits of most first- and second-generation Italians. Words such as /féntsa/ 'fence', /fárma/ 'farm', /garbíččo/ 'garbage', /kékka/ 'cake', /puššáre/ 'to push', /skwizáre/ 'to squeeze', /smeššáre/ 'to smash', and the like, have replaced Standard Italian lexical items. Needless to say, similar contact phenomena have been observed in other HLs.

Teachers are, therefore, usually confronted with children who know a dialectal version of the HL, and such a situation clearly calls for specialized pedagogical practices (Danesi, 1983b, 1984b). Above all else, the teacher's attitude is of paramount importance. An acceptance of the home dialect will prevent the formation of negative associations with the speaking of nonstandard forms of a language. Given the acceptance of this basic pedagogical principle, the rest follows logically; that is, the methodology used should develop within children a conscious awareness of the differences between the home dialect and the standard version of their HL without attaching any negative connotations to them. It has, in fact, been revealed (Keyser & Brown, 1981) that as the children learn to distinguish between standard and nonstandard versions of their HL at school, they become more eager and willing to use the HL at home, often sensitizing their parents and grandparents ''linguistically'' in the process.

6. CONCLUSION

To sum up, after a decade of intensive research on ancestral language training in the Canadian elementary school system, it can now be said with conviction that HL training is an important factor in drawing out the immigrant children's potential to become biliterate. In the not too distant past, the school's treatment of such children was probably a factor in their lack of success. It was assumed that the children's failure was due to their imperfect bilingualism. The ''balance effect'' theory was often cited to claim that there is only so much space in the child's brain for language, and that if this space is divided between two languages neither one will develop properly and cognitive confusion will result. The HL educational experience has shown the opposite to be true; that is, bilingualism can be a positive force in the intellectual development of immigrant children when their HL is promoted in school.

It is true, however, that the effectiveness of a specific HL program will be influenced by a number of instructional and psychoeducational variables. For example, the degree of ambivalence felt toward the HL is a crucial factor in predicting psycholinguistic outcomes. Moreover, there exists research suggesting that bilingual training is not necessary for all immigrant children (Bhatnagar, 1976; Ramsey, 1970; Ramsey & Wright, 1969). But, in general, the findings on ancestral language training should allay the fears of those educators who believe that the appropriate educational treatment of immigrant children in school consists in the intensive teaching of the dominant language.

As a final comment, I would like to emphasize that HL training has made it quite clear that by recognizing the value of biliteracy, the school system will tend to increase personality development rather than stifle it by attempting to eradicate the child's bilingualism. In fact, it is not an exaggeration to claim that bilingual educational programs, such as the HL program, have made a significant impact on the very concept of education. These programs have shown quite conspicuously that academic progress is a function of personality development. By enhancing children's perceptions of themselves and their heritage, the school system can help ensure their academic success.

REFERENCES

Ashworth, M. (1979). More than one language. In K. A. McLeod (Ed.), *Multiculturalism, bilingualism and Canadian institutions* (pp. 80–88). Toronto: Faculty of Education, University of Toronto.

Baetens Beardsmore, H. (1982). *Bilingualism: Basic principles*. Clevedon: Multilingual Matters.

Benderly, B. L. (1981, April). The multilingual mind. *Psychology Today*, pp. 9–12.

Bhatnagar, J. (1976). Education of immigrant children. *Canadian Ethnic Studies, 8*, 52–70.

Carey, S. T. (1984). Reflections on a decade of French immersion. *Canadian Modern Language Review, 41*, 246–259.

Cummins, J. (1976). The influence of bilingualism on cognitive growth: A synthesis of research findings and explanatory hypotheses. *Working Papers on Bilingualism, 9*, 1–43.

Cummins, J. (1978a). The cognitive development of children in immersion programs. *Canadian Modern Language Review, 34*, 855–883.

Cummins, J. (1978b). Educational implications of mother tongue maintenance in minority-language groups. *Canadian Modern Language Review, 34*, 395–416.

Cummins, J. (1979). Linguistic interdependence and the educational development of bilingual children. *Review of Educational Research, 49*, 222–251.

Cummins, J. (1980a). Ancestral language maintenance: The roles of school and home. *Multiculturalism, 4*, 23–27.

Cummins, J. (1980b). Psychological assessment of immigrant children: Logic or intuition? *Journal of Multilingual and Multicultural Development, 1*, 97–111.

Cummins, J. (1980c). The construct of language proficiency in bilingual education. In J. E. Alatis

(Ed.), *Georgetown University Round Table on Languages and Linguistics* (pp. 12–19). Washington, DC: Georgetown University Press.

Cummins, J. (1981a). Educational success for Canadian minority language children: The role of mother-tongue development. *Canadian Journal of Italian Studies, 4,* 299–315.

Cummins, J. (1981b). *Bilingualism and minority-language children.* Toronto: OISE Press.

Cummins, J. (1983). Mother-tongue development as educational enrichment. In J. Cummins (Ed.), *Heritage language education* (pp. 40–43). Ottawa: Minister of Supplies and Services.

Cummins, J. (1984a). Heritage languages and Canadian school programs. In J. R. Malles & J. C. Young (Eds.), *Cultural diversity and Canadian education* (pp. 477–500). Ottawa: Carleton University Press.

Cummins, J. (1984b). *Bilingualism and special education: Issues in assessment and pedagogy.* Clevedon: Multilingual Matters.

Cummins, J., & Mulcahy, R. (1978). Orientation to language in Ukrainian–English bilingual children. *Child Development, 49,* 1239–1242.

Danesi, M. (1982). L'interferenza lessicale nell'italiano parlato in Canada (Toronto). *Les Languages Néo-Latines, 241,* 163–167.

Danesi, M. (1983a). Early second language learning: The heritage language educational experience in Canada. *Multiculturalism, 7,* 8–12.

Danesi, M. (1983b). Curriculum development and organization. In M. Ip (Ed.), *Proceedings of the Heritage Language Association of British Columbia* (pp. 1–15). Vancouver: British Columbia Heritage Language Association.

Danesi, M. (1984a). Italo-Canadian: A case in point for loanword studies. *Geolinguistics, 10,* 79–90.

Danesi, M. (1984b). Tecniche di insegnamento dell'italiano a livello primario in Canada. *Il Veltro, 28,* 62–67.

Danesi, M. (1985). Phonological adaptation mechanisms in the assimilation of English loanwords into Italo-Canadian. *Information/Communication, 4,* 10–25.

Dawson, D. (1982). Ethnic bilingual/bicultural programs in Canadian public schools. *Canadian Modern Language Review, 38,* 648–657.

Doyle, A. B., Champagne, M., & Segalowitz, N. (1977). Some issues in the assessment of linguistic consequences of early bilingualism. *Working Papers on Bilingualism, 14,* 21–30.

Fishman, J. A. (1971). *Sociolinguistics: A brief introduction.* Rowley, MA: Newbury House.

Fishman, J. A. (1976). *Bilingual education: An international sociological perspective.* Rowley, MA: Newbury House.

Fishman, J. A. (1977). Bilingual education for the children of migrant workers: The adaption of general models to a new specific challenge. In M. De Grève & E. Rossel (Eds.), *10e Colloque de l'AIMAV* (pp. 97–105). Brussels: Didier.

Fishman, J. A. (1980). Minority language maintenance and the ethnic mother-tongue school. *Modern Language Journal, 64,* 167–172.

Fleming, J. (1983). Heritage languages and the policy of multiculturalism. In J. Cummins (Ed.), *Heritage language education: Issues and directions* (pp. 11–14). Ottawa: Minister of Supplies and Services Canada.

Francescato, G. (1981). *Il bilingue isolato.* Bergamo: Minerva Italica.

Genesee, F. (1978–1979). Scholastic effects of French immersion: An overview after ten years. *Interchange, 9,* 20–29.

Jones, J. (1984). Multilingual approach reflects Canadian mosaic. *Language and Society, 12,* 33–38.

Keyser, R., & Brown, J. (1981). *Heritage language survey results.* Toronto: Metropolitan Separate School board.

Krashen, S. D. (1984). Immersion: Why it works and what it has taught us. *Language and Society,* *12*, 61–64.

Laferrière, M. (1980). Language and cultural programs for ethnic minorities in Quebec: A critical review. *Multiculturalism, 4*, 12–17.

Lambert, W. E. (1975). Culture and language as factors in learning and education. In A. Wolfgang (Ed.), *Education of immigrant students* (pp. 55–83). Toronto: OISE Press.

Lambert, W. E. (1978). Cognitive and socio-cultural consequences of bilingualism. *Canadian Modern Language Review, 34*, 537–547.

Lambert, W. E., & Tucker, G. R. (1972). *Bilingual education of children: The St. Lambert experiment.* Rowley, MA: Newbury House.

Lapkin, S., Swain, M., & Argue, V. (1983). *French immersion: The trial balloon that flew.* Toronto: OISE Press.

Morrison, T. R. (1980). Transcending culture: Cultural selection and multicultural education. In K. A. McLeod (Ed.), *Intercultural education and community development* (pp. 8–16). Toronto: Faculty of Education, University of Toronto.

Paulston, C. B. (1977). Theoretical perspectives on bilingual education programs. *Working Papers on Bilingualism, 13*, 130–177.

Peal, E., & Lambert, W. E. (1962). The relation of bilingualism to intelligence. *Psychological Monographs, 76*, No. 546.

Popp, L. A. (1976). The English competence of French-speaking students in a bilingual setting. *Canadian Modern Language Review, 32*, 365–377.

Ramsey, C. (1970). *Language backgrounds and achievement in Toronto schools* (Research Report No. 85). Toronto: Toronto Board of Education.

Ramsey, C., & Wright, E. N. (1969). *Students of non-Canadian origin: The relation of languages and rural–urban background to academic achievement and ability* (Research Report No. 76). Toronto: Toronto Board of Education.

Skutnabb-Kangas, T. (1984). *Bilingualism or not: The education of minorities.* Clevedon: Multilingual Matters.

Skutnabb-Kangas, T., & Toukomaa, P. (1976). *Teaching migrant children's mother tongue and learning the language of the host country in the context of the socio-cultural situation of the migrant family.* Helsinki: The Finnish National Commission for UNESCO.

Stern, H. H. (1978). French immersion in Canada: Achievements and directions. *Canadian Modern Language Review, 34*, 836–854.

Stern, H. H. (1984). The immersion phenomenon. *Language and Society, 12*, 4–7.

Swain, M. (1980). French immersion programs in Canada. *Multiculturalism, 4*, 3–6.

Swain, M., & Cummins, J. (1979). Bilingualism, cognitive functioning and education. *Language Teaching and Linguistics Abstracts.* Cambridge University Press Monographs.

Taylor, M. M. (1974). Speculations on bilingualism and the cognitive network. *Working Papers on Bilingualism, 2*, 68–124.

Tedesco, D. (1980). Problemi psicolinguistici della seconda generazione di emigrazione. *Rassegna Italiana di Linguistica Applicata, 12*, 253–278.

Titone, R. (1972). *Le bilinguisme précoce.* Bruxelles: Dessart.

Titone, R. (1979). Bilingual education today: Issues and perspectives. In R. Titone (Ed.), *Bilingual education* (pp. 31–46). Milano-Roma: Oxford Institutes Italiani.

Titone, R. (1983). Psycholinguistic variables of child bilingualism: Cognition and personality development. *Canadian Modern Language Review, 39*, 171–181.

Titone, R. (1984). Some personality dimensions in bilingual children. *Rassegna Italiana di Linguistica Applicata, 16*, 71–90.

Tosi, A. (1980). Bilingualismo e immigrazione: una nota sociolinguistica al piano europeo di mantenimento delle lingue nazionali nella comunità di emigrati. *Rassegna Italiana di Linguistica Applicata, 12,* 243–264.

Tosi, A. (1984). *Immigration and bilingual education.* Oxford: Pergamon Press.

Trites, R. A., & Price, M. A. (1978–1979). Specific learning disability in primary French immersion. *Interchange, 9,* 73–85.

Trites, R. L. (1976). Children with learning disabilities in primary French immersion. *Canadian Modern Language Review, 33,* 193–207.

CHAPTER 6

The Use of Creole as a School Medium and Decreolization in Haiti

ALBERT VALDMAN

1. INTRODUCTION: THE PLACE OF THE NATIVE LANGUAGE IN EDUCATION IN A CREOLE CONTEXT

Education in a multilingual context must have a dual objective: on the one hand, it must respect the dignity of the student and promote the vernacular culture by raising the status of the native language; on the other hand, it must allow students a certain level of participation in modern life and insure that they have some chance of social betterment by giving them access to their society's dominant language and to the major languages of international communication used in their region.

These two requirements are by no means easy to reconcile, and the task is made no simpler by a monolingual tradition which has long held sway in the schools and which considers them to be incompatible. Recourse to the vernacular language for basic instruction and free access to the dominant language are particularly difficult to harmonize in creole-speaking communities. This is due to the very nature of creole languages, or at least of those which are destined to be used side by side with their *lexifier* language. This term refers to a creole's former target language in the very special second-language learning situation of the plantation social context. The lexifier language provides the creole

This chapter is an adapted and translated version of an article published in *Language Problems and Language Planning, 10*(2), Summer, 1986, pp. 115–139. I would like to express my gratitude to Thomas Klingler for the translation.

ALBERT VALDMAN • CREDLI, Indiana University, Bloomington, Indiana 47405, USA.

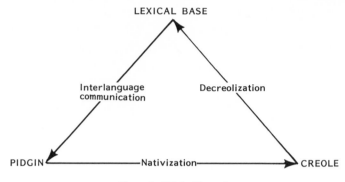

Figure 1. Pidgin life cycle.

with its units of expression: lexicon and grammatical forms.[1] The creole languages which find themselves in this situation—they in fact make up the majority—are condemned to an irremediable fate: having originated from the major languages of international communication in the modern world (English, French, Portuguese), they are doomed inevitably to merge with them through the process of decreolization.

The creole life cycle (Hall, 1962), represented in Figure 1, illustrates the trajectory of creole languages which develop in close contact with their lexifier language. Simplifying matters somewhat, it is possible to say that creole languages derive from an approximative version of a dominant language which was used to fulfill relatively limited communicative needs in an interlinguistic situation. In the presence of certain social factors, such as the demographic preponderance of nonnative speakers of the dominant language (Chaudenson, 1986), and the loss of the native languages of these speakers, this approximative version stabilized and became a language in its own right. It developed an autonomous linguistic structure clearly distinct from that of its lexifier language, while at the same time adopting virtually all of its vocabulary (see Table 1; Stein, 1984, p. 34). From a sociolinguistic perspective, the status of a creole language always remains subordinate to that of its lexifier. At least two consequences follow from this: (1) the creole language is perceived as a deviant form of the lexifier language by all members of the multilingual community in which the lexifier enjoys the status of dominant language; this attitude is reflected, for example, by the term *patois,* frequently used to refer to French-based

[1] We distinguish between the *content* of a language, or its semantic structure, and its *expression,* the means by which its content is manifested. Linguistic change affects expression less quickly than content, which is why many Haitian Creole terms still reflect their French origin, even though they have undergone deep transformations of meaning or grammatical function.

Table 1. Origin of Words Beginning with the Letter
k in Haitian and Seychelles Creole[a]

Origin	Haitian	Seychelles
French	92.3	85.6
English	0.3	3.7
Spanish or Portuguese	1.2	0.8
African	2.7	1.8
Caribbean	1.0	—
Malagasy	—	1.0
Indian	—	2.4
Other or unknown	2.5	4.3

[a] All numerical values are percentages.

creoles;[2] (2) the creole language is subject to structural pressure from the lexifier language, eventually disintegrating and thus losing its independence as an autonomous linguistic system; it ultimately forms with its lexifier a range of continuous variation called the post-creole continuum. This process, known as *decreolization,* makes any clear division between the creole and its lexifier impossible; at best, forms may be classified as basilectal (situated near the creole pole), acrolectal (situated near the pole constituted by the lexifier), or mesolectal (intermediate between the two poles).

It is common among creolists studying English-based creoles, most of which are heavily decreolized, to claim that languages of the same type which derive from French have better resisted this process (DeCamp, 1971). In fact, however, French-based creoles do not show the homogeneity often attributed to them, and moreover, their variability is due precisely to the effects of decreolization. In time, French-based creoles are in danger of succumbing to the same fate as their English counterparts. (For an overall view of English-based pidgins and creoles, see Hancock, 1985, and Todd, 1986.)

For communities where the use of a French-based creole (Créole) figures among the educational options, decreolization poses a delicate problem. Since Standard French and the local creole are mutually unintelligible, one might conceive of a bilingual type of instruction in which the vernacular would assume the function of a transitional working language, and in which the transition to French would take place as soon as students had acquired sufficient knowledge of the language, as well as the ability to read and write. But decreolization, by lessening the distance between French and the variety of Créole used in school textbooks, threatens to make this variety of their native language

---

[2] This name is used, in particular, for the French-based creoles which are in the process of dying out in the Lesser Antilles formerly under British rule: Dominica, Saint Lucia, and Trinidad.

opaque to monolingual speakers of Créole. As I try to show in this chapter, this is precisely the situation which is currently taking shape in Haiti, where an ambitious educational reform is opening the school gates to Creole, the developing vernacular language. But due to the complex diglossic situation between Haitian Creole and its lexifier language, the former tends to merge with the latter as it becomes standardized and instrumentalized.

I begin in section 2 by outlining the linguistic situation in Haiti, and I review the sociopsychological factors which determine speakers' attitudes toward the two languages of the country. In section 3 I describe the parameters of variation within Haitian Creole by identifying certain variables whose geographical and social variants are ordered according to the corresponding forms in French. It would be impossible to examine the role of Haitian Creole in the Haitian educational system without considering the question of developing an orthography for the vernacular language, especially insofar as the positions adopted by the developers and the linguistic communities reflect their attitudes concerning the relation between the two languages (section 4). I discuss in particular the notion of "transition to French," according to which Creole orthography should conform to that of the dominant language. Section 5 is devoted to the examination of recent written texts which reveal a conflict between two norms, one based on the daily speech of the monolingual rural masses, the other influenced by the use of the vernacular by privileged bilingual groups. This conflict, as I show, goes back to the earliest attempts to provide Creole with a written form and appears in the first written texts. Finally, in section 7 I describe the process of standardization and instrumentalization as it can be observed in the conscious efforts of editors and material developers, and in the use of Creole in communicative situations.

2. THE LINGUISTIC SITUATION IN HAITI

In his seminal article, Ferguson (1959) offers the coexistence of Haitian Creole and French in Haiti as a prototypical case of diglossia. In fact, however, the current linguistic situation in Haiti makes it difficult to place the coexistence of these two languages in the framework of classical diglossia. It is more appropriate to view the country as consisting of two linguistic communities, the urban middle class, which is indeed diglossic in the Fergusonian sense, and the rural masses, who are essentially monolingual speakers of Haitian Creole. Although middle-class children acquire French and Haitian Creole in the home, their use of the two languages is more or less complementary. For their rural counterparts or the urban lumpenproletariat, Haitian Creole assumes all language functions. Ever since Haitian Creole has gained wide access to radio, certain stations with a large rural audience, such as Radio Lumière, controlled by Protestant groups, and Radio Soleil, a service of the Haitian Catholic church, have been broadcasting programs primarily in the vernacular. School constitutes the primary vector for the penetration of French among the monolingual Creole-speaking masses. But this vector can have only a limited effect, since only about a third of rural school-aged children actually go to school, and most of them leave after 2 or 3 years of schooling.

At the national level, French has been recognized as the official language of the Republic since the Constitution of 1918, drafted under the aegis of the American occupation forces. In 1964, the first Duvalierist Constitution recommended the use of Creole in certain cases for "the protection of the material and moral interests of citizens who do not possess a sufficient knowledge of French." In 1979, by a presidential decree, Haitian Creole was officially recognized as classroom medium and as school subject at the primary school level. In the 1983 Constitution it was upgraded to the level of national language with French; the latter language, however, was to "serve" as official language. Finally, the last Constitution (1987) conferred on Haitian Creole the status of official language, equal to that of French.[3]

If we take the inequality of the languages of a community to be the central feature of diglossia, this relation characterizes the Haitian situation quite well. French, which is spoken by a minority, is dominant over Creole, the language shared by all Haitians and the only means of communication for approximately 90% of the population. But the various modifications made in official acts of linguistic policy since 1964 symbolize the upgrading of Haitian Creole and show that the linguistic situation in Haiti differs in its dynamic aspect from the stability inherent in classical diglossia. The notion of linguistic conflict proposed by Catalonian sociolinguists (Aracil, 1965; Ninyoles, 1960; Vallverdú, 1979) seems better able to describe the relationship that holds between French and Creole. According to authors who work with the notion of linguistic conflict—which I prefer to call by the more descriptive name of conflictual diglossia—this situation is resolved either by assimilation or by normalization. The first type of resolution leads to the glottophagic extension of the dominant language and, eventually, to the disappearance of the vernacular. The second al-

---

[3]There does exist one organization, the ONAAC (Office Nationale d'Alphabétisation et d'Action Communautaire), which succeeded the ONEC (Office National d'Education Communautaire), created around 1960. Although the ONAAC undertakes educational activities among adult illiterates, neither the ONAAC nor the ONEC have participated directly in standardization and instrumentalization programs. The three Haitian Creole spelling systems are the work of individuals or foreign groups. However, the IPN (Institut Pédagogique National) is now equipped with specialists authorized to assume tasks of standardization and instrumentalization within the framework of the current educational reform. The CLA (Centre Linguistique Appliquée) of Port-au-Prince, a branch of the State University of Haiti, is currently carrying out specialized research which contributes directly to standardization: lexicographical studies, studies of linguistic variation (in particular, the Linguistic Atlas of Haiti), and discussions of standardization strategies (Vernet, 1980).

ternative leads to the valorization of the vernacular and, possibly, to a variety
of language planning measures designed to make it suitable for use in prestigious domains (administration, education, etc.) formerly reserved for the dominant language. It is in the latter direction that Haitian Creole is headed; still,
the particular conditions of its origin and the continued presence, in the community where it is spoken, of its lexifier language make its progress difficult
and the completion of the normalization process improbable under current economic, political, and social conditions.

Conflictual diglossia is manifested by a profound ambivalence toward the
coexisting languages on the part of the competing groups of the community:
the privileged classes who have a command of the dominant language and the
dominated classes who use the subordinate language almost exclusively. Among
middle-class bilinguals in Haiti this ambivalence takes the form of affective ties
which attach an individual to his or her native language. It is also manifested
by the valorization of the so-called African heritage which includes voodoo and
Haitian Creole. But among bilinguals this valorization of the vernacular goes
hand in hand with strong feelings of loyalty toward the cultural heritage of the
colonial past, of which the French language is the most salient aspect. Indeed,
a crucial element in the explosion of Haitian nationalist sentiment in the 1930s
and 1940s was the claim to a dual cultural identity, whose vehicles were French
and Haitian Creole. This dual identity was raised up as a bulwark against what
was perceived to be American cultural imperialism and the spread of English,
the instrument of this cultural invasion.[4] All Haitians share the same symbolic
values associated with French and Creole; the differences between bilinguals
and monolinguals show up in relation to their relative level of access to the
dominant language.

3. VARIATION IN HAITIAN CREOLE

According to Fleischmann (1984), the linguistic behavior of bilingual Haitians is governed by what he terms ''diglossic phantasm.'' Fleischmann, who
carried out a sociolinguistic survey among speakers in the process of integration
into the lower working class of Port-au-Prince, believes that monolingual speakers
are implicated in conflictual diglossia even though they do not know French.
They might, for example, affect pseudo-French, using terms that sound more
French than the corresponding authentic words:

---

[4] In the linguistic domain, this current was revealed in the elite's opposition to the McConnell–
Laubach orthography, perceived as a veritable Trojan horse of English.

(1)

Standard French	Haitian Creole	Pseudo-French
remerciement	remesye	remesisman
en général	an jeneral	an generalman
décision	deside	desidasyon

But the primary way in which monolingual speakers participate in diglossia is through the choice of variants from among the vernacular's relatively small set of variable features.[5] Indeed, the homogeneity of Haitian Creole is striking when one considers that the rural population is very spread out and that many areas are not served by roads, and are thus cut off from the rest of the country. Most of the geographical variables are phonological and lexical (Orjala, 1970; Valdman, 1978). Generally, a central form used in the Port-au-Prince region and spreading to the other regions of the country contrasts with peripheral variants found in the north, in the south, or on the island of Gonave:

(2) *Geographical variation oriented toward Standard French*

Standard French	Central (Port-au-Prince)	South	North
arachide	pistach		amizman
panier	makout		dyakout
bougie	bouji		chandèl
marmite	mamit		kanistè
plaisanter	jwe	badinen	jwe
"progressive verb marker"	ap	ape/pe	ap

The variants shown in (2) are neutral in relation to the Haitian-Creole–French axis, which is not the case, however, for a large number of variables for which the central form approximates the corresponding French form, while the peripheral form remains distinct from it:

(3) *Geographical variation oriented toward Standard French*

Standard French (SF)	Central variant	Peripheral variant
soif	swaf	swaf/swèf
déjà	deja	dija
sage	saj	say/chay/chaz/saj
ail	lay	laj
orange	zoranj	zorany

[5] By *variable* we mean a linguistic feature that is subject to variation, such as the French *un* of *brun* (brown), which is pronounced [œ] or [ẽ], depending on the speaker. The particular realization of a variable is a *variant:* thus the two variants of the variable *un* are [œ] and [ẽ].

A fourth set of variables involves a contrast between urban and rural variants. The former are to be found among urban bilinguals, while the latter characterize monolingual speakers; obviously, any speaker may alternate between the two variants:

(4) *Social variation (urban versus rural)*

SF	Urban	Rural
riz	duri	diri
soeur	sèu(r)	sè
deux	deu	de
famille	famiy	fanmiy
jambe	janb	janm
cendre	sand	sann

The variants listed under (4) arise from differences in phonological inventory or from differences in the distribution of certain phonemes. Monolingual speakers generally do not have the front-rounded vowels (/y ø œ/) or sequences of nasal vowels + voiced stops (/b d g/), and they tend to nasalize vowels in the context of a nasal consonant. These features—in particular the front-rounded vowels—are subject to hypercorrection, that is, to the use of the "high" (socially preferred) variant in contexts where it is not permitted in the high form. Thus a little girl, when asked what term she used to refer to the ribbon she wore in her hair, answered *son neu* (sõ nø) (it's a ribbon), which represented the perfectly correct form of the high variant (the low variant being *ne* [sõ ne]). But when I asked her for the equivalent of *nez* (nose), she produced *neu:* she had generalized the use of the rounded vowel and had substituted it for an invariable form pronounced *nen* in both the high and low varieties of Haitian Creole.

4. THE QUESTION OF SPELLING

Diglossic phantasm also arises in the course of discussions about the choice of an orthographic system: among some bilinguals it takes the form of a rejection of any spelling of Haitian Creole that renders the language unrecognizable to readers who are familiar with French spelling. Many cultured Haitians claim that they are unable to read autonomous spelling systems based on the phonology of contemporary spoken Haitian Creole. They prefer an etymological representation which relates Creole words to their corresponding French cognates.[6] In (5) we contrast one of the autonomous orthographies, the so-called

[6]Georges Sylvain (1901), the author of a collection of fables adopted from LaFontaine, is to be credited for having attempted to develop a systematic etymologically based orthography, an undertaking which was, unfortunately, doomed to failure, as our samples in (5) show. The etymo-

IPN (Institute Pédagogique National) notation, which serves as Haiti's official orthography, with two of the most systematic etymological orthographies:

(5) *Autonomous versus etymological spelling*

IPN (autonomous)	Sylvain (etymological)	Berry (etymological)
tout chen genyen	toutt chien gangnin	tout chin gain'ien
pis	piç'	puce
avék moso	avec moceau viann	avèc morceau
vyann nan gyòl (djòl) li	nan guiol li	vienne nan guiol li
yon lòt chen, lèd, volè, gwo je	Gnou lott chien, laidd, vòlè, gros gé	Youn laute chin, laide, voleur, gro jé

For the monolingual learner, any orthographic convention which deviates from a one-to-one correspondence between phoneme and graphic sign renders the orthographic code potentially more abstract and thus more difficult to master, especially where writing is concerned. Thus in order to restore the *r* of *morceau* and final *e*'s which do not correspond to any spoken sound, the learner must memorize the graphic forms of these particular words.

Among supporters of the various competing autonomous orthographies, arguments for or against a particular system revolve around a reduced number of choices of graphic conventions (see [6]):

(6) *Moot points in the elaboration of phonological orthographies*

IPA	McConnell–Laubach (Anglo-Saxons 1943)	IPN-official (French 1975)	Faublas-Pressoir (Haitians 1945)
ẽ	ê	en	in
in	in	in	i-n
ĩ	î	in	in
ẽn	ên	enn	inn
ɛn	èn	èn	èn
ã	â	an	an
an	an	àn	a-n
wa	wa	wa	oua
wo	wo	wo	ouo
jo	yo	yo	yo
pje	pyé/pié	pye	pié

logical spelling of Berry (1964), developed in response to the systematic orthographies of Mc-Connell–Laubach and Faublas–Pressoir, reveals confusion concerning the choice of strategy in adult education in Haiti.

McConnell and Laubach, who proposed the first autonomous orthography for Haitian Creole, simply adapted the phonological transcription of forms of the language by the IPA (the alphabet of the International Phonetics Association) contained in the first serious description of the language (Sylvain, 1936).[7] Their system hardly deserves the accusation of being a Trojan horse for the spread of English nor the nickname of Anglo-Saxon orthography, which were used against it by some members of the bilingual elite at the time. They in fact chose *ch* for /š/ (instead of English *sh*) and even adopted *i* to represent the semivowel /j/ before a vowel. The McConnell–Laubach orthography rejected only three French spelling conventions: the use of combinations of vowels + *n* for nasal vowels, the digraph *ou* to represent /w/, and the combination *oi* for the sequence /wa/. The circumflex accent was chosen in place of the tilde to indicate vowel nasalization because printers in Port-au-Prince did not have the latter symbol. The examples in (6) show clearly that only the diacritical solution which uses a circumflex accent to distinguish a nasal vowel from its oral counterpart allows for the unambiguous and perfectly univocal representation of Haitian Creole nasal vowels.

Although the Faublas–Pressoir system—the only one designed by a team composed exclusively of Haitians—is the closest to French, the three phonologically based autonomous systems differ little from each other. It would therefore be difficult to conduct any experiments to demonstrate empirically that any one of them would be more effective in teaching monolinguals to read and write, on the one hand, or would facilitate the transition to French, on the other. For more than 40 years the polemics surrounding the choice of an orthography have revolved around the notion of the transition to French, as if simply endowing Haitian Creole with an orthographic code modeled directly on that of French would facilitate the learning of the dominant language by a population that is almost totally cut off from it (Dejean, 1980). It nonetheless remains true that, as Pressoir (1947, p. 68), speaking on behalf of many illiterates, pointed out, "in the minds of the people, reading is tied to the study of French, or to the more or less vague hope of one day being able to speak and write French." One is inclined to believe that the diglossic phantasm encourages illiterate monolingual speakers of Haitian Creole to prefer a frenchifying spelling because it gives them the illusion of opening the way to the mastery of French.

The semiofficialization of the IPN orthography has had the effect of toning down discussions about orthography.[8] But the symbolic value that certain so-

---

[7] Actually, as early as 1872 an autonomous systematic orthography had been developed for Guyanese Creole by A. de Saint-Quentin (1872). This orthography, which unfortunately was not known in Haiti, is almost identical to the Faublas–Pressoir orthography.

[8] Strictly speaking the IPN orthography does not have official status. The 1979 decree only recommends its use and specifies, moreover, that its use is experimental. Aside from didactic texts

cial groups attach to etymological orthography shows up in other ways. French-ifying spellings appear on billboards, which are beginning to offer messages in the vernacular, in advertisements and announcements written on walls, and in the rare articles written in Creole that appear in the Port-au-Prince daily press. The following excerpt (7) from *Panorama,* a Port-au-Prince daily newspaper, offers a quite representative example of the foregoing, from both the point of view of linguistic forms and the point of view of spelling:[9]

(7) *Foc cé li*

> Tiré à 30.000 exemplaires oun numéro Bon Nouvèl à 50 centimes ba ou matière réflexion pour toute oun mois. Cé là dans l'nous ouè travail super salauds qui pas reculé devant aucun infamie pour avili pays a lan z'yeux étranger.
>
> Dévelopman tèt anba Mézanmi, nan kesksyon chak koukouil kléré pou jé l'la. Min ginyin ki pi grav pasé lot. Gin yon zon koté m'konn passé chak jou pou m'al lékol. Grangou ac mizè vlé fini ak maléré nan zon sa a.
>
> (*Panorama* 11-2-85)

This article praises *Bon Nouvèl,* a monthly magazine published exclusively in Creole with a circulation of over 30,000, which regularly exposes the excesses of certain officials. Note that the passage quoted by *Panorama* follows the Faublas–Pressoir orthography, with the exception of spelling errors introduced by *Panorama: koukouil* for *koukouy* 'firefly', *passé* for *pasé* 'than' (in the comparative ''more . . . than'' sense), and *ac* for *ak* 'with'.

5. CONFLICT OF NORMS IN THE STANDARDIZATION OF HAITIAN CREOLE

To sum up what has been said thus far, even illiterate monolinguals who are incapable of producing a simple utterance in French participate in diglossia in that the only language available to them is one they hold in low esteem. In formal situations, and especially when writing, there is considerable pressure upon them to use those variants which are nearest to French, the dominant language and the desired, but rarely accessible, target. As for the favored class, its interests lead it in the same direction.

Confronted with this situation, language planners might opt for a frenchi-fying norm, arguing that it would conform to the attitudes of the concerned parties. Thus Pressoir (1947, p. 66) criticizes the authors of the McConnell–

produced by the IPN, national organizations, which distribute very few publications in Haitian Creole, do not use this orthography.

[9] The meaning of this text is relatively accessible to French readers, except for the title, *Foc cé li,* literally ''it must be it,'' which, among other things, refers to the most ordinary staple food in Haiti, cornmeal porridge.

Laubach orthography for choosing a depreciated variety of Haitian Creole, as well as for the use of the ''Anglo-Saxon'' letters *y* and *w:*

> not knowing our idiom well enough to grasp its nuances, [McConnell] tries only to render the vowels of ''gros créole'' [basilectal Haitian Creole], without taking into account doublets which are used not only in the speech of cultivated Haitians, but also in the language of a considerable number of proletarians mixed in the mass of those who speak ''gros créole.''

Pressoir is alluding here to front-rounded vowels which, as we have seen, constitute a stereotypical feature of frenchifying Creole.

The other alternative is to forge a norm which might be qualified as basilectal. Bernabé (1983), drawing his inspiration from the principle of *maximal deviance,* proposes a constructed norm for Martinique: not only is the acrolectal variant rejected, but Bernabé resorts to creation or to borrowing from a related variety to fill gaps in the vernacular. Thus, *prolétè* gives way to *madÿendÿen* and *révolution* to *wanboulzay* (Prudent, 1983). As Prudent (1983, p. 38) notes, this strategy ''leads straight to purism and to the separation from the speech usage of the masses.'' The Mauritian Baissac offers a less interventionist solution (1880, pp. LI–LII):

> Thus if Creole can today say equivalently: *Quand vous va reconte li, dire li ça mo te pale av vous,* or *L'heure wou azouinde li, cause li ça qui mo té cause sembe wou,* it appears obvious to us that the second version is truer than the first. Creole must have begun by saying *l'heure* rather than *quand; joindre* rather than *rencontrer; causer* rather than *parler;* and *ensemble* rather than *avec.* Likewise, the form *ou li to manman* is later than *a côte to manman?; pourquoi vous batte-moi* is later than *Qui fère ou batte moi?; Passequi to té fronté* is later than *cause to ti fronté,* etc . . . etc . . .

The point, of course, is not to retain the oldest form, but the one which differs most from the corresponding form in Standard French.

The problem of choosing a norm emerged in Haiti as soon as the need was felt to endow the vernacular with a writing system. The two samples below, illustrating written Haitian Creole usage of the late colonial and early postindependence periods, clearly show decreolization in process:

(8) *Decreolization in early texts*

> (a) Two versions of a song collected by educated members of the colonial elite:

Moreau de Saint-Méry, 1797	Idylles et Chansons de Saint-Domingue, 1811
Lisette quitté la plaine	Lizette *toi* quitté la plaine
Mon perdi *Bonher* à *moué*	Mo perdu *Bonheur* à *moi*
Gié à moin semblé	Gié à *moi* tourné
fontaine	fontaine
Depi mon pa miré *toué.*	Dipi mo pa miré *toi.*

> . . . La nuit guand mon
> dans cabane
> Dans dromi mon quimbé
> *toué.*

> La nuit quan mo dan
> cabane
> Dan dromi ma songé
> *toi.*

(b) Comte de Rosiers, l'Entrée du Roi en sa capitale en janvier 1818.[10]

A force nou brûlé d'envie et d'impatience, mo craire tête à toute monde va tourné folle, quant à coeur à moé li après palpité, li dans délire tant comme prémié fois gié à moé té contré quienne à toé . . . *n'a pas pitit composé li va composé* dans tête à li, tant mo vlé toute zoizeaux pé dans bois pou io tendé mo chanté.

(c) Proclamations of General Leclerc, 1802.

(i) Brumaire An 10
Consuls la Répiblique Francé a tout zabitans
Saint-Domingue, Zabitants, et vous tous qui dans
Saint-Domingue. Qui ça vous tout yé, qui
couleur vous yé, qui côté papa zote vini, nous
pas gardé ça: nous savé seleman *que* zote tout
libre, *que* zote tout égal, douvant bon Dieu
dans zyé la Répiblique . . .
(ii) Pluriôse An 10
Lire Proclamation primié Consul Bonaparte voyez
pour zote. Zote à voir *que* li vélé nègues resté
libre . . . Li va mainteni commerce et culture,
parce que zote doit conné *que* sans ça, colonie
pas cable prospéré. Ça li promé zote li va
rempli li fidellement.

Text (8b), taken from a play in which, following the example set by Molière, characters of the popular classes speak to each other in the vernacular, differs from (8c) in certain syntactic expressions which French does not possess. The most salient feature of (8b) is the emphatic structure which makes use of a preposed nominal copy of the verb: *n'a pas pitit composé li va composé dans tête à li* ("it won't be little the composition that he will compose in his head"). This expression is absent from earlier texts and thus serves as a link between the 1818 sample and contemporary Haitian Creole. Another feature which could be qualified as basilectal is the absence of a complementizer in *mo vlé toute zoizeaux pé* ("I would like for all of the birds to be silent"); in the frenchifying Haitian Creole of today the complementizer *ke* (often pro-

---

[10] This is the title borne by Juste Chanlatte, the official poet at the court of King Christophe. I learned of this important text, a "vaudeville opera" in honor of the monarch, through a reproduction of the only copy available in Haiti in the Sunday edition of the Port-au-Prince daily, *Le Nouvelliste*. In addition to a first act in which two representatives of the common people of the Northern Kingdom's capital (Cap Haïtien) converse exclusively in Haitian Creole, the play contains an excerpt in dialectal French modeled on that of the peasants in Moliere's *Dom Juan*, and another in approximative French which is intended to render the speech of an English officer. The same kind of variability, an example of decreolization, characterizes the earliest texts written in English-based creole (see Rickford, 1985).

nounced with a final mute *e*) would be inserted at the beginning of the noun clause.

Text (8c), the first sample known to us of the use of Haitian Creole for administrative purposes, may be seen as a predecessor of recent initiatives to broaden the vernacular's domains of use. These initiatives are clearly basilectal in orientation, and have for the most part been undertaken by what Haitians call the private sector. These are denominational groups which, while maintaining a certain religious aim, contribute at least as much as government organisms do to the education of the monolingual rural masses within the framework of community development.

Nearly all Haitian Creole writings in this tradition—of which pastor McConnell's work opens the modern period—have either a religious or a utilitarian character—translations of the Old and New Testaments, of the catechism, and the like, and guides to hygiene and rural development. Protestant groups were the first to recognize the importance of the use of the vernacular in winning souls. In 1944–1945 they launched the monthly *Limié Fòs Progrè,* published exclusively in Haitian Creole, and in 1965 began to publish a second monthly, *Boukan.* The Catholic church caught up in 1967 with the founding of *Bon Nouvèl,* a monthly whose current circulation is about 30,000, the highest of any Haitian periodical.

While it is true that certain religious figures of foreign origin played an important role in this movement—notably McConnell, a Northern Irishman, and the Dutch-speaking Belgian Ceuppens, founder of *Bon Nouvèl*—the tasks of translating, adapting, and creating were for the most part performed by Haitians (Carrié Paultre, editor of *Boukan* and author of edifying novels; Roger Désir, the main translator of the Bible; Pauris Jean-Baptiste, compiler of proverbs and author of several collections of stories and a novel, to name just the most widely known). One of the distinguishing features of this basilectally oriented movement is the use of an autonomous orthography, first the McConnell–Laubach system, then the Faublas–Pressoir spelling—in which most Haitian Creole writing is published—and, today, the semiofficial IPN orthography. This tendency is joined by lay writers who write for a cultivated public: Sylvain (1901), who adapted the fables of LaFontaine in *Cric? Crac!*; Fouché (1950) and Morisseau-Leroy (1953), who in the 1950s adapted the Greek plays *Oedipus the King* and *Antigone,* using an etymological orthography; and, more recently, Céléstin-Mégie (1975) and Franketienne (1975), authors who have made names for themselves in all literary genres, including the novel, and who adhere strictly to systematic orthographies.

The educational reform of the Ministry of National Education marked an important turning point in the standardization and instrumentalization of Haitian Creole. Not only has this massive effort on the part of the state meant a significant increase in written Creole—texts for teaching reading and writing, books on mathematics, the natural sciences, history, and geography, and teachers' manuals—but, supported by specialized personnel with training in the various language sciences, it also provides a level of technical specialization and a certain reflection which was lacking in the private sector. However, these government initiatives are not accompanied by the use of the vernacular in the administrative domain. Paradoxically, the only administrative texts which we have been able to gather are press releases aimed at the general public and translated from French by the information service of the American Embassy in Port-au-Prince (U.S.I.S.). These texts vary considerably in their normative orientation, undoubtedly according to the chosen translator/adaptor, but, like (8c), they show the danger than threatens Haitian Creole when it penetrates the administrative sphere. The texts that we have chosen as examples illustrate the two commonly used autonomous orthographies:

(9) Typical administrative texts

    (a) Basilectal: Faublas–Pressoir:
        Yon lòt bagay ankò Ambasad la ta vle fè nou *chonje:*
        depi kons*il* la dakò pou bay viza-a, l ap *rinmèt* moun
        lan yon to kat. Se kat-sa-a *pou* li prezante nan Kon-
        s*il*a-a pou yo ka *rinmèt* li paspò yo ak tout viza-a . . .

    (b) Intermediate: IPN
        . . . senk lot moun ki t'ap eseye rantre *anbachal*
        Ozetazini. Gad Kot ameriken yo fè yon rapò sou yon
        ti bato *ke* you bato patrouy yo jwenn sou lanmè
        Ozetazini a minwi pase. Kidonk, yo te considere yo
        kankou "etranje *ke* yo gen dwa *ekspulse*".

    (c) Acrolectal: IPN
        An juen 1984, Ajans Ameriken pou Devlopman Intèna-
        syonal siyen yon akò ak Kwa *R*ouj Ayisyen pou yon valè
        de preske yon demi milyon dolà pou projè kominote
        *U*ben Nan *Vil Sekondè* . . . Depi juen pou rive j*us*
        desanm 1984 . . . Si nou ajoute fanmi yo, nou kapab
        di *ke* 16.500 moun benefi*ci*e direkman *de* projè-*an* nan
        twa vil yo.

    The texts produced as part of the educational reform opt for a basilectal norm, as is indicated by the following variants used in a reading textbook, *Pol ak Anita: ditou* 'at all' instead of *dutou; ze* 'egg' instead of *zeu; lè* 'when' instead of *lèu; misye* 'man' instead of *msyeu; koumanse* 'commencer' instead of *komanse; moute* 'to begin' instead of *monte.*

    Text (9a) opts for *chonje/sonje* 'to remember' containing an assimilation marked as a rural feature, nasalization in *renmèt/remèt* 'to transmit', and the absence of a front-rounded vowel in *konsil* and *konsila* 'consulate'. Texts (9b) and (9c) are characterized by acrolectal morpho-syntactic features: the use of the complementizers *ke* and *de* where basilectal Haitian Creole expresses the relation of dependence by parataxis. Text (9c) also shows variables which are realized by front-rounded vowels (*jus/jis* 'just', *uben/iben* 'urban'). The last two texts borrow freely from French: *Ozetazini* instead of *peyi zetazini* 'United States'; *ekspulse* 'to expel'; *vil sekondè* 'minor town'; *beneficie [sic]* 'to bene-fit'. In contrast text (9b) contains basilectal *kankou/tankou* 'as' and the typically vernacular expression *anbachal* 'covertly, illegally'. Finally, only text (9a) ad-heres rigorously to an adopted orthographic system, while the other two contain frenchifying "mistakes" such as *considere* for *konsidere* 'to consider'; *benefi-cie* for *benefisye; Rouj* for *Wouj* 'red'.[11] Considering the symbolic value which is attached to spelling—in particular to letters such as *c* and *r*—these deviations are very revealing.

6. STANDARDIZATION AND INSTRUMENTALIZATION AT WORK

One of the remarkable aspects of the standardization of Haitian Creole is the degree of homogeneity achieved by a written language which lacks nor-mativizing institutions (academies, state organizations, and academic tradition, etc.). Not a single text exists which contains clearly regional features, such as the expression of the possessive by means of the function word *a* (*papa a mwen* vs. *papa mwen* 'my father'), characteristic of northern speech. We can observe how this standardization works by comparing certain texts submitted to the monthly *Bon Nouvèl*, the main producer of written Creole in Haiti, and which has a large audience, to their final published versions.[12]

The editorial staff of *Bon Nouvèl*, though their orientation is basilectal, make an attempt to strike a middle ground between two extreme varieties of Haitian Creole: one that is purified of all clearly frenchifying features and one that eliminates any features that are strongly marked as regional or too rural

---

[11] In Haitian Creole the distinction between /w/ and /r/ (realized as a dorso-velar resonant) is neu-tralized before rounded (grave) vowels. A phonologically based orthography would call for the use of *w* for the last two words. In writing these words with *r*, the Faublas–Pressoir system takes a step toward an etymologizing representation. Since the deletion of *r* in postvocalic position is one of the features which distinguishes Haitian Creole words from their corresponding French forms, this phoneme—and its graphic representation—takes on symbolic value. In French the letter *k* is found only in words borrowed from foreign languages or of Greek origin. It is therefore perceived as marginal in relation to the spellings *c* and *qu*, which are more frequent and which, moreover, complement each other systematically in the representation of /k/. In a short-lived attempt to frenchify the Faublas–Pressoir orthography, *k* was replaced by *c* and *qu*. (Pompilus, 1973).

[12] I would like to thank the staff of *Bon Nouvèl*, and in particular its editor, Pè Anri, for having made available to me the originals of the texts received by the periodical in 1984 and during the first months of 1985.

(this constitutes what is called *rèk* 'coarse, crude' speech). In the absence of any codification of Haitian Creole, these judgments are obviously intuitive, but they nonetheless serve as indicators.

On the phonological level, none of the original texts we examined contained front-rounded vowels, which reinforces our claim that these constitute a highly stereotyped frenchifying feature. In contrast, the line drawn for nasalization appears to be very fine: the editors insert nasal vowels for *plèn/plenn* 'plain' and *abandone/abandonnen* 'abandon', but take an opposite stance for *premye/prenmye* 'first', *lamizè/lanmizè* 'misery, poverty', and *telefone/telefonen* 'to telephone.' This last case is surprising—perhaps it is simply a slip—because it is an instance of a general rule which nasalizes the final *-e* of a verb stem after a nasal consonant. In any event, vowel nasalization constitutes one of the elements of Haitian Creole phonology which is subject to considerable variation and for which it would be premature to impose uniform standards.

On the level of morpho-syntax, standardization eliminates the relational morphemes *de* and *ke: atik (de) Enot Terrier* 'the article by Enot Terrier'; *mwen mande (ke) bon Dye kenbe ou fenm* 'I ask that God keep you', which becomes *mwen mande pou Bon Dye*. The editors correct the southern form *ape/pe* of the progressive marker *ap,* as well as characteristic "errors" in the use of the nominal particularizer; they remove it in *yo pa ka achte sik-la* 'they can't buy any sugar', where the noun has the value of a partitive, but they insert it in *jou 6 desanm (-nan)* 'December 6' and *devan katedral (-la)* 'in front of the cathedral,' where the noun refers to a presupposed entity.[13]

On the lexical level the modifications that have been adopted underline the dilemma which confronts language planners in a creolizing diglossic situation. The editors of *Bon Nouvèl* try to eliminate terms borrowed from French whenever alternatives exist: thus *koman* is replaced by *kijan* 'how', *sa pa regade yo* 'that's none of their business' by *sa pa gade yo*, or *nèg Matinikè* 'Martinican' by *nèg Matinik*. But the danger of decreolization, which is headed off here, turns up again elsewhere. In attempting to achieve greater precision of expression, the editors usually managed to stick to Haitian Creole, as when *mete yo nan yon ti chanm* 'put them in a small room' becomes *fèmen yo . . . .* ; *touye yo* 'kill them' is replaced by *pete fyèl yo* 'crush their gallbladders'; or *yo pati* 'they have left' gives way to *yo derape* 'they are setting out, they are on their way'. But in other cases precision is gained at the price of frenchifying: *sistèm esklavai* for *sistem esklav* 'slavery system', *pwofitè yo* for *nèg k ap viv sou do ti pov komesan yo* 'guys who live at the expense of the small merchants', or

---

[13] In Haitian Creole the particularizer has several different realizations depending on the preceding phonological context. If *la* is posited as the underlying form, then *l* is deleted after a vowel, the vowel nasalizes after a nasal vowel, and *l* optionally becomes *n* after a nasal consonant. Actually, this rule does not provide a complete explanation of the variation, since the realization of the particularizer constitutes a social and stylistic variable in the process of evolution.

yo flanke yo nan prizon for *yo fèmen yo nan prizon* 'they put them in prison'.

In a nation with an illiteracy rate of over 80%, the written word is only one of the factors which will determine the development of the vernacular. Not only is the transistor radio available to even the most disadvantaged peasants today, but cassette recordings constitute the most practical means of communication between Haitians of the interior and members of the North American diaspora. We must therefore take into consideration the nature of radio speech. The norms which are targets for immigrants in Brooklyn, Miami, and Boston, on the one hand, and for the producers and announcers of various radio stations, on the other, have a significant influence on the evolution of Haitian Creole. Cassette recordings, for example, are the intermediary through which English, the third contender in the linguistic competition in Haiti, is likely to have a noticeable effect.

In the absence of studies of radio speech, a commentary on a single radio broadcast sample must suffice. This sample is particularly significant in that it was produced by A., a figure who plays an important role in the production of written Creole. He combines the roles of author, developer of pedagogical materials, and language planner.

In (10) and (11) we contrast a text written by A. which shows the search for internal creation in order to express scientific—in this case linguistic—concepts with statements about certain psychiatric aspects of Carnival, made spontaneously in the course of a radio broadcast:

(10)

> Laplipa lekòl lengis yo, laplipa gwoup lengis yo, pou plis presizyon, yo derefize pale de "mo". Gen yon lengis franse, misye André Martinet ki pale li menm de "monèm". Yon monèm dapre *mouche* André Martinet se: yon gwoup fonèm ki gen sans. Nou deja konnen: yon "fonèm" se yonn nan tout kolonn son yo jwenn nan fondalnatal yon lang . . .

(11)

> . . . tout bagay ki pwent*u* . . . senbolikman li re*u*prezante . . . donk on sòt d*eu* rapò antr*eu* fiy (femme) e gason (homme) menm si moun nan pa panse a sa d*u* tou . . . menm enkonsyaman nan on sans pwofon se sa l senbolize bagay sa yo menm si nou pa konsyan d*eu* sa.

Despite many borrowings from French to render technical terms, A. gives (10) a basilectal tone through the use of the basilectal term *mouche* 'mister', the variant *derefize* for *refize* 'refuse', and the ordinary terms *kolonn* 'large quantity' and *fondalnatal* 'fundamental' to express the concepts of entirety and of core or foundation, respectively. In (11), in contrast, we find a collection of French words connected by Creole syntax and characterized, moreover, by numerous cases of the use of front-rounded vowels.

The apparently contradictory behavior of A. is to be found among the majority of proponents of a basilectal norm. It by no means reflects their inconsistency but rather the unconscious social pressures which govern the use of Haitian Creole among members of the bilingual subcommunity. It is most likely that these same authors use fewer acrolectal variants when they speak with monolinguals. It is just as likely, on the other hand, that monolinguals, when speaking with bilinguals, accommodate to them by aiming at a more mesolectal norm than the one that governs their interactions with members of their own group.

7. CONCLUSION

Paradoxically, the extension of Haitian Creole to new domains of use leads to decreolization and threatens its autonomy in relation to French. We have seen that many factors favor the use of forms resembling those of the dominant language:

1. For many social and geographical variables, the valorized variant—found either in the central zones or among privileged groups—proves to be the one which differs least from the corresponding form in the dominant language.
2. The need for precision in written Haitian Creole encourages authors and producers of written texts to borrow from the dominant language, especially since, in the absence of planned instrumentalization, the creation of new terminology is insufficient to keep pace with the expansion of the vernacular's uses.
3. In formal situations or when speaking to their peers, bilingual Haitians make use of frenchifying variants. Thus when they read and, in particular, when they listen to the radio, monolinguals are exposed to a great number of frenchifying variants. Furthermore, given the symbolic value of French for the monolingual masses, they are encouraged to attempt the highest level of frenchifying appropriate to a particular speech situation.

The decreolization of Haitian Creole could be checked by a vigorous program of standardization and instrumentalization. An organization should be created which would be capable of instituting certain norms for written texts and for broadcast speech and which would be given the means necessary for a massive production of texts illustrating these norms. The private sector, which has always taken the initiative in these domains, does not have sufficient means at its disposal to initiate and maintain such actions on a large scale. As for government organizations, they are not ready to fill the gaps, despite the recent expansion of their activity.

Commenting on lexical and stylistic development in written Haitian Creole, Bentolila and Ganni (1983, p. 55) state:

> texts written in Haitian Creole today have the value of *proposals,* whatever may be the basis of the choices made. What is important is the capacity of the newly literate to use these propositions to create their own linguistic practices and, according to their communicative intentions, adapted forms of written discourse.

It is unrealistic to expect a population that is for the most part illiterate and deprived of economic and political power to take charge of the instrumentalization of its own vernacular. This responsibility falls to the privileged classes, some of whom—the ones we have grouped together under the term private sector—have fully assumed it. For the undertaking to be successfully carried out, these groups must be joined by others, as well as by government organizations. Otherwise, the written forms of Haitian Creole are apt to decreolize, becoming too distant from the varieties spoken by monolinguals. They then may begin to wonder whether their interests would not be better served by educating their children directly in the dominant language, rather than by the transitional use of a version of the vernacular language which they no longer recognize as their own.

REFERENCES

Anon. (1811). *Idylles et chansons ou essais de poésie créole. Par un habitant d'Hayti.* Philadelphia: J. Edwards. 2nd Edition (Repr. 1821?). *Idylles ou essais de poésie créole, par un colon de Saint-Domingue.* Cahors: Combarieu, imprimeur de la Préfecture.

Aracil, L. (1965). *Conflit linguistique et normalisation linguistique dans l'Europe nouvelle.* Nancy: Centre Universitaire Européen.

Baissac, C. (1880). *Etude sur la patois créole mauricien.* Nancy: Imprimerie Berger-Levrault et Cie.

Bentolila, A., & Ganni, L. (1983). Langues créoles et éducation. *Espace Créole, 5 (Recherches actuelles pour les aires créolophones),* pp. 43–58.

Bernabé, J. (1983). *Fondal-natal: Grammaire basilectale approchée des créoles guadeloupéen et martiniquais* (3 vol.). Paris: L'Harmattan.

Berry, P. C. (1964). *R & D in applied psychology and linguistics for mass education.* Croton-on-Hudson, NY: Hudson Institute. (Appendix: Writing Haitian Creole: Issues and proposals for orthography. Hudson Institute, documents HI-458-D and HI-458-D-A.)

Céléstin-Mégie, E. (1975). *Lanmou pa gin baryè* (Première Période). Port-au-Prince: Editions Fardin.

Chaudenson, R. (1985). Norme, variation, créolisation. *AILA Review/Revue de l'AILA, 2* pp. 69–88.

Constitution de la République d'Haïti. (1983). Le Moniteur, samedi 27 août 1983. Titre III, Article 62.

DeCamp, D. (1971). Toward a generative analysis of a post-creole speech continuum. In D. Hymes (Ed.), *Pidginization and creolization of languages* (pp. 349–370). Cambridge: Cambridge University Press.

Dejean, Y. (1980). *Comment écrire le crèol d'Haïti?* Outremont (Québec): Collectif Paroles.

Ferguson, C. A. (1959). Diglossia. *Word, 15,* 325–340.

Fleischmann, U. (1984). Language, literacy, and development. In C. R. Foster & A. Valdman (Eds.), *Haiti: Today and tomorrow. An interdisciplinary study* (pp. 101–118). Lanham, MD: University Press of America.

Fouché, F. (1950). *Oedipe-Roi.* Port-au-Prince. Editions Fardin.

Franketienne. (1975). *Dèzafi.* Port-au-Prince: Editions Fardin.

Hall, R. A., Jr. (1962). The 'life cycle' of pidgin languages. *Lingua, 11,* 151–56.

Hancock, I. F. (Ed.). (1985). *Diversity and development in English-related creoles.* Ann Arbor, MI: Karoma Press.

Konstitisyon Repiblik Ayiti 1987. Copy provided by the Ministry of Information and Coordination. Tit I, Atik 5.

Mirville, E. (1980). Kijan yo fè mo nèf an Kreyòl. In A. Valdman and Y. Joseph (Eds.), *Créole et enseignement primaire en Haiti* (pp. 182–188). Bloomington, IN: Indiana University, Creole Institute.

Moreau de Saint-Méry, M. L. E. (1797). Description topographique, physique, civile, politique et historique de la partie française de l'isle de Saint-Domingue (pp. 81–82). Philadelphia: The author (2 vol.). Paris: Dupont, 1797–1798 (Repr. 1958, Paris: Société de l'Histoire des Colonies Françaises, 3 vol.).

Morisseau-Leroy, F. (1953). *Antigone en créole.* Pétionville: Morne Hercule. (Repr. Liechtenstein: Kraus Reprint Corp., 1972).

Ninyoles, R. L. (1960). *Conflict linguistic valencia.* Barcelona: Ed. 62.

Orjala, P. R. (1970). *A dialect study of Haitian Creole.* Unpublished Ph.D. dissertation, Hartford Seminary Foundation.

Pompilus, P. (1973). De l'orthographe du créole. *Conjonction, 120,* 15–34.

Pressoir, C.-F. (1947). *Débats sur le créole et le folklore.* Port-au-Prince: Imprimerie de l'Etat.

Prudent, F.-L. (1983). Le discours créoliste contemporain: apories et entéléchies. *Espace Créole 5 (Recherches actuelles pour les aires créolophones),* pp. 31–42.

Saint-Quentin, A. de. (1872). Notice grammaticale et philologique sur le créole de Cayenne. In A. de Saint-Quentin. *Introduction à l'histoire de Cayenne* (pp. 99–169). Antibes: Marchand.

Stein, P. (1984). *Kreolisch und Französisch.* Tübingen: Max Niemeyer. Verlag (Romanistische Arbeitschefte 25).

Sylvain, G. (1901). *Cric? Crac! Fables de la Fontaine racontées par un montagnard haïtien et transcrite en vers créoles.* Paris: Ateliers haïtiens.

Sylvain, S. (Comhaire-Sylvain). (1936). *Le créole haïtien: Morphologie et syntaxe.* Wetteren: de Meester. Port-au-Prince: The author.

Rickford, J. R. (1985). The diachronic and sociolinguistic significance of some early creole texts (unpublished).

Todd, L. (1986). *Modern Englishes: Pidgins and Creoles.* Oxford: Blackwell.

Valdman, A. (1978). *Le créole: structure, statut et origine.* Paris: Klincksieck.

Valdman, A. (Ed.). (1980). *Créole et enseignement primaire en Haïti.* Bloomington, IN: Indiana University.

Vallverdú, F. (1979). *La normalitzacio lingüistica a Catalunya.* Barcelona: Ed. Laia.

Vernet, P. (1980). *Techniques d'écriture du créole Haïtien.* Port-au-Prince: Centre de Linguistique Appliquée.

CHAPTER 7

Catalan and Castilian in School
A First Evaluation

MIGUEL SIGUAN

1. INTRODUCTION

Catalan, which in the Middle Ages was the means of expression of an important political community and vehicle of a magnificent literature, managed to resist adverse historical circumstances over several centuries and retain its character as a language for everyday use. This was to last until the nineteenth century, when it underwent a Renaissance linked with Catalonia's economic development and a renewed political consciousness. At this time, Catalonia has ample political autonomy and its own government. As far as language is concerned, not only does Catalan share with Castilian or Spanish the nature of official language throughout Catalonia but the Catalan government and public institutions have also come out strongly in support of the Catalan language and the culture in which it finds expression.

In spite of all this, the survival of Catalan remains a problematic question.

The first fact of note is obviously the greater weight attached to Castilian, which is not only the official language of the whole of Spain but also the means of communication and expression of a community numerically much greater

MIGUEL SIGUAN • Institut de Cièncias de l'Educacion, University of Barcelona, Barcelona 7, Spain.

than that of Catalan speakers. Thus, although Barcelona is the center for printing books in Catalan and the number of books printed in Catalan is relatively high, Barcelona still prints many more books in Castilian. Although newspapers, magazines, and films are produced in Catalan, the public in Catalonia buys many more papers and magazines in Castilian and watches many more films in Castilian than in Catalan. In addition, the number of hours of TV coverage in Castilian is higher than that given to Catalan, although a Catalan public TV channel is in operation.

Secondly, demographic statistics must be borne in mind. While it is true that Catalonia's industrial development has strengthened its political personality, it is nonetheless true that this has led to massive immigration especially from the south of Spain and, therefore, to an ever-increasing influence of Castilian. This has occurred to such a degree that at present almost half the population of Catalonia speaks Castilian as mother or family tongue, a proportion which at the same time is very widely spread out. While in the city of Barcelona certain balance exists between the two linguistic cultures, in rural areas Catalan clearly predominates, while in the Barcelona industrial belt the predominance of Castilian is absolute.

In these circumstances one can talk of a diglot situation in favor of Castilian, although it is a singular one in that some classic indicators of diglottism are not fulfilled, or if they are, it is in a paradoxical fashion.

Thus it is true that insofar as Catalonia forms part of the Spanish state, Castilian is the language of political power and therefore enjoys greater prestige, while Catalan is the language of a linguistic minority. The fact that the presence of Catalan is much stronger in the country than in the city is also a typical feature of many bilingual situations. But at the same time, the fact that Catalan is the majority language for the middle classes, including the intellectuals and a considerable part of the bourgeoisie, while Castilian is more frequent among industrial workers, especially the least skilled, and among clearly underprivileged social groups, would tend to support the idea of a reverse situation in which Catalan is the language of greater prestige.

There is, on the other hand, another indicator less used in studies of bilingualism but, in this case, very revealing as to a balance in favor of Castilian. We refer to the proportion of bilinguals among speakers of both languages, a proportion which in effect is very diverse. Practically all Catalans understand and speak Castilian, whereas only a part of Castilian speakers can do the same with Catalan. (In very general terms, it can be affirmed that of the inhabitants of Catalonia for whom Castilian is their first language, 25% understand and speak Catalan, 50% understand it but do not speak it, and 25% neither understand nor speak it.) In these conditions, communication between two or more speakers where one is a Castilian speaker tends to take place spontaneously in Castilian.

As regards the place of Catalan in the educational system, the situation can be briefly summarized as follows.

The government of the Generalitat, to which full authority has been handed over in educational matters by the Statute of Autonomy, proposes in its linguistic education policy that by the end of secondary schooling (Enseñanza General Básical) schoolchildren should be able to use both languages normally both for oral and written communication. Given that the situation from the outset implied the predominance of Castilian or, rather, the total absence of Catalan in education, its efforts have been mainly directed at strengthening the role of Catalan in order to make this aim possible. Elements in this policy have included introduction of Catalan in teacher-training establishments, in-service training in Catalan for teachers, stimulation of schools prepared to undertake teaching in Catalan, as the like.

More specifically, the presence of Catalan and Castilian in education is regulated by a series of provisions of which the first, that establishes the compulsory nature of the teaching of Catalan at all levels and modes of teaching, dates from 1978 and is therefore prior to the political autonomy of Catalonia and to the statute regulating it.

The whole of the provisions in force at present can be summarized by saying that a wide variety of linguistic approaches can be adopted, ranging from the school with teaching mainly in Castilian to that with teaching mainly in Catalan. In either case, at least 3 to 5 hours per week must be given over to the language used least (according to individual cases), at all levels, grades, and modes of teaching. The existence of this minimum and the efforts of the Catalan government to increase the use of Catalan as a taught language therefore constitute the most obvious characteristics defining the present situation.

To this can be added the generalized opinion that the introduction to learning should be done in the child's mother tongue. This introduction was traditionally understood as the acquisition of reading and writing, but in our day the spread of preschool education has varied the approach to the problem. The fact that children whose mother tongue is Catalan work together in the preschool classroom with children whose mother tongue is Castilian and that teachers address themselves to each one in his or her own language gives rise to early familiarity with the second language. This occurs to such an extent that the introduction does not present special difficulties, even for children beginning to read in the second language.

Finally, the last very important fact to bear in mind is that although different types of schools exist in Catalonia today, according to the predominance of one language or the other in teaching, this does not mean the existence of two different educational systems for two linguistically different communities, as happens in other countries, but that students with different mother tongues can be found in any one school.

How have these provisions been put into practice, and what are the results obtained?

Some time ago a volume entitled *Lenguas y Educación en el Ámbito del Estado Español*[1] (Siguan, 1983). was published, collecting together the papers presented at the seminar on this subject held annually for the past 8 years in Sitges by the Instituto de Ciencias de la Educación of the University of Barcelona. At present this constitutes the most complete and up-to-date information available on the subject. Among much other interesting data to be found therein, there is one paper, presented by the Education Committee of the Catalan Government Ministry of Education, which reveals that, in 1982, of the total number of E.G.B. (secondary education) centers in Catalonia, 78% offered teaching in Castilian and 21.76% offered teaching wholly or partly in Catalan.

The volume also contains the summary of a study evaluating the results obtained (Generalitat de Catalunya, 1983), carried out by the study group of the Education Committee's Catalan Teaching Service, entitled "Four Years of Catalan in School: Factors and Results." The complete study, entitled *Four Years of Catalan in School* (Generalitat de Catalunya, 1983), was also published later, and the present commentary is based on this study.

2. METHODOLOGY

Before tackling the commentary on the results obtained, it is necessary to outline in some detail the methodology used in the study.

2.1. Objectives

The aim of the study was to evaluate the level of knowledge of Catalan and Castilian reached by pupils entering the fourth year of E.G.B. and to relate this level to the degree of exposure to the two languages in school and to the set of other variables which might influence the levels reached by the pupils.

2.2. Characteristics of the Sample

Because the schools differ widely according to the proportion in which they use the two languages in teaching and because the proportions of speakers of each language, according to schools and locations, are also very different, it was decided to set up a sample bearing in mind these two variables and distinguishing two levels in each of them:

[1] *Languages and Education in the Area of the Spanish State.*

- Degree of catalanization of the school: teaching mainly in Catalan; teaching mainly in Castilian; intermediate situations.
- Degree of catalanization of the location of the school: location with mainly Catalan speakers; locations relatively balanced.

By combining the two criteria, nine kinds of schools were established. All the schools in Catalonia were then classified according to these nine categories, and six schools in each category were chosen at random, giving a sample of 54 schools spread over the whole of Catalonia. All the pupils studying the fourth course of E.G.B. in these schools were examined, with the exception of those who had been pupils in the school for less than 2 years and some others, who for different reasons could not take the test. Finally, 1,539 pupils remained, and these constituted the sample tested.

As should be clear from what I have just outlined, it is not a representative sample of the whole of Catalonia's school population, but representative of the different kinds of schools in order to be able to compare the results obtained.

2.3. Characteristics of the Pupils Sampled

For these 1,539 pupils, a series of data were obtained which were considered to be factors influencing the results achieved. These data were correlated with the results. The data were: sex; place of birth (whether in Catalonia or not); father's and mother's places of birth; socioprofessional level of the parents (upper, middle, lower); mother tongue (Catalan, Castilian, or both); linguistic atmosphere of the school (predominance of one or other of the two languages in the school under consideration, with the average of the linguistic characteristics of the pupils in the same school taken as a guideline); attitude to the languages (deduced from the pupil's replies to the questionnaire); and evaluation by the pupils themselves of their competence in either language. Finally each pupil received a mark for "learning capacity," which was his or her average school mark for the previous course.

2.4. Linguistic Tests

Each pupil was given a set of parallel tests in Catalan and Castilian aimed at evaluating his or her competence in each of the two languages. Given that linguistic competence has very diverse aspects, the choice of the set of tests to measure it, as well as the weight attached to each one of them in the final evaluation, always has an element of arbitrariness. In the case of this study, its authors made an attempt to cover a broad spectrum of linguistic competence and not to limit themselves to the more traditionally "school type" aspects. The details of the different tests employed can be consulted in the publication I have quoted, and I limit myself here to enumerating them:

- Oral comprehension: isolated words and sentences.
- Reading comprehension: isolated words and sentences.
- Oral expression: lexis, communicative competence.
- Written expression: production of a text (composition).
- Phonology: ability to utter certain phonemes.
- Interferences: lexical, semantic, and morpho-syntactic.
- Spelling.
- Phonetics: type of accent.

3. LINGUISTIC RESULTS OF THE TEACHING

The results of the research can be summarized as follows: children whose mother tongue is Castilian and who attend a school in which teaching is normally given in Castilian acquire the level of competence in this language which is considered normal according to the educational program; but those who attend a school in which teaching is normally given in Catalan, in spite of the fact that their exposure to Castilian in school is much lower, practically reach the same levels. Their level of acquisition of Catalan, however, varies greatly according to the kind of school they attend. Those who attend a school where teaching is mainly given in Castilian get rather or very poor results both in oral and written expression in Catalan, despite receiving the regular teaching of Catalan prescribed by the statutes. Only those who attend a school where teaching is mainly in Catalan acquire a knowledge of Catalan comparable with that of Castilian.

As for children whose mother tongue is Catalan, if they attend a Castilian school, they reach a level of knowledge of Castilian which, measured by means of language tests, is comparable with that achieved by their Castilian-speaking classmates. If they attend a Catalan school, in spite of the fact that they receive only the prescribed minimum of teaching of and in Castilian, they achieve a similar or only slightly lower level of competence in this language.

Their level of competence in Catalan depends, however, on the kind of school they attend. If they attend a Castilian-language school they maintain their command of oral competence and acquire a good comprehension of the written language, but their Catalan vocabulary increases less than their Castilian and, above all, their ability to write in Catalan is lower than their ability in Castilian. Only children whose mother tongue is Catalan and who attend a school where teaching is given mainly or partly in Catalan acquire comparable written competence in the two languages.

In other words, the educational system in Catalonia from a linguistic point of view is symmetrical, but its results are not. In mainly Catalan schools, the pupils acquire linguistic competence in Castilian which is much higher than the linguistic competence in Catalan acquired by pupils in mainly Castilian schools.

This asymmetry naturally has its explanations outside the school. Children whose mother tongue is Catalan come to school with a certain background in Castilian which they have received from social interactions, and throughout their school years, their social surroundings will continue to compel them to use Castilian more or less frequently in a wide variety of circumstances. On the other hand, children whose mother tongue is Castilian, in most cases, come to school in complete ignorance of Catalan, and throughout their school years the pressure on them from their surroundings to use it will be slight.

The results of the Generalitat de Catalunya study permit us to formulate this asymmetry in another more original but no less illustrative way.

As I have said, children whose mother tongue is Catalan not only achieve results in Castilian which are comparable as a whole with those achieved by Castilian-speaking children, but the marks achieved by each child in each of the two languages are relatively similar, and both, in turn, are correlated with general academic level. Expressed in simple terms, this means that among children whose mother tongue is Catalan, the best pupils get good marks both in Castilian and Catalan, and, inversely, the worst pupils get bad marks in language tests both in Catalan and Castilian.

This conclusion is more evident in pupils from Catalan-speaking schools, but to a certain degree it also appears in those mainly taught in Castilian. In other words, the so-called swing effect, by which the gain in competence in one language takes place to the cost of the other, does not occur. On the other hand, this effect does not occur in children whose mother tongue is Castilian or else only among those who attend mainly Catalan-speaking schools. For the others, marks in Catalan are practically independent of their marks in Castilian.

The reason for this initially surprising fact does not seem difficult to deduce. Influenced by his or her surroundings, the child whose mother tongue is Catalan becomes practically bilingual and has at his or her disposal two linguistic instruments which he or she can handle practically without difficulty. From this point onward the child's progress in the two languages, especially in those aspects of competence measured by tests—vocabulary, syntax, spelling, may be relatively parallel and related to his or her intellectual abilities and attitude to school. On the other hand, the child whose mother tongue is Castilian, with a limited knowledge of Catalan and reduced scope for practice, acquires a level of competence in Catalan which depends on the frequency to which he or she is exposed to this language in daily experience and his or her attitudes toward it, rather than on his or her intellectual abilities or school behavior patterns.

4. CONSEQUENCES FOR LINGUISTIC POLICY IN EDUCATION

From the results outlined it can be deduced that the mainly Catalan-speaking school achieves its aim that its pupils should have a high degree of competence in both languages by the end of their schooling; the mainly Castilian-speaking school, on the other hand, despite offering consistent teaching of Catalan, fails to achieve this aim in that the level of competence in Catalan achieved by its pupils whose mother tongue is Castilian is clearly insufficient. Only if Catalan, besides being a language taught as a subject, is to some degree a language in which teaching is imparted, is there a stimulus to use it in oral and written communication and thus increase competence.

The consequence for educational policy seems clear: in order to achieve the proposed aim of command of the two languages by the end of E.G.B., the presence of Catalan in schools where teaching is done mainly in Castilian must be increased. This is the basis of the recent measures to which I have made mention above. It is true, however, that this consequence can be argued out from differing standpoints.

It is admissible to accept that the results of the study I have outlined, especially the favorable results for Castilian-speaking pupils in Catalan schools, can be explained by certain characteristics of the population studied which cannot necessarily be generalized. It is a fact that in the Catalan schools where the study was carried out, the pupils are in the majority Catalan-speaking, which facilitates the learning of this language by those who speak Castilian. In a school where most or all of the pupils are Castilian speakers, even if a considerable part of the teaching is done in Catalan, this facilitation by means of spontaneous communication will not take place. It can also be assumed that Castilian-speaking families who send their children to Catalan-speaking schools have, on the whole, a favorable attitude to this language, which will influence the linguistic learning of their children. This cannot be guaranteed on the part of all of the population.

The subject of family attitude ties in with a more general consideration. In a democratic political system, decisions on linguistic policy must take into account the opinion of the electorate represented by the political parties and expressed at the polls. When it comes to fixing the rate of expansion of Catalan in teaching, these opinions have to be taken into account. However, the present rate of expansion is quite moderate and has so far met with no resistance of any note.

The results of the study I have outlined admit interpretation of another kind; that is, they reveal that the school can influence but not substantially change the existing linguistic situation and that to a large degree it may simply perpetuate it. Only if the situation of Catalan in Catalonia's social life as a whole changes will the school be able to achieve more outstanding results in this field.

Reasoning of this kind fuels the present arguments about schooling in Catalonia. As this chapter does not directly aim at educational policy, I do not deal with those arguments here. What I attempt, however, is to show that the study's data admit another kind of analysis, and that the results of this analysis may also be of interest when it comes to setting out educational policy.

5. BILINGUALISM AND INTELLECTUAL ACTIVITY

Both the study we are reporting on and the experience of different educators reveal that the children who come into early contact with a second language—children whose mother tongue is Catalan and who on coming to school are already familiar with Catalan, children whose mother tongue is Castilian and who attend a Catalan preschool center—acquire this language apparently without effort and this acquisition does not interfere with their intellectual development or their learning process in school.

The first manifestation of this fact is shown by the learning of reading. Once the child familiar with the two languages has learned to read in one language, he or she transfers this reading competence to the other language practically without effort. It even appears that the fact of children learning to read first in their own language or in their second language does not have an appreciable influence. The reason is that the reading operation has an intellectual component common to learning in the two languages. To this must be added the fact that the arbitrary rules that link letters and sounds are relatively similar in the two languages.

Moreover, the study appears to show, although this fact would require more precise demonstration, that for those children who quickly acquire the second language, the fact that they have their teaching given in their first or second language does not affect their academic results. In other words, Catalan-speaking children who attend a school in Castilian get academic results similar to those of their Castilian-speaking classmates. Similarly, Castilian-speaking children who attend schools in which teaching is mainly given in Catalan get marks similar to those of their Catalan-speaking classmates. Therefore, it is untrue, as some have thought, that teaching in a second language necessarily affects the intellectual development and academic performance of the schoolchildren unfavorably.

In other words, when Catalans claim that their children should be taught first and foremost in Catalan, they have many arguments on which to base their claim, but not on that which says that by not being taught in Catalan their children's intellectual or academic development is being seriously harmed. In the same way, Castilian speakers can happily send their children to Catalan schools without any fear in this respect.

6. SOCIOCULTURAL CONDITIONING FACTORS

What I have just deduced from the results obtained in the Generalitat de Catalunya study coincides with the results from well-known studies, particularly the experiments with the so-called immersion method popularized by the work of Lambert. As is well known, a certain number of English-speaking families resident in French Canada decided that their children should have a perfect command of French, and to this end they set up an educational center in which their children would receive an education given totally in French from the first day onward. The results of this early immersion were wholly positive: the children learned French and became bilingual without their English suffering harm or ceasing to improve, and their academic results were comparable to those they would have received in an English-medium school. Such was the basis for the popularity of the immersion method.

In time, Lambert himself, its most fervent defender, warned that the method was not recommendable in all cases. For example, if French-speaking families living in French Canada were obliged to send their children to exclusively English-medium schools in the name of the advantages of immersion, they would logically and rightly protest. Given the importance of English in public life, English-speaking children living in French Canada are in no danger of losing their language despite attending a French school. The opposite, however, is not the case.

Lambert deduced from this that immersion as a method is only recommendable when the child maintains a private and public use of his first language which ensures its survival. This is a perfectly reasonable recommendation. In a situation in which a strong and a weak language coexist, the immersion of the children who speak both represents no danger for their first tongue, whereas the immersion in the strong language of the child who speaks only the weak one clearly puts the survival of the child's first language at risk.

But the truth is that the dangers of immersion and the early acquisition of a second language in general are not limited to the danger of loss of the first language because of the imbalance between the two.

Bilingual education in general may have very diverse effects, in some cases positive and in others negative, according to the sociocultural circumstances. The question deserves close examination. Let us consider the Spanish-speaking population in the United States—Chicanos, Puerto Ricans, Dominicans, and others—who occupy mainly the lower strata of society, for whom schooling and, above all, acquisition of English in school ought to be the main route toward their integration into American society. But for these pupils, school does not fulfill this function, and their low level of knowledge of English represents the first obstacle to this integration.

In the light of this fact, and in order to avoid this failure, bilingual education programs were set in motion which were to permit a gradual acquisition of the second language, a genuine bilingualism, and thereby an easy integration into the new society. The defenders of bilingual teaching firmly believed that, apart from the right of the Hispanics to conserve their own language, it would be easy to show that the pupils who followed bilingual programs achieve better results than the pupils who followed programs exclusively in English. However, the numerous studies carried out have not proved conclusive in this sense. It is not clear that pupils in bilingual programs get much higher academic results, but it does appear that a clear balancing effect is the outcome: the pupils who acquire the most English are those least exposed to Spanish, whereas those most familiar with Spanish, because they come into contact with it more, are those who make the least progress in English.

There is, however, one highly significant exception. In the majority of studies carried out in Florida, where the Hispanics are middle-class immigrant families from Cuba, this balancing effect does not occur: the pupils with the highest grades in English are also the ones with the highest grades in Spanish.

Given that the languages involved are the same, the differences in the results we have just noted must have a sociocultural root which acts against the most underprivileged.

A first explanation, proposed by Cummins (1979, 1981), is of a linguistic character. The acquisition of a second language requires that the first should already be basically established. If the second is introduced when the first is still weak and insecure, its introduction will have disrupting effects. Given that children with a low cultural level also show poor linguistic development, the introduction of a second language when they reach school age will easily have negative effects.

Expressed as a purely linguistic explanation, this does not prove very convincing. The children who grow up in a family in which two languages are spoken come into early contact with a second language, before the first has been consolidated, without this having negative consequences. The fundamental reason must therefore be sought in the particular characteristics of the children's linguistic development, according to the sociocultural milieu they grow up in.

Interdependence between linguistic development and social class also occurs in monolingual children, as has been demonstrated by Bernstein (1971). Whether we agree with him or not as to the nature and root cause of these differences, I believe it is easier to accept that the middle-class child comes to school with a mode of language and a use of language similar to that prevailing in the school, whereas the child from a lower social class comes to school with a mode of language and a way of using it which are significantly different, and this difference represents an initial handicap which is difficult to overcome or can only be done imperfectly.

To the extent that this is true, and I for one am convinced that it is (Siguan & Mackey, 1987), the main difficulty for the Chicano or Puerto Rican child in the United States is not so much that the school speaks English, as that the mode of language used in the school is "school English," a way of speaking and of using language for which the child can find no basis in his or her own linguistic usage. The child would encounter the same difficulty if Spanish was spoken in the school—the functions of language there would be equally unfamiliar—but it is obviously increased by having to speak in English. This also explains the balancing effect. Clearly, the child who makes more use of his or her own language will make less progress in English, but it is also true that progress made in "school English" cannot influence the child's colloquial Spanish and make it improve. The children of Cubans in Florida who speak Spanish at home are familiar with a mode of language similar to "school English," because a middle-class father speaks to his child in a similar way to that in which a teacher speaks to his or her pupils. This means that not only does it prove easier for these children to learn school English, but also any progress in either of the two languages can have repercussions on progress in the other.

All this could be summarized by saying that children for whom bilingual teaching or teaching in a second language proves negative or prejudicial are precisely the ones who in monolingual teaching or teaching in their own language would also come up against difficulties because they are held back by a linguistic handicap.

Differences in modes and ways of using language crop up among different social classes and also occur between different cultures. These differences are greatly accentuated when there are both strong social and cultural differences between the two linguistic groups involved—more so if one of the linguistic groups is solidly integrated and the other is more or less culturally disintegrated.

At present, two cultures rub shoulders in the countries of the Maghreb—Moslem Arab and Western, or French-speaking, to be more exact. Education is to a good degree bilingual in French and Arabic. Different researchers, among them Fitouri (1983), recently have noted that educational bilingualism has clearly differing effects according to social levels. For the children of families of a certain sociocultural level, whether they are solidly traditionalist Moslems or open to French culture, the introduction of French represents a positive factor in their academic progress and, therefore, an enrichment. But for immigrants from the countryside and city slum dwellers, practically cut off from their traditional past, the introduction of French represents the final obstacle on the road of school failure, a failure which is but the reflection of their cultural situation; that is, they are shorn of their traditional culture but incapable of becoming integrated into cultural modes imported from the outside.

I do not wish to say that the situation of Castilian speakers in the Barcelona industrial belt or Catalan speakers in isolated rural communities is comparable to that of the Chicanos or inhabitants of the Maghreb. Each situation where languages are in contact is different, and each has its own special factors. But what I do want to say, with all possible emphasis, is that any educational system which has to take two languages into account has very strong sociolinguistic conditioning factors and that one and the same linguistic policy in education may produce very divergent results, according to the situations in which it is applied. In order to understand and clarify these influences, careful studies are required.

On this point, the amount of information offered by the Generalitat de Catalunya study is slight and could hardly be otherwise, as this was not the study's projected aim. But I believe the time has come to attempt a study of this kind and to map out research which will try to clarify the influence that the teaching of language has on the intellectual development and academic results of pupils as a function of the latter's sociocultural situation. The information thus obtained would be important for educational planning in Catalonia, but it would also reach a much wider audience at a time when the presence of different languages in the educational process has become a burning issue all over the world. Serious research into the subject is lacking and, moreover, concentrated in only a few places. Systematic research work carried out here would easily become an obligatory point of reference.

I do not wish to end this commentary without making an observation which I feel is unavoidable. As the result of a political change, Catalonia has gone from a situation in which Castilian was the only vehicle for teaching to one in which the two languages share in the teaching, each with different formulae. This change has taken place relatively quickly and with an intensity and scope at present unparalleled in Europe. Despite the fact that one cannot say that the change has taken place without differences of opinion or problems, since these exist, these differences of opinion have not crystallized in the form of tension nor have these problems become collective conflicts. The proof of maturity, which has been and continues to be given, constitutes, in my modest opinion, an excellent omen for the future of the process.

REFERENCES

Bernstein, B. (1971). Class, codes and control. In *Theoretical studies towards a sociology of language* (Vol. 1). London: Routledge and Kegan.

Cummins, J. (1979). Linguistic interdependance and the educational development of bilingual children. *Review of Educational Research, 49*(2), 222–251.

Cummins, J. (1981). *Bilingualism and minority language children.* Toronto: Institute for Studies in Education.

Fitouri, C. (1983). *Biculturalisme, bilinguisme et education.* Neuchatel: Delachaux.

Generalitat de Catalunya (1983). *Cuatre anys de Catala a l'escola.* Barcelona.

Siguan, M. (Ed.) (1983). *Lenguas y educacion en el ámbito del estado español.* Barcelona: Barcelona University Press.

Siguan, M., & Mackey, W. F. (1987). *Education and bilingualism.* London: UNESCO/Kogan Page.

CHAPTER 8

Implications of Defining Literacy as a Major Goal of Teaching the Mother Tongue in a Multicultural Society
The Dutch Situation

SJAAK KROON AND JAN STURM

1. INTRODUCTION

In the February 1985 issue of *College English*, published by the American National Council of Teachers of English as a forum for discussion of the teaching of English and the content of language arts programs, Deborah Brandt presents a review article which is—at least in our opinion—rather strikingly entitled *Versions of Literacy* (Brandt, 1985). The use of that caption seems to suggest a somewhat provocative perspective on the perilous problem of becoming literate in modern, that is to say, Western societies, mainly characterizable as plurilingual and multicultural.

Formally speaking, Brandt reviews as few as four, though rather voluminous, writings on literacy, ranging from 128 pages to 448 pages and published between 1980 and 1984. However, when counting all the publications mentioned in her text (including the footnotes), which are in one way or another related to the field of literacy, one can find no less than eight publications since 1981, among them five extended readers and a wide-ranging research report. Obviously, the problem of literacy is not at all a simple one; neither does Brandt's review suggest that solutions are near at hand.

SJAAK KROON • Department of Language and Literature, Tilburg University, P.O. Box 90153, 5000 LE Tilburg, The Netherlands.   JAN STURM • Dutch Department, Nijmegen University, P.O. Box 9103, 6500 HD Nijmegen, The Netherlands.

Reflecting on and discussing Brandt's analyses, which mainly concern the
state of affairs in the USA and the UK, and relating them to our knowledge of
and experiences in the Dutch situation—which is a real microcosm compared
with the Anglo-Saxon macrocosm, not to speak of the whole world—we are
inclined to assume that the range of her observations is broader than suggested.
As far as our knowledge of the state of affairs goes, especially in The Netherlands, the following statements of hers, which we have slightly paraphrased,
seem to be true (Brandt, 1985, p. 128):

1. The convergence of multidisciplinary attention upon literacy is evident.
2. Authors writing about the subject include linguists, psychologists, sociologists, educationalists, organizers of literacy programs, anthropol-
   ogists, and last but not least, literary critics and liberally educated
   laymen.
3. Experts in the literacy problem seem to converse with each other only
   rarely. To put it somewhat provocatively: experts cannot really exchange or integrate their developing knowledge and insight into the
   subject, due to the diversity of their reference frameworks, as documented in a variety of discourses from, for instance, broad political
   and literary speculation via narrowly defined psychometric and skill—
   approach-based prescriptions to detailed ethnographic descriptions. This
   precludes any certain and truly interdisciplinary conclusions about the
   nature of literacy.

Nevertheless, in an obvious attempt to take a positive attitude, Brandt does at
least gather a consensus from the literature she reviews. Accounting for those
"shared messages"—as she calls them—she summarized as an overall and
penetrating opinion "that literacy has less to do with overt acts of reading and
writing than it does with underlying postures toward language" (Brandt, 1985,
pp. 128–129). Unfortunately, given Brandt's obvious expertise and extensive
reading in the research area, our hopes that she would be capable of formulat-
ing some more "shared messages" are not fulfilled. She instead merely poses
some "shared questions" about the same knotty matters, some of them being
rather rhetorical in character, as indeed the remainder of her article implicitly
shows. Learning unambiguous lessons from the literature on and research in
the field of literacy seems to imply taking a decided stance, ultimately based
on political priorities, and that is exactly what is usually not done in scientific
discussions. As a consequence policymakers have full discretion to use research
results in whatever way they like. Needless to say, policy-making in literacy
has far-reaching consequences for all people involved, especially the so-called
illiterates.

However, Brandt's questions are well worth taking into consideration in order to delineate a developing trend that we also hope to illustrate with regard to the Dutch situation. She asks:

> Is literacy to be defined in terms of its potential or in terms of its actual practice? Can the results of becoming literate be distinguished from the prerequisites for becoming literate? Do cultures, subcultures, even individuals differ merely in the uses they make of reading and writing, or must we more accurately say that they develop different literacies, complete with different frameworks for thinking about written language and about what it means to read and write it? If different literacies do exist, what are the implications of their diversity for reading and writing in school? (Brandt, 1985, p. 129).

It must be clear that it is not our intention to answer these questions, either in general, or with regard to the Dutch situation. We only aim at sketching a rough outline of a theoretical framework for discussing literacy, taking into account some basic concepts current in educational sociology and the sociology of knowledge (i.e., power, domination, social control, and liberation) as well as in sociolinguistics and educational linguistics. Keeping in mind the questions formulated by Brandt, we devote the first section of our chapter to that outline. In the second section we try to delineate the state of affairs in The Netherlands with regard to multilingualism and language teaching. Although we strive for as descriptive an account as possible, the plain fact that we did not systematically examine the relevant research literature (again) for this occasion, but relied heavily on our present knowledge in that field, causes a certain amount of selectiveness. In this section we briefly answer the following three questions:

1. What different languages (including indigenous and ethnic minority languages) and dialects are spoken in The Netherlands at the moment?
2. What is the legislative educational framework like in The Netherlands regarding language teaching, especially the teaching of the mother tongue?
3. What kind of relevant educational-linguistic research has been done or is in progress, especially in the field of plurilingual education, and what kind of relevant curriculum projects in the field of plurilingual education have been developed or are in progress?

In a third section we explore the relations between the first and second sections in the sense that we try to evaluate the Dutch situation against the background of the tentative theoretical framework developed in the first section. Our conclusions are very cautious and open to discussion, for they are not based on empirical evaluation research but are the results of armchair research and—as we hope—sound reasoning. Therefore, strictly speaking, our "argument will often not be able to progress further than common-sense observations" (cf. Stubbs, 1980, p. 8). On the other hand, we are only trying to make the Dutch situation comparable to others in an international context in order to exceed the limited scope of our national view and to check the acceptability and applicability of our theoretical framework.

2. ASPECTS OF PROBLEMS IN DEFINING LITERACY

As Stubbs (1980, pp. 10–11) poses,

> it is useful to remember that . . . *literate* is simply ambiguous in everyday English, as . . . is clear from usages such as: (1) to be fully literate, you have to know the classics; (2) students are not literate these days: they can't spell.

Surprisingly, Stubbs does not explain why he considers this ambiguity limited to *everyday* English: according to our observations the dominant definition of "literacy," at least in Dutch society, including the areas of schooling, educational policy, and research especially related to language teaching, contains the full potential meaning of these statements as well as any intermediate meanings between these two extremes. The former (representing one pole of a continuum) refers to "wideness of education" (Stubbs, 1980, p. 14), originally the indigenous prerogative of the aristocracy. The latter (being the other pole) refers to the ability to read and write at least on a "mechanical" level, which, in the nineteenth century, with the start of popular education and the introduction of compulsory education with the minimum requirement of literacy for all, was a powerful means of moral regulation of the masses (Grace, 1978). In the words of Johnson (to quote just one example of the massive evidence in this connection):

> The early Victorian obsession with the education of the poor is best understood as a concern about authority, about power, about the assertion (or the reassertion) of control. This concern was expressed in an enormously ambitious attempt to determine, through the capture of educational means, the patterns of thought, sentiments and behaviour of the working class. Supervised by its trusty teachers, surrounded by its playground wall, the school was to raise a new race of working-class people—respectful, cheerful, hard-working, loyal, pacific and religious. (1970, p. 119)

Wondering whether this observation, by and large, holds true in our times, one should, for instance, note Anyon (1980), and especially her observations on language arts pedagogy, which inescapably lead to the conclusion that

> in each of the classrooms . . . students are learning class specific behavior for both understanding and adapting to the world of work and the larger society. Students appear to be developing a potential relationship to different forms of work, including domestic labor, and in doing so they are acquiring a specific form of symbolic capital. (Citation to be found in Fitzclarence & Giroux, 1984, p. 471.)

Dutch research on classroom practice endorses these conclusions (Sturm, 1984a).

By stressing the relevance of power and (social) control (Young, 1971) and their covert relationship with literacy and schooling in general, we do not mean to suggest that nothing has changed in the last 150 years. The aristocracy lost its dominant social position a long time ago, and its definition of the hierarchy of legitimate knowledge (in which knowledge of the Classics was paramount) has been partly replaced by a technocratic definition, albeit Stubbs' observation makes it clear that it has not disappeared completely. What is more, the "Victorian obsession" with education is to be interpreted as an issue of that technocratic definition itself, protecting the newly captured bourgeois power (Grace, 1978, pp. 9–27). Nevertheless, as an analysis of some publications on literacy can show, the continuum mentioned does exist these days.

What is really at stake here is the position of schools (being the definite mediators of "literacy") as "sites in which contradictory cultures and social relations are subordinated to the imperatives of a dominant culture, one that functions as the mediating link between dominant class interests and everyday life" (Fitzclarence & Giroux, 1984, p. 467). Unfortunately we do not have the opportunity here either to explore this position (clearly developed by the so-called new sociology of education; Young, 1971) in detail, or to illustrate much more concretely "the way in which schools legitimate dominant forms of culture through the hierarchically arranged bodies of knowledge that make up the curriculum, as well as the way in which certain forms of linguistic capital and individual rather than collective appropriation of knowledge get rewarded" (Fitzclarence & Giroux, 1984, p. 467).

From this position we would like to draw attention to the inescapable internal contradiction that is implicated in the current claim to educate for literacy by teaching the mother tongue (of all pupils) especially in multicultural societies. Acknowledging the intimate and for the time being inextricable relationship between mother tongues and cultural identities, that claim confronts the language teacher especially with the dilemma of "either legitimating or resisting dominant forms of ideology and culture." If a language teacher is going to take seriously the need to develop workable alternatives in order to implement that claim, he or she has to recognize "the struggle [he or she will get] involved in over defining what counts as legitimate language and knowledge forms, over what constitutes the distinction between normality and deviance, and over the struggle as to what counts as acceptable social practice." Furthermore he or she will have "to investigate historically the nature of the teaching field itself and how it has evolved under conditions through which racial, gendered and class-specific practices have become part and parcel of the teaching profession" (Fitzclarence & Giroux, 1984, pp. 475–476).

The language teacher definitely cannot trust in the policymakers' official support, as it is ultimately in their interest to sustain the dominant culture, which by definition is deeply rooted in the administrative structure.

Therefore, teaching literacy through teaching the mother tongue (at least in our opinion, agreeing with the broader plea for a tranformative critical pedagogy) implies, first of all, developing

> forms of knowledge and classroom social practices that *work with* the [language] experiences that students bring to school. . . . This demands taking seriously the language forms, style of presentation, dispositions, forms of reasoning and cultural forms that give meaning to student experiences. . . . [Secondly, this nevertheless also implies] the need to *work on* the [language] experiences that students bring to the school. . . , [in the sense that it becomes clear] what students need to learn outside of their experiences, so that they can break the chains of domination and subordination as they work on their own personalities, as well as on the objective forces that bear down on them daily. (Fitzclarence & Giroux, 1984, pp. 473–474)

Returning to Brandt's article, referred to in the preceding section, we find that the most important book she reviews seems to be Heath's rather provocative research report on language, life, and work in communities and classrooms, entitled *Ways with Words* (Heath, 1983). Brandt is very positive in her assessment of Heath's work. Nevertheless, Heath's conclusions, as formulated and summarized on page 368 of her book, are not very encouraging, although she worked (as Brandt, 1985, p. 137, formulates)

> along with students and teachers to find ways to make the gulf [between the children's families and the school] the object of conscious attention and study, [aiming and devising] educational approaches that allowed students to act [in a] literate [way] by integrating the ways of community and school.

Literally, Heath (1983, p. 368) writes:

> But structural and institutional changes in the schools and patterns of control from external sources, such as federal and state governments, have forced many of the teachers described here to choose either to leave the classroom or to transmitting only mainstream language and culture patterns.

Heath's experiences reflect that dominant definitions of literacy are very hard to kill, despite the best educational intentions. Therefore, it seems to be appropriate to look askance at official proposals to strive for literacy by teaching the mother tongue.

It seems to be more realistic—and at least fairer with respect to the often officially, but merely rhetorically, acknowledged eager expectations of class-specific, gendered, or racial as well as linguistic and cultural minority groups— to consider every proposal and attempt to rethink the definition of literacy related to the practice of mother-tongue teaching and schooling in general, as a covert endeavor to counteract and attack vested interests as experienced by dominant groups. This is the case unless the attempt is clearly based on the claim (in Heath's words) "that a radical restructuring of society or the system of education is needed for [that] kind of cultural bridging . . . to be large scale and continuous" (Heath, 1983, p. 369).

Equally, the growing awareness of the multicultural character of modern society, as proclaimed by the (Dutch) government, seems to be best interpreted merely as a neat administrative reaction, allowing some individuals from minority groups to ensconce themselves in the existing power structure. As a result, the often highly esteemed cultural and linguistic identity of such groups is doomed to disappear or to deteriorate to pure folklore.

3. THE DUTCH SITUATION WITH REGARD TO MULTILINGUALISM AND LANGUAGE TEACHING

3.1. Linguistic Diversity in The Netherlands

In his survey of the linguistic situation in Italy, Balboni (1984) supposes that this country, seen from abroad, looks rather monolithic. On closer examination, however, as Balboni convincingly shows, the situation appears to be quite different. As a matter of fact, a great number of languages and dialects coexist within Italian society. Quite the same seems to be true as far as The Netherlands is concerned. Seen from abroad this small country on the North Sea border might also appear to be a homogeneous language area. Contrary to expectations, being a small, highly industrialized and urbanized country with hardly any natural boundaries, a very dense population and highly developed transportation and communication networks, The Netherlands is at the moment—and, in fact, has always been—a multilingual country. This means that in The Netherlands, apart from Standard Dutch, a lot of indigenous and non-indigenous languages and dialects are spoken. The first group consists of regional varieties, with or without language status; the second group consists of language varieties used by ethnic minorities that, for various—but mainly economic—reasons have chosen The Netherlands, and especially its big cities and industrial areas, as their permanent or temporary place of residence.

Overviews of indigenous dialects that are spoken in the Dutch language area (including the Dutch-speaking part of Belgium) are given by Donaldson (1983) and Van Hout (1984). As far as the nature of Dutch dialects is concerned, Van Hout stresses that although neighboring dialects show only slight linguistic distance and are therefore mutually intelligible, over some distance, because of the accumulation of differences at all levels of the language system, they fairly rapidly become mutually unintelligible. Hence, according to Van Hout, the structural differences between Dutch dialects seem to be better comparable to the geographical diversity found in, for example, Germany, France, and Italy than to that found in the USA.

Although the gradualness of linguistic transitions in the Dutch language area makes a clear-cut classification of the dialects within it rather difficult, Van Hout (1984, p. 4) points out six main dialect groups (see Figure 1):

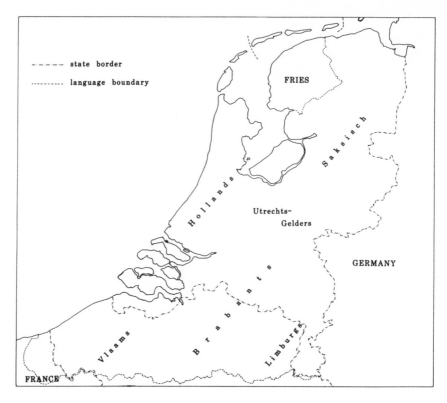

Figure 1. Main dialect groups in The Netherlands and Flanders (Van Hout, 1984).

In the North-West are situated the Holland dialects ["Hollands"] which are the most cognate with the Netherlandic standard language from the linguistic point of view. Next there are the North-Central Utrecht-Guelders dialects ["Utrechts-Gelders"], the North-East Saxon dialects ["Saksisch"], the North-West Flemish dialects ["Vlaams"], the South-Central Brabant dialects ["Brabants"], and finally there are the South-East Limburg dialects ["Limburgs"].

The only regional variety with language status in The Netherlands is Frisian, including its own dialects. Frisian is now an indigenous minority language, originating from the languages spoken in the Middle Ages along the continental shore of the North Sea from Amsterdam to the Elbe. In the nineteenth century, due to the efforts of the so-called Frisian Movement, headed by an educated elite and inspired by the climate of Romanticism, Frisian was more or less standardized, and, relatively speaking, its appreciation and status are still growing. Frisian and Frisian dialects are at the moment spoken as a home language (next to Standard Dutch and Dutch dialects) by about 60% of the

550,000 inhabitants of the province of Friesland (see Zondag, 1982a, and Van Hout, 1984).

A more detailed map of indigenous variation in the Dutch language area is given in Donaldson (1983, p. 8). It is based upon a combination of judgments by dialect speakers on the similarity of neighboring dialects and isoglosses that were found by dialectologists (see Figure 2).

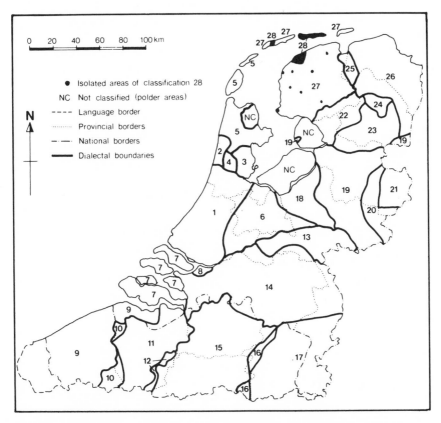

Figure 2. Dutch dialects in detail. Key: 1 = South Hollands; 2 = Kennemerlands; 3 = Waterlands; 4 = Zaans; 5 = West Frisian—North Holland; 6 = Utrechts; 7 = Zeeuws; 8 = Westhoeks; 9 = West Flemish and Zeeuws Flemish; 10 = Dialect of the area between West and East Flemish; 11 = East Flemish; 12 = Dialect of the area between East Flemish and Brabants; 13 = South Gelders; 14 = North Brabant and North Limburgs; 15 = Brabants; 16 = Dialect of the area between Brabants and Limburgs; 17 = Limburgs; 18 = Veluws; 19 = Gelders-Overijssels; 20 = Twents (former county); 21 = Twents; 22 = Stellingwerfs; 23 = South Drents; 24 = Central Drents; 25 = Kollumerlands; 26 = Gronings and North Drents; 27 = Frisian; 28 = Bildts, Town Frisian, Midlands, Amelands. N. B. Very generally speaking, the higher the number, the greater the distance from standard Dutch. Adapted from a map by Jo Daan in the *Atlas of The Netherlands,* plate x-2, 1968 (Donaldson, 1983).

So far, unfortunately, there has been no nationwide sociolinguistic survey on the basis of which it would be possible to say exactly how many people in The Netherlands use a variety other than Standard Dutch. In 1976, however, a survey of parents ($n = 1,370$) and teachers ($n = 537$) of primary school children was conducted. Of the parents, 46% thought their children were speakers of a dialect, and a majority of the teachers thought that even more than 50% of the pupils in their classes were dialect speakers (CMM, 1976). Results from other, small-scale sociolinguistic surveys confirm these figures. Combining these findings, it seems reasonable to assume that about 50% to 60% of Dutch primary school children and about 70% of the rest of the population have a Dutch dialect, or Fisian, or a Fisian dialect as a home language. This does not mean that these dialect speakers have no command of the standard language at all but quite the reverse: dialect speakers in The Netherlands are in most cases also, at least to a certain degree, speakers of the standard language. Besides, a growing number of people turn out to be speakers of a variety that is somewhere in between the ''real'' dialect and the ''real'' standard: people often speak a dialect with some characteristics of the standard language, or they speak Standard Dutch with some dialect features. And, to complete the picture, it has to be said that Standard Dutch is often pronounced with a clear dialect accent (Trudgill, 1975).

As far as ethnic (and in most cases also cultural and linguistic) minorities in The Netherlands are concerned, a recent overview is provided by Extra and Vallen (1985b). Combining earlier publications such as Appel (1981) and Vermeer (1981) with more recent data, they distinguish five main ethnic groups (see Table 1):*

1. People whose origins lie in the former Dutch colonies. These are (1) natives of Surinam (185,000) and the Dutch Antilles (42,200) who started to come to Holland in the late 1960s and the early 1970s, and (2) repatriates from the former Dutch Indies, the present Republic of Indonesia (285,000), including 35,000 Moluccans who came to Holland in the post World War II years. Apart from the Moluccans, who are often stateless, most of these people have Dutch nationality.

2. People from Mediterranean countries. Most of them are so-called immigrant workers from Turkey (156,000) and Morocco (107,000) who came to Holland in the early 1960s and 1970s, but there are also people from Spain, Italy, Yugoslavia, Portugal (including the Cape Verdian Islands), Greece, and Tunisia, to a total of 72,700 inhabitants.

3. Political refugees from various countries such as Hungary, Czechoslo-

---

*More recent figures on ethnic minorities in the Netherlands are to be found in G. Extra and T. Vallen (1988), ''Language and ethnic minorities in the Netherlands,'' in: *International Journal of Sociology of Language, 73*, pp. 25–110.

Table 1. Sizes of the Most Important ($n > 1000$) Ethnic–Cultural Minorities in
The Netherlands in January 1983 [a]

Source country	Number
Ex-colonies	
Surinam	185,000
Dutch Antilles	42,200
Moluccan	35,000
Dutch Indies (excluding Moluccan)	250,000
Mediterranean countries	
Turkey	154,200 (January 1984: 156,000)
Morocco	101,500 (January 1984: 107,000)
Spain	22,100
Italy	20,600
Yugoslavia	13,900
Portugal (including Cape Verdian Islands)	9,300
Greece	4,100
Tunisia	2,700
Refugees	
Hungary	4,000
Czechoslovakia	2,000
Poland	1,500
Turkish and Armenian Christians	3,700 (January 1984)
Chile	2,000
Vietnam	6,000
Other countries	4,800 (January 1984)
Chinese (excluding Surinam and Vietnam)	
People's Republic of China ⎤	
Taiwan ⎟	
Malaysia ⎬	30,000
Singapore ⎟	
Hong Kong ⎦	
Other countries	
Federal Republic of Germany	42,900 (January 1984: 45,000)
United Kingdom	39,300 (January 1984: 42,000)
Belgium	23,600 (January 1984: 24,000)
United States	11,000
France	6,500
Ireland	2,100
Denmark	1,200
Other American countries	8,000
Other Asian countries and Oceania	30,000
Other African countries	4,000
Caravan dwellers	17,000

[a] From Extra and Vallen (1985b).

vakia, Poland, Chile, Vietnam, Turkey (Turkish and Armenian Christians), and other (Latin and Central American) countries, to a total of 24,000 inhabitants.

4. Chinese people from the People's Republic of China, Taiwan, Malaysia, Singapore, and Hong Kong, to a total of 30,000 inhabitants.

5. Immigrants from other countries in Western Europe, the Americas, Asia, Oceania, and Africa, and caravan dwellers, to a total of 189,900 inhabitants.

According to these figures, about 7% of the more than 14 million inhabitants of The Netherlands are of nonindigenous origin (Extra & Vallen, 1985b). And the same is true for most of the various languages and dialects that are spoken by and within the different minority groups that were mentioned. Unfortunately, however, there are hardly any research findings with regard to linguistic heterogeneity within these groups in The Netherlands. Therefore, we have to limit ourselves here to just a few examples. People from Morocco can, for example, be speakers of Moroccan-Arabic or speakers of Berber or Bedouin dialects; people from Surinam can, for example, be speakers of Sranan Tongo, Sarnami Hindustani, Javanese, Haka, a lot of Indian dialects, or Surinamese-Dutch; people from Turkey can, for example, be speakers of Turkish, Armenian, Zani, Azeri, Tserkessi, or Kurdish; Chinese people can, for example, be speakers of Mandarin, Cantonese, Wenzhou, Shanghai dialects, and so on.

Besides, one should notice that the transition to Dutch by ethnic minority groups *could* lead to the development of new varieties of Dutch such as Turkish-Dutch or Arabic-Dutch and to language shift or language loss in ethnic minority languages (see Lambert & Freed, 1982).

3.2. Legislation with Regard to Linguistic Diversity and Education

The Dutch educational system is founded on the freedom of education which is guaranteed by the constitution (article 23). Roughly speaking, this means that every group (or even individual) who is able to get together a certain number of potential pupils has the right to establish its own school and to set it up with respect to denomination, organization, teaching materials, and the like, according to its own ideas. Within certain legal margins (e.g., regulations concerning the subjects to be taught, the minimum number of lessons to be devoted to a certain subject, the qualifications required of teachers, and examination standards), the school can then expect to be fully subsidized by the government—if the school appears to be capable of survival, of course (Sturm, 1984b).

The Dutch parliament concerns itself mainly with the structure of the educational system, rather than with the content of education, unless the interests of society as a whole are at stake. Notable and clear examples of parliamentary debate and legislation concerning the contents of education are, among others, about linguistic diversity and education. Nevertheless, there are only a few articles and paragraphs in Dutch legislation with regard to (language) teaching in a multilingual society.

Regulations with regard to Dutch dialects are mentioned in the Dutch Education Law since 1937; reference to the Frisian language was introduced in 1955 (see Zondag, 1982b, for an overview). In its most recent (1980) formulation (operative since August 1, 1985), which now includes nonindigenous minority languages, the Dutch Elementary Education Law, article 10, paragraph 4–5 says:

> 4. At the schools in the province of Friesland instruction is also given in the Frisian language, unless, at the request of the proper authority, the Provincial Authorities have granted exemption from this obligation.
> 5. Wherever, besides the Dutch language, the Frisian language or a dialect is in active use, the Frisian language or the dialect may also be employed as a medium of instruction. In order to facilitate the transition and adaptation to the Dutch educational situation for pupils with a non-Dutch cultural background, the language of the country of origin may also be used as a medium of instruction.

In other words, since 1980, Frisian has been a mandatory school subject and an optional medium of instruction in all primary school classes in the province of Friesland; exemptions can be made, on request, for nonindigenous pupils and pupils whose home language is a non-Frisian dialect. There are proposals to introduce Frisian as a medium of instruction in special education and as a mandatory school subject in secondary education as well. Dutch dialects and nonindigenous minority languages, on the other hand, can be used as a nonmandatory medium of instruction.

As far as nonindigenous minority languages are concerned, some further specifications are found in article 11, paragraphs 1–5:

> 1. For the benefit of pupils with a non-Dutch cultural background the proper authorities may decide to make instruction in the language and culture of the country of origin of these pupils part of the school curriculum. After consultation of the Council of Education it will be determined by Order in Council to which pupils the aforegoing sentence applies.
> 2. Classes in which the instruction referred to in the 1st paragraph is given may also be attended by pupils registered at other schools, if at these schools instruction of this kind is not available.
> 3. The pupils referred to in the 1st paragraph are only required to attend the classes mentioned if their parents wish them to do so.
> 4. Of the time devoted to the instruction, referred to in the 1st paragraph, at the utmost 2.5 hours are included in the minimum numbers of hours of instruction which, under article 12, 4th paragraph, pupils are to receive per week.
> 5. In contravention of article 12, 4th paragraph, pupils attending the classes referred to in the 1st paragraph may receive a maximum of 6 hours of instruction per day.

Obviously, in paragraphs 2–5, mainly restrictions on mother-tongue teaching for ethnic minority children are formulated.

As a matter of fact, as Extra and Vermeer (1984) show, there are striking differences in the treatment by law of Frisian as an indigenous minority language (and other dialects) and nonindigenous minority languages; these differences seem to be ultimately based upon political, not psychological or linguistic, criteria (see also Spolsky, 1971). Whereas Frisian is declared a mandatory school subject in the province of Friesland for which exemption has to be requested, nonindigenous minority languages and other dialects can be taught only with several restrictions. Home language teaching as a school subject is only possible if (1) the authorities think it is useful; (2) the pupils involved fulfill certain conditions (i.e., if they are children of migrant workers from Mediterranean or other European countries, children of political refugees or Moluccans—no home language teaching is provided for Surinamese, Antillian, or Chinese children—and if there are at least 10 children per group); and (3) their parents wish them to be taught in their mother tongues—which are not in all cases really *mother* tongues. There are some time restrictions as well.

As far as the teaching of Dutch as a second language is concerned, legislation is still lacking. Although the Ministry of Education and Science declared the teaching of Dutch as a second language to be an issue of central importance in its 1981 policy plan, schools still have to make an appeal to a so-called Facility Regulation in order to get any additional temporary support for the teaching of Dutch as a second language to immigrant children. As far as Dutch as a second language is in fact taught, apart from some experiments (see Extra & Verhoeven, 1985), this generally takes place in small groups separated from the rest of the class. Most immigrant children, however, attend (or are immersed in) regular Dutch classes.

3.3. Research and Curriculum Development in the Field of Multilingual Education

Extra and Vermeer (1984, p. 199) sum up four models for the organization of education for children speaking a minority language (L1) that differs from the dominant majority language (L2) (see Figure 3).

All these models do, to some extent, exist within Dutch primary schools. Model A (segregation) can be found in so-called national schools that are totally oriented toward repatriation. Model B (assimilation) is very often used for indigenous and nonindigenous language minorities in low concentrations. Model C (transition) is promoted for nonindigenous language minorities, but, in practice, L1 is in most cases introduced only after a couple of years in primary education, and there is no relationship between L1 teaching and regular teaching in/of L2. Model D (maintenance) is often promoted by minority groups;

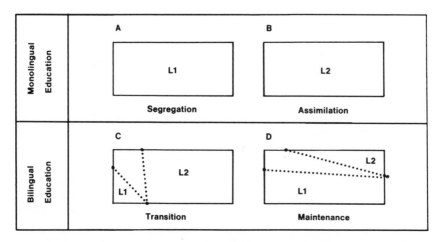

Figure 3. Four models for teaching to language minorities. Horizontal: time at school grade 1 to grade *n;* vertical: degree of attention to L_1 and L_2 (Extra & Vermeer, 1984).

however, as we have seen, the Frisians are the only group that succeeded in putting this demand into legislation.

As overviews show (e.g., Appel, Cruson, Muysken, & De Vries, 1980; Appel & Muysken, 1983; Extra & Vermeer, 1984; Extra & Verhoeven, 1985; Extra & Vallen, 1985a,b; De Moor, 1985), not much research has been done in The Netherlands on the effects of these different teaching models. Besides, research results that are available generally do not differ much from trends suggested by international investigations, which often play an important role in setting up Dutch research. Generally speaking, there seems to be no one-to-one relationship between research and curriculum development in the field of plur-ilingual education. We therefore limit ourselves here to just mentioning some research trends, and after that we discuss three important curriculum development projects.

As far as indigenous minority languages and Dutch dialects are concerned, attention should be paid here mainly to the Friesland Project and the Kerkrade Project.

The Friesland Project investigated the degree of school success of primary school children with Frisian as a home language as compared to a Dutch-speaking group from the province of Utrecht.

The main finding of the project was that children who have Frisian as a home language and who were taught under different educational conditions do not differ much from each other with respect to proficiency in reading and writing Dutch after 3 years of schooling. Additionally, pupils from bilingual schools also learned to read and write Frisian. As far as reading and writing proficiency in Dutch are concerned, the Frisian groups also do not differ much from the group of Dutch-speaking children from Utrecht (see Wijnstra, 1976, 1980, for an extensive report).

The most important Dutch research project into dialects and education has been the so-called Kerkrade Project, a sociolinguistic and educational investigation into the problem of dialect-speaking children in primary education in Kerkrade, a town in the southern part of the province of Limburg, where a dialect is spoken which rather strongly deviates from Standard Dutch. The project was designed within the framework of the sociolinguistic difference conception (Vallen, Stijnen, & Hagen, 1985).

The most important, though not very sensational, results of the research phase (1973–1977) of the Kerkrade Project can be described as pertaining to the attitudes of teachers and pupils concerning dialect and Standard Dutch, dialect and verbal interaction in the classroom, and communicative and grammatical aspects of the use (especially written) of Standard Dutch by dialect-speaking pupils. It should be mentioned here that the project team devoted a lot of energy to informing teachers about its research. The last phase of the Kerkrade research was designed as a curriculum development project (for extensive reports see Hagen, 1981; Kuijper, Stijnen, & Van den Hoogen, 1983; Stijnen & Vallen, 1981).

As far as ethnic minority languages are concerned, research is mainly being carried out into the acquisition of Dutch as a second language by immigrant children under different schooling conditions and with different teaching methods.

As to the first subject, in a longitudinal study, Appel (1984) investigated the acquisition of Dutch by Turkish and Moroccan immigrant children (age 6–12) using an experimental transitional bilingual program with a considerable amount of minority language teaching as compared to an immersion approach in regular schools with hardly any minority language teaching ($n = 24$ and 33, respectively). He concludes "that, in general, minority-language teaching does not have to harm or hinder second-language acquisition; it might even stimulate (i.e., create facilitating conditions for) the learning of the minority language" (Appel, 1984, p. 150).

As to the second subject, De Bot and Janssen-Van Dieten (1984), in a large-scale survey of about 1,000 pupils (age 6–16), could not find any clear explanatory relationships between language proficiency and different methods of second-language teaching in Dutch schools (i.e., a grammar-based versus a communicative approach). They suggest that systematic observation in classrooms could perhaps shed more light on what (second language) teachers are really doing, because the existing heterogeneity within and between different groups of pupils seems to give rise to such a variety of approaches of L2 teaching that capturing them with large-scale research instruments is not at all possible.

Until now little research has been done about the preferences of ethnic minority groups with regard to the models of language teaching that were mentioned before. Interviews with representatives from Moroccan, Portuguese, Surinamese, and Turkish ethnic organizations about their ideas on mother-tongue teaching, however, show a clear preference on the part of these groups for a kind of mother-tongue teaching that supports language maintenance and that leads to a growing ethnic awareness and ability to stand one's ground as an ethnic group member in Dutch society (see Werkgroep Taalpolitiek en Etniese Minderheden, 1984).

Several research projects concerning language and ethnic minorities have recently been started within the Tilburg University Department of Language and Minorities. They cover the following areas: Dutch spoken by and to speakers of other languages than Dutch; the use of minority languages; language and education and language attitudes. An overview of some preliminary results of most of these projects is given in various contributions in Extra and Vallen (1985a).

As has been mentioned before, generally speaking, curriculum projects in plurilingual education are currently not being built directly on research projects.

In our opinion, three Dutch curriculum projects, reflecting three distinguished administrative and educational reactions to potential societal disintegration, merit consideration here. We briefly describe:

- The curriculum project Towards a Frisian Curriculum (TFC).
- The curriculum development phase of the so-called Kerkrade Project.
- The newly designed Educational Priority Area Curriculum Project.

The TFC project can be interpreted as a reaction to:

- The historical and rather ancient Frisian movement toward independence, cherished mainly by a cultural elite, though from time to time inextricably interwoven with strongly felt sentiments of political and economic deprivation compared with Dutch society as a whole.
- A more recently felt educational and pedagogical need for linking classroom practice to the community habits of knowing and language use the pupils bring with them to school, in order to raise the desired output of formal education (cf. Cosin, Dale, Esland, Mackinnon, & Swift, 1977).
- The very recent idea that fostering language abilities in standard language, second language, and even foreign languages will be best served by developing them first in the so-called home language (cf. Meestringa, 1985, pp. 7–8).

The TFC project started in 1975 and has recently been completed. It was designed as a school-based curriculum project. Though the project has published a series of documents dealing with many aspects and problems of teaching the Frisian language (one of which is supplied free of charge to all schools in the Frisian area), the impact seems to be rather slight, despite support from the Frisian administration and the attention paid to the project in the local media. As recently published research did show, only 10% of the Frisian schools can be characterized as oriented toward full bilingualism (Meestringa, 1985).

The curriculum development phase of the Kerkrade Project was based on the research findings of the earlier phases of this project. Just when the development phase of the project was getting underway in 1981, the economic crisis became the focus of attention, and, as a result, funds for development projects became scarce. Therefore, a small-scale and school-based pilot project was started. The fact that the real school situation appeared to be linguistically much more heterogeneous than supposed, together with resistance on the part of teachers and parents to use the dialect as a medium of instruction or, to a lesser degree, to tolerate dialect at least in classroom interaction, coerced the project team to readjust the project aims. In the broader context of developing a new pedagogical approach, labeled thematic teaching, they hoped to bridge the gap between language at home and language at school in one way or another (Hos, Kuijper, & Van Tuijl, 1982). Research did indeed show an increasing participation in classroom interaction and slightly improved school results on the part of the pupils speaking a dialect (Kuijper, Stijnen, & Van den Hoogen, 1983).

In the 1980s, the problem of pupils who did not become academically literate has appeared on the agenda of the Dutch educational policymakers in a new form (cf. Coleman, 1968). Due to the economic crisis and extreme unemployment that has especially affected the immigrant workers and caused "new poverty" in general (forming a fertile soil for growing racism), a new Educational Priority Policy Program is being designed. And again, research on language and language acquisition and development is expected to produce workable alternatives for what is felt to be failing education, especially concerning literacy (or much more unpronounced—failing families and local communities; cf. Halsey, 1977). Under the strong pressure of time, the results of this research were anticipated, so that the accent is now on developing so-called multi- or intercultural teaching programs, of which guidelines for teaching the mother tongue are considered constituent components. The well-known, though not even partially resolved, problem of underachieving working-class children in general seems now to be considered a relatively minor problem in that context.

Because the newly designed Educational Priority Area Curriculum Project is in an early stage, nothing can now be said on the effects, except that there is a lot of work to do for linguists, educationalists, sociologists, psychologists, and the like.

4. CONCLUSIONS

Against the background of the theoretical outline sketched in the first section—roughly defining literacy as an educational concept mainly oriented to protecting vested societal interests, though leaving marginal scope for alternative interpretations and practices, especially in multicultural perspective—we are inclined to evaluate the Dutch situation, described in the second section, in a somewhat ambiguous way. This ambiguity is reflected in our seven conclusions, containing some dilemmas as to teaching "the mother tongue" in a multicultural society.

1. Concerning literacy, from a historical point of view, there are at least two discernible dominant definitions—forming the endpoints of a continuum—both treating the written word as a force to integrate youngsters into a specific societal group and to segregate groups from each other. At one end of the continuum one finds the most highly valued definition of literacy. It has to do with wideness of education, operationalized as a knowledge of the ancients and/or national classics and reflecting an aristocratic definition, as readjusted by the rising bourgeoisie during the nineteenth century, in order to fit in with their meritocratic culture. At the other end of the continuum is a definition of literacy, which has to do with moral regulation of the masses, mainly operationalized as mechanical reading and writing skills in standard language. In between these two poles there are, as a matter of fact, several transitional forms, depending on the stage of societal (i.e., historical, socioeconomic, cultural, political, etc.) development in a specific country or society.

2. Not being indigenously and potentially literate in the dominant sense, speakers of indigenous and nonindigenous minority languages or dialects have to shed the idiosyncrasies of their languages and the cultural practices of their social or ethnic group to cross over to the dominant ways of literacy, as defined in and fostered by written standard language (cf. Brandt, 1985, p. 137).

3. The Netherlands is a multilingual country. The use of the phrase "mother-tongue education," when actually referring to the teaching of Standard Dutch only, should therefore be avoided. Such a phrase is misleading and, as a matter of fact, incorrect because Standard Dutch is frequently not the mother tongue of the pupils who are attending Dutch schools. Mother-tongue teaching thus appears to be just a euphemism for teaching the national language in its standardized form (Rosen, 1982), concealing and in the meantime enfeebling the pursuit of an alternative meaning of "literacy" as an aim of real mother-tongue

teaching, as reflected in research and curriculum development projects in multilingual education.

4. Defining "literacy" as a major goal of teaching the mother tongue must be interpreted either as (1) a mere blind, promoting the flexibility of the process of societal integration of, among other things, (ethnic) minority groups in order to maintain vested interests, along which failures of reading and writing are not in the end failures of technology but failures of group membership (Brandt, 1985, p. 138), or as (2) an incentive to reconsider fundamentally the nature of literacy, leading in the end to a radical restructuring of the educational system (Heath, 1983, p. 369).

As a matter of fact, educational and other authorities are historically bound to follow the first interpretation. Granting mother-tongue teaching facilities to minority groups must therefore ultimately be considered as a means of fostering integration of those groups into dominant societal structures.

5. The 1980 Dutch Elementary Education Law states that "education should start from the principle that pupils grow up in a multicultural society" (article 9, paragraph 3). Following this article, the policy plan of the Ministry of Education and Science on Cultural Minorities in Education promotes the development and implementation of inter- or multicultural education by saying: "education should stimulate the acculturation of the minority groups and other members of Dutch society by means of intercultural education" (see also Batelaan, 1985). Dutch legislation with regard to mother-tongue teaching also seems at first sight to be in tune with these principles. A closer examination, however, of the paragraphs on the position in education of other languages and dialects than Standard Dutch makes clear that the ultimate aim of language teaching in Dutch classrooms for all pupils is acquiring literacy in Standard Dutch.

6. The analysis presented in this chapter should be seen in the light of Halsey's illuminating observation that "it can be plausibly agreed that intellectuals have never conducted a successful social revolution, though they have often played a crucial part in undermining belief in the legitimacy of political orders which are subsequently overthrown" (Halsey, 1977, p. 123).

7. As our present contribution makes clear, we do not intend researchers (especially educational linguists; Spolsky, 1978) and curriculum designers (in this specific order) to stop their activities with regard to mother-tongue teaching in multilingual contexts.

REFERENCES

Anyon, J. (1980). Social class and the hidden curriculum of work. *Journal of Education, 162*, 67–92.

Appel, R. (1981). Language problems of minority groups in the Netherlands. In A. R. Vermeer (Ed.), *Language problems of minority groups.* Proceedings of the Tilburg Conference, 18 September 1980 (pp. 7–26). Tilburg Studies in Language and Literature 1. Tilburg: Tilburg University.

Appel, R. (1984). *Immigrant children learning Dutch; Sociolinguistic and psycholinguistic aspects of second-language acquisition.* Dordrecht: Foris.

Appel, R., & Muysken, P. (Eds.). (1983). *Themanummer Taal-en Minderheden. Interdisciplinair Tijdschrift voor Taal- en Tekstwetenschap, 3.*

Appel, R., Cruson, C., Muysken, P., & de Vries, J. W. (Eds.). (1980). *Taalproblemen van buitenlandse arbeiders en hun kinderen.* Muiderberg: Coutinho.

Balboni, P. E. (1984). The teaching of mother tongues other than Italian in Italy. In W. van Peer & A. Verhagen (Eds.), *Forces in European mother-tongue education.* Proceedings of the International Symposium on Mother-Tongue Teaching, Tilburg University, 16 December 1983 (pp. 165–180). Tilburg: Tilburg University/SLO.

Batelaan, P. (1985). Intercultural education in Europe. Policy, developments, dilemmas. *IMEN Newsletter, 2,* 31–38.

Brandt, D. (1985). Versions of literacy. *College English, 47,* 128–138.

CMM. (1976). *School en Dialect. Een discussienota.* 's-Hertogenbosch: CMM.

Coleman, J. (1968). The concept of equality of educational opportunity. In B. R. Cosin, I. R. Dale, G. M. Esland, D. Mackinnon, & D. S. Swift (Eds.), *School and society: A sociological reader* (2nd ed., pp. 216–223). London: Routledge & Kegan Paul.

Cosin, B. R., Dale, I. R., Esland, G. M., Mackinnon, D., & Swift, D. S. (Eds.). (1977). *School and society: A sociological reader* (2nd ed.). London: Routledge & Kegan Paul.

De Bot, K., & Janssen-Van Dieten, A. (1984). Het onderwijs Nederlands aan Turkse en Marokkaanse leerlingen. Een poging tot evaluatie. *Levende Talen, 395,* 520–525.

De Moor, E. (1985). Arabisch en Turks op school. Discussies over eigen taal—en cultuuronderwijs. Muiderberg: Coutinho.

Deprez, K. (Ed.). (1984). *Sociolinguistics in the low countries.* SSLS 5. Amsterdam/Philadelphia: John Benjamins.

Donaldson, B. C. (1983). *Dutch. A linguistic history of Holland and Belgium.* Leiden: Martinus Nijhoff.

Extra, G., & Vallen, T. (Eds.). (1985a). *Ethnic minorities and Dutch as a second language.* Dordrecht: Foris.

Extra, G., & Vallen, T. (Eds.). (1985b). Language and ethnic minorities in The Netherlands: Current issues and research areas. In G. Extra & T. Vallen (Eds.), *Ethnic minorities and Dutch as a second language* (pp. 1–10). Dordrecht: Foris.

Extra, G., & Verhoeven, L. (1985). Tweetaligheid en tweetalig basisonderwijs. *Pedagogische Studiën, 1,* 3–24.

Extra, G., & Vermeer, A. (1984). Minderheidstalen in het basisonderwijs. In W. van Peer & A. Verhagen (Eds.), *Forces in European mother-tongue education.* Proceedings of the International Symposium on Mother-Tongue Teaching, Tilburg University, 16 December 1983 (pp. 197–219). Tilburg: Tilburg University/SLO.

Fitzclarence, L., & Giroux, H. A. (1984). The paradox of power in educational theory and practice. *Language Arts, 61,* 462–477.

Grace, G. (1978). *Teachers, ideology and control: A study in urban education.* London: Routledge & Kegan Paul.

Hagen, A. (1981). *Standaardtaal en dialectsprekende kinderen. Een studie over monitoring van taalgebruik.* Muiderberg: Coutinho.

Halsey, A. H. (1977). Government against poverty in school and community. In B. R. Cosin, I. R. Dale, G. M. Esland, D. Mackinnon, & D. S. Swift (Eds.), *School and society: A sociological reader* (2nd ed., pp. 235–243). London: Routledge & Kegan Paul.

Heath, S. B. (1983). *Ways with words: Language, life, and work in communities and classrooms.* Cambridge: Cambridge University Press.

Hos, H., Kuijper H., & van Tuijl H. (1982). *Dialect op de basisschool. Het Kerkradeproject: van theorie naar onderwijspraktijk.* Enschede: SLO.

Johnson, R. (1970). Educational policy and social control in early Victorian England. *Past and Present, 49,* 119.

Kuijper, H., Stijnen, S., & van den Hoogen, J. (1983). *Onderwijs tussen dialect en standaardtaal. Onderzoek in en beschouwingen over de innovatiefase van het Kerkradeproject.* Nijmegen: NCDN.

Lambert, R., & Freed B. (Eds.). (1982). *The Loss of language skills.* Rowley, MA: Newbury House.

Meestringa, T. (1985). Engels in de Friese Basisschool? *De Pompeblêden, 56,* 3–9.

Peer, W. van, & Verhagen, A. (Eds.). (1984). *Forces in European mother-tongue education.* Proceedings of the International Symposium on Mother Tongue Teaching, Tilburg University, 16 December 1983. Tilburg: Tilburg University/SLO.

Rosen, H. (1982). Sociolinguistics and the teaching of the mother tongue. *Gramma, 6,* 49–61.

Spolsky, B. (1971). The language barrier to education. Interdisciplinary approaches to language. *CILT Reports and Papers, 6,* 8–17.

Spolsky, B. (1978). *Educational linguistics: An introduction.* Rowley, MA: Newbury House.

Stijnen, S., & Vallen, T. (1981). *Dialect als onderwijsprobleem. Een sociolinguistisch-onderwijs-kundig onderzoek naar problemen van dialectsprekende kinderen in het basisonderwijs.* 's-Gravenhage: Staatsuitgeverij.

Stubbs, M. (1980). *Language and literacy: The sociolinguistics of reading and writing.* London: Routledge & Kegan Paul.

Sturm, J. (1984a). Deficit and difference: A false dichotomy in an educational perspective. In K. Deprez (Ed.), *Sociolinguistics in the low countries* (pp. 193–209). SSLL5. Amsterdam/Philadelphia: John Benjamins.

Sturm, J. (1984b). *Report on the development of mother tongue education in The Netherlands since 1969.* In W. Herrlitz, A. Kamer, S. Kroon, H. Peterse, & J. Sturm (Eds.), *Mother tongue education in Europe. A survey of standard language teaching in nine European countries* (pp. 238–276). Studies in Mother-Tongue Education 1. Enschede: SLO.

Trudgill, P. (1975). *Accent, dialect and the school.* London: Edward Arnold.

Vallen, T., Stijnen, S., & Hagen T. (1985). The difference hypothesis in the Kerkrade project: Measurement of verbal abilities and intelligence. In K. Deprez (Ed.), *Sociolinguistics in the low countries* (pp. 169–191). SSLS 5. Amsterdam/Philadelphia: John Benjamins.

Van Hout, R. (1984). Sociolinguistics in the Netherlandic language area. In K. Deprez (Ed.), *Sociolinguistics in the low countries* (pp. 1–41). SSLL5. Amsterdam/Philadelphia: John Benjamins.

Vermeer, A. (1981). Survey of linguistic minorities in Holland. In A. R. Vermeer (Ed.), *Language problems of minority groups.* Proceedings of the Tilburg Conference, 18 September 1980 (pp. 111–113). Tilburg Studies in Language and Literature 1. Tilburg: Tilburg University.

Vermeer, A. R. (Ed.). (1981). *Language problems of minority groups.* Proceedings of the Tilburg Conference, 18 September 1980. Tilburg Studies in Language and Literature 1. Tilburg: Tilburg University.

Werkgroep Taalpolitiek en Etniese Minderheden (1984). *Opvattingen over taalbehoud en taalverlies een onderzoek onder etnies-kulturele migrantengroepen.* Utrecht: Instituut voor ontwikkelingspsychologie RUU.

Wijnstra, J. M. (1976). *Het onderwijs aan van huis uit friestalige kinderen. Verslag van een evaluatie-onderzoek in een meertalige regio.* 's-Gravenhage: Staatsuitgeverij.

Wijnstra, J. M. (1980). Education of children with Frisian home language. *International Review of Applied Psychology, 29,* 43–60.

Young, M. F. D. (Ed.). (1971). *Knowledge and control: New directions for the sociology of education.* London: Collier/MacMillan.

Zondag, K. (Ed.). (1982a). *Bilingual education in Friesland.* Franeker: Wever.

Zondag, K. (1982b). Background to the educational system of the Netherlands and Friesland. In K. Zondag (Ed.), *Bilingual Education in Friesland* (pp. 1–35). Franeker: Wever.

CHAPTER 9

Literacy Problems in Hungary

GYÖRGY SZÉPE AND MÁRTA DOVALA

1. INTRODUCTION

Hungary, which is situated in eastern central Europe, has a population of 10.7 million spread over 93,000 square kilometers. The population is considered to be "monolingual": 95% belong to the Hungarian nationality, according to the latest census (which should be accepted with reserve like any other data gained by census methods); the rest know Hungarian too, to a certain extent. The non-Hungarians are divided into regular "nationalities," that is, Germans, Slovaks, Romanians, and Yugoslavs, which comprise three ethnic groups (Serbs, Croats, and Slovenes) and two language groups (Serbo-Croatians and Slovenians), and into an "ethnic group," that is, the Gypsies. Gypsies can be divided into three linguistic groups: Gypsies speaking a Hindustani idiom, of which there are several varieties, Beash speaking a Transylvanian Rumanian dialect, and those who speak Hungarian.

Other ethnic or linguistic fragments are usually not mentioned in this context, for example, a Ukrainian-speaking village, Polish fragments, Yiddish-speaking Jews (the Sefardim group is just vanishing), and a few Armenians; there are also the newcomers: Bulgarians (until the 1940s), Greek refugees (in the late 1940s), Chilean refugees (in the 1970s), and Polish migrant workers with their families (in the 1980s).

On the other hand, there are 4 to 6 million Hungarians (or Hungarian-speaking people) living in other countries, mainly in the five adjacent states: Czechoslovak FR (Slovak Republic), Yugoslav FR (Croat Republic, Slovene

GYÖRGY SZÉPE • Research Institute for Linguistics, Hungarian Academy of Sciences, P.O. Box 19, H-1250 Budapest, Hungary.   MÁRTA DOVALA • Department of Language and Communication, The Teachers' College, Kaszap utca 6-10, H-6000 Kecskemét, Hungary.

Republic, Voyvodina Autonomous Province), Soviet Union FR (Ukrainian Republic), Romania, and Austria. Hungarian immigrants can be found in Western Europe, North America, South America, Australia, and elsewhere.

Now let us return to Hungary. In 1984, 42 out of 100 active workers were working in industry, 18 in agriculture and forestry, 8 in transport and communications, 10 in commerce, 2 in the water supply, and 20 in other fields (Központi Statisztikai Hivatal, 1984). The country, which is more or less industrialized, has since 1949 been a socialist state with rather centralized administration, economy, and educational system.

The cost of education and research is covered by the state mostly from the national budget, but to a lesser extent project and foundation financing—as well as the exploitation of local resources—exists and has existed for the last 5–10 years. The proportion of the national budget devoted to education is around 6% (Központi Statisztikai Hivatal, 1984).

2. EDUCATIONAL SYSTEM

For the present task one should also have some data on the educational system.

The first phase is the nursery school, for children between the ages of 3 and 6. It is not obligatory, but nevertheless, in 1984, 89.8% of this age group attended nursery school; of the rest, 3.8% attended a 192-hour course in preparation for school.[1]

Then there is an eight-class primary school: the first four classes (ages 6–10) are taught by a school mistress, and the following four (ages 10–14) by teachers specialized in subjects like Hungarian language and literature. This is a compulsory free school, remarkably homogeneous all over the country (education is compulsory until age 16). For the present chapter, information on secondary and higher education is not necessary.

There is also a system of special education, both at the level of primary and nursery schools.

Another system takes care of adults, to a very small extent at primary school level and to a larger extent at the level of various secondary schools.

Mother-tongue education is omnipresent within these systems, under different labels or in different organizational forms. (For our ideas on mother-tongue education, see Szépe, 1978, 1984.)

---

[1] In addition to these data, 4.8% had grade repetition of some kind and 1.6% of the age group had no connection with any educational institution (see Veres & Lengyel, 1984, p. 31, table 16; for the preparatory course, see Faragó, 1975).

2.1. Nursery School

Mother-tongue education in the nursery school (Dovala, 1985a, pp. 66–78; Gosztonyi-Dovala, 1983; Losoncz, 1981) is an "overall program" which extends over each field of nursery school education, There is no separate field for the mother tongue. The main goal is to develop the communicative skills of children: speaking, hearing, and understanding, the use of metacommunicative devices, and the like. This is implemented within a more or less planned process of interaction, steered by a nurse and other persons who could be labeled as auxiliary personnel. The nurse tries to influence the communication in a "nondirective" way. There are two activities which display the highest chance for live communication: "playing"—which also contains the acquisition of different social "roles"—and the so-called literary period, containing tale-telling, acting out dramatized tales, and puppet-show activity. "Picture-reading," that is, looking at pictures and talking about them, is a relatively new feature (see Sugárné Kádár, 1985, pp. 76–136).

The nursery school does not teach either reading or writing, but it tries *to prepare* the child for the acquisition of both activities. Reading is prepared for through, for instance, eye-training, as when children identify and name objects (from a picture) from left to right. Then there is an elaborate system of pattern recognition training where, for instance, incomplete drawings of objects are to be identified (Pirisi, 1975).

The learning of writing is also prepared for in the nursery schools through a series of practices serving to develop hand muscles. From 3 years of age on, kids "scribble" with a pencil (Bakonyi & Szabadi, 1971), but no direct writing exercises are required in the average nursery school.

There are, however, some experiments on the development of early reading through the serial recognition of pictures, where words (i.e., chains of letters) were substituted for pictures. The experiment was successful; it made the acquisition of reading skills easier in the first class of primary school (Gledura, 1981).

Another experiment was conducted on phonemic distinction by dint of specially designed drills. This experiment also had beneficial effects in the first year of primary school, when children had to analyze written words into letters (letters are mostly phonemically unambiguous in Hungarian) (Török & Vekerdi, 1981).

For non-Hungarian-speaking children, there are three types of nursery schools in the country:

1. The nursery school organized in the language of the "nationality" has almost the same program as any Hungarian nursery school with this difference: the working language is not Hungarian, but three times a

week Hungarian is the medium of activity. One has to admit that these kids are usually bilinguals, with a slight predominance of Hungarian (!) over the nationality language of their parents.

2. The "language-teaching nursery school" is a Hungarian nursery school with organized activities occurring 3 times a week in the language of the nationality; German is by far the most popular of this type, because German is not only a nationality language in Hungary but the best known foreign language. Other foreign languages taught sporadically in Hungarian nursery schools are English and Russian, and sometimes other languages are also present.[2]

The decision between the use of type 1 or 2 lies in the competence of the local educational authority, and it is highly conditioned by the availability of bilingual nurses—who are trained in several secondary and postsecondary institutions—and auxiliary personnel.

3. Quite recently, one of the Gypsy dialects (usually the prestigious Lovāri) has also been employed as a means of communication, jointly with Hungarian; but there has been no training of Gypsy educators so far.[3]

Here we have to stop for a moment in order to mention a large-scale linguistic-educational survey of *Gypsy* children, terminated in 1985, within the Department of General and Applied Linguistics of the Research Institute for Linguistics of the Hungarian Academy of Sciences. Research has been done on the bilingual and monolingual communication of Gypsy children, their vocabulary, text-formation, dialogue-formation, and, generally speaking, their intellectual-verbal development (Réger, 1986).

2.2. Educational Methodology at the Primary School Level

In 1984, 90% of 6-year-old Hungarian children were enrolled in the first "normal" class of the primary school. The rest went either to special schools for the handicapped or to the so-called correctional first class of the primary school, which enables children to be reintegrated after 1 year to the mainstream normal classes or to be transferred to the special schools. (On "remedial" first class of the primary school, see Gosztonyi, 1978.) There are no correctional classes in nationality languages; on the other hand, many children in these Hungarian-speaking correctional classes are of Gypsy origin.

---

[2] In 1983 there were 593 children in type (a), and 11,906 children in type (b) nursery schools (see Kökény, 1984, p. 18).
[3] This experiment is being conducted by a special unit within the National Institute of Education (Mrs. G. Rácz, personal communication, 1985).

The first class in the primary (elementary) school traditionally has had as its main task the acquisition of reading and writing. These two tasks plus a more or less novel language register—transmitted by the school, the textbooks, and also by the teacher—render the first class a very hard job, in spite of the complex preparation for it by the nursery school or the special preparatory courses (Dovala, 1985b).

In 1970, 11.4% of first-class children failed because of their "insufficient" reading and writing achievement (Kurucz & Veres, 1975, p. 15, table 11). The reasons for this failure are due to either the immaturity of these children for school work or the unsatisfactory preparation given by the nursery school (which, at that time, was undergone by only two-thirds of this cohort of first-class children), and probably also the then prevailing "phonic-analytical-synthetical" method of reading education (Dovala, 1985a, pp. 72–73). Since that time, this monopolistic method of central Europe has undergone some changes and has lost its dominant position. This traditional method now has been enriched with some elements of the so-called global method in reading education: a "global preparatory period" has been inserted in the first weeks. This accelerates the acquisition of reading by providing a better motivation for children through their "quasi-reading" experience. Control tests really prove that some progress is being made with this modified method, while some teachers give accounts of quite a few problems to be solved, among which is the fact that pupils get polarized: children with better abilities progress faster, whereas slower ones stop abruptly, even in the course of the global preparatory period. For the latter children, differentiated reading education during the lessons, or extra classes (4 hours coaching a week), is given. Even now, about 70% of the children display difficulties in reading during the phoneme–grapheme learning period: they change the order of letters or disregard suffixes. So much for the actual majority method.

The oldest minority method is the global method of reading education. After a hopeful experiment, which was terminated in the 1940s, a psychologist and a primary school teacher renewed this method in the 1970s (Kuti & Ligeti, 1978; Ligeti, 1982). The revival—enriched by novel elements—can be considered a success; it now is an alternative (optional) method in the first classes, by means of which it has been possible to get rid of some of the difficulties we have enumerated above when describing the global preparatory period of the traditional method. But there are still some problems to be solved. The main problem lies in the morphological structure of Hungarian words, which display base-vowel alternation, very elaborate suffixation, and several other phenomena which cannot be treated—that is, analyzed, read, written—unless one splits words into smaller units. In order to solve this problem successfully, the appropriate abilities should be developed, that is, procedures of morphemic "breaking down" and "constructing." If the child is unable to split words into parts, the procedure of analysis should be practised on objects and toys.

A younger minority method, utilized for the first 4 years of primary school, is the experiment in the education of language, literature, and communications (Zsolnai, 1982). This is a project which covers all mother-tongue education for the age group 6–10, and reading is only one minor part of the project. Learning to read and write is treated as a part of educating to communicate. A combined method is used, containing some aspects of the so-called pure methods, but there are also some other ingredients—first of all, intensive practice of correct pronunciation of the koine. Some elements have also been taken over from special programs designed for handicapped children, as well as from the so-called speed-reading. Best results have been achieved among children, Gypsies included, living in socially and culturally unfavorable conditions.

These three "methods" (plus a fourth one which stands close to the majority method) have been compared by a large-scale follow-up investigation organized by the National Institute of Education (Petriné Feyér & Végh, 1984). All four approaches had almost the same results by the end of the first year: about 90% of children could master the global recognition of words. Some differences could also be found:

1. The combined—majority—method achieved best results in the "correctness of reading," that is, not making mistakes when reading aloud.
2. The global method produced most reading mistakes, for example, changing the order of letters and syllables. It produced a generally uncertain reading of suffixes, and longer words were usually read by dint of splitting them into shorter words, but pupils were better at understanding the texts, that is, processing the visual information.
3. The third approach—which has been by far the best organized educational research project in the country—was the most successful because it de-emphasized the task of reading and embedded it in a systematic training of speech and functional communication. The team concerned with the project, consisting of primary school teachers who partially turned into researchers, use a combination of methods adjusted to the individual pupil; they have, for example, two parallel readers for the first years, of which one is more and the other less "global."

2.2.1. Writing Skills

The teaching of writing begins in a delayed form in all the previously mentioned approaches; the time of the delay differs from 1 to 6 months. The longest delay has proved to be the most successful.

Here we have to stop once again. There is a large-scale investigation into school maturity, conducted by a team from the University of Szeged (Nagy,

1980, see especially pp. 147–160). The research has produced some interesting results. From our viewpoint the most surprising was the following: all but one of the abilities of Hungarian 6-year-old children met the requirements of school maturity laid down by the researchers. These requirements were to be accumulated over a period of 4 years in children between the ages of 4 and 8. The only exception was writing ability: only 20% of Hungarian children were mature enough for writing at the age of 6. After another year of maturation, however—at the age of 7—the vast majority were able to learn writing. This research has also produced novel data on the knowledge of vocabulary and logical operations of this age group.

Let us return to the problem of writing education. Hungarian handwriting has been overstandardized, following the example of the German *Schütterlin* standing letter shapes. In the last 40 years, children have been vexed by the geometrical drawing of letters, which was abandoned by everybody when reaching adolescence, because the shapes of these Luttor (à la *Schütterlin*) letters were considered childish. A graphic artist has designed two new variants for Hungarian handwriting: a "standing" type (but provided with binding parts acceptable for adult writing) and one resembling the italic-type handwriting used in British schools. Both variants have been tried out in teaching, accompanying the global reading education program (see Virágvölgyi, 1981).

2.2.2. Mother-Tongue Education

Children of national minorities learn reading and writing in their own language if they attend a nationality school, where the medium of teaching is their respective idiom (Jakab & Mokuter, 1975, and especially Fekete, in that volume). The acquisition of Hungarian reading begins in the second class through a contrastive method (that is, by taking into consideration the reading knowledge acquired in the first class in the mother tongue). In the "language-teaching" (nationality) primary school, reading and writing are taught in Hungarian in the first class; the nationality language is taught 3 hours a week, and in this framework minority-language children begin to read in their nationality language in the second class.

In the few schools where Gypsy (usually Lovāri) is an auxiliary language, there is no reading and writing in the first half of the first school year—"speech development" is given instead (of course, in Lovāri). After 6 months, children start reading and later even writing with the aid of beautifully designed Gypsy primers (Karsai & Rostás Farkas, 1984).[4] This is not a formally organized

[4]The artist who deserves praise for the extraordinary visual presentation is Ildikó Péli, who belongs also to the Gypsy community.

experiment but rather an attempt to try out this way of schooling for Gypsies who, for various reasons, had been mostly dropouts.

2.2.3. Reading Skills Follow-Up

Reading education is only in its initial phase in the first class of primary school. There are endeavors at follow-up, until the age of 14, both within the school—within the mother tongue, Hungarian, and language and literature[5]—and outside the school, within a movement conducted by very dedicated young sociologists and educators.[6] "Reading" in this context is ambiguous: the technique of reading is but one part of the activity. Information and text, elementary literary education, social studies ("sociography" in the Eastern European tradition), as well as discussion are also parts of this extracurricular follow-up program. In some cases even elementary research in ethnography, onomastics, and dialectology are included.

2.2.4. Achievement Testing

Reading achievement has always been measured in some way or other in Hungary, but there were no American-type testing controls until the late 1960s, when we joined the International Educational Achievement (IEA) survey system (Báthory & Fülöp-Kádár, 1985). We took part in three international surveys: Hungarian pupils scored fantastic in the sciences, did rather poorly in English, and their results in reading—that is, understanding a text read in their mother tongue—were a disaster. The texts investigated may have been a bit culture specific, that is, alien to Hungarian kids, therefore the actual results could have been somewhat better if the specificity of cultural environment had been taken into consideration. But the shock caused by that kind of failure in reading education in Hungary had a beneficial effect upon research, development, and innovation in the field.

2.2.5. Foreign Language

The first foreign language in the primary school is Russian. It starts in the fourth class, when Hungarian children can already read and write Latin char-

---

[5] The network of school libraries contribute a lot to this work; their periodical is *Könyv és Nevelés* ["Book and Education"].

[6] The reading movement extends to young people and adults via the Hazafias Népfront Olvasó Mozgalom ["Peoples Patriotic Front Readers Movement"]. Its periodical, *Olvasó Nép* ["The Reading People"], has a special section devoted to reading education.

acters and minority-language children can read both in Hungarian and in their mother tongue. Only those who belong to the Serbo-Croatian minority master Cyrillic characters by that time. Hungarian pupils begin "oral Russian" in the fourth grade; reading also follows with a considerable delay. Since Cyrillic characters differ from the Latin ones, they do not cause "homogeneous inhi- bitions." The acquisition of writing with Cyrillic characters seems to be more difficult because Russians write in a different style ("ductus"), more similar to that of italic handwriting (see Virágh, 1982, and Papp, 1982).

Since Hungarian orthography is considered to be "phonemic," that is, graphemic segments mostly have a bi-unique correspondence with phonemic segments, Hungarian pupils have hardly any difficulty in acquiring German, Italian, Spanish, or Esperanto spelling. Even French seems to be rather acces- sible, but English usually causes writing problems.

3. ILLITERACY

After completing the work on this chapter, we received the results of a survey on some aspects of Hungarian language use, organized by the Mass Communication Research Center in Budapest (Terestyéni, 1987). This was the first survey conducted in the framework of public polling but also exploiting different techniques from sociological research methods. The most surprising result was the discovery of a very large percentage of people who never read or write, partly because they are never required to do so in their work and partly because they may have forgotten how (see Table 1). It is very difficult to explain the results of a survey based on a representative sample, beyond its own scope. It is, however, very likely that the 1.8% of illiteracy reported by the 1980 census in Hungary is (1) an understatement, and (2) a somewhat undifferentiated report on the state of affairs.

Let us remark that the aforementioned survey included elementary arith-

Table 1. Information-Processing Activity during Work[a]

Occurrence	Reading	Writing	Calculating	Drawing
Never uses it	44	60	39	86
Seldom uses it	20	15	15	6
Often uses it	36	25	46	8

Note. $N = 637$. All values are percentages.
[a]From Terestyéni, 1987, p. 19, Table 1.

metic operations in its survey parameters; this is in consonance with the definition of literacy suggested by UNESCO.[7]

It should also be pointed out that in this chapter we did not deal with two translated uses of literacy/illiteracy: in the field of music education, where it means reading notes, and in the field of computer practice, where it may be a simple extension of a terminology built up with several elements taken from linguistics.

4. CONCLUSIONS

In a descriptive chapter like this, we do not offer particular conclusions. We have, however, tried to summarize our concluding statement in the following way: one has to open a door wide for the acquisition of reading and writing, where work and fun should be combined at the initial stage and can be organized in the school in several equivalent ways. But the success of the whole literacy (alphabetizational) process depends on the functional follow-up organized both within the educational system and in society at large.

This short statement can be made somewhat more complex if we allow for the importance of the "virtues of illiteracy" (in clear reference to Bright, 1984, Ch. 9), that is, the relative values in communicational skills (and attention and memory) of people in preliterate societies—values which may be lost through alphabetization.

This leads us to seriously meditate upon the unexpected results in functional (secondary) illiteracy of the survey organized by the Mass Communication Research Center. Much more social sensitivity should be shown both in the teaching of reading and writing and in the follow-up—formal or informal—even in countries where the progress of social revolution in the field of culture is a permanent issue.

Do we perhaps also need our Freire? or, rather, Montessori, Decroly, and Freire,[8] jointly within a framework which has solid foundations in quite a few fundamental sciences, like linguistics, psychology, and anthropology (communication).[9] But education will always remain the coordination (organization) of various fields for the benefit of people who need or want to acquire something.

---

[7] The definition is: "A person is *functionally illiterate* when he cannot engage in all those activities in which literacy is required for effective functioning of his group and community and also for enabling him to continue to use reading, writing and calculation for his own and the community's development" (UNESCO, 1983, p. 3).

[8] These names are the best known—in my country—for reading education addressed to the very young, the handicapped, and poor people.

[9] An endeavor has been made to meet these requirements; see Szépe, 1978, 1984, as well as further papers on Hungarian mother-tongue education: Szende and Szépe, 1978; Bánréti 1979, 1981; Zsolnai, 1982. For documentation see Angyal, 1984a,b. For the background of recent initiatives, see Rét, 1978.

REFERENCES

Angyal, É. (1984a). Report on the development of the mother tongue education in Hungary. In W. Herrlitz, S. Kroon, H. Peterse, & J. Sturm (Eds.), *Mother tongue education in Europe* (pp. 211–236). Enschede: International Mother Tongue Educational Network.

Angyal, É. (1984b). Bibliography on mother tongue teaching in Hungary. In W. Herrlitz, S. Kroon, H. Peterse, & J. Sturm (Eds.), *Major publications on mother tongue education in Europe* (pp. 66–74). Enschede: International Mother Tongue Educational Network.

Bakonyi, P., & Szabadi, I. (Eds.). (1971). *Az óvodai nevelés programja* [The program of nursery school education]. Budapest: Tankönyvkiadó.

Bánréti, Z. (1979). *Gyerek és anyanyelv* [Child and mother tongue]. Budapest: Tankönyvkiadó.

Bánréti, Z. (1981). *Kamasz és anyanyelv* [Adolescent and mother tongue]. Budapest: Tankönyvkiadó.

Báthory, Z., & Fülöp-Kádár, J. (1985). Educational evaluation studies in Hungary. *Evaluation in Education, 9,* 109–215.

Bright, W. (1984). *American Indian linguistics and literature.* Berlin/New York/Amsterdam: Monton.

Dovala, M. (1985a). Primary education in Hungary. In *Research into primary education.* Hamburg: UNESCO Institute for Education.

Dovala, M. (1985b). Der ungarische Primarbereich im Lichte neuerer curricularer Entiwicklung. *Bildung und Erziehung, 38,* 311–325.

Faragó, L. (Ed.) (1975). *Az iskolára előkészítő foglalkozások vezetése* [Guidance of school preparatory activities]. Budapest: Tankönyvkiadó.

Fekete, B. (1975). Az anyanyelvi és a magyar nyelvi íráskészségek alakulása szerb-horvát tanítási nyelvü általános iskoláinkban [The development of writing abilities in mother tongue and in Hungarian in the Serbo-Croatian schools in Hungary]. In R. Jakab & I. Mokuter (Eds.), *Nemzetiségi iskola-anyanyelvi nevelés* [Nationality school and mother tongue education] (pp. 90–105). Budapest: Országar Pedagógiai Intézet.

Fülöp, K., & Lengyel, Z. (Eds.) (1982). *Az orosz nyelv tanítása az általános iskola 4. osztályában* [The teaching of Russian in the 4th class of the primary school]. Szeged: Juhász Gyula Tanárképző Főiskola.

Gledura, L. (1981). "Olvasás" az óvodában ["Reading" in the nursery school]. In J. J. Nagy (Ed.), *Vizsgálatok az alsó tagozatos anyanyelvi nevelés gazdagítása érdekében* (pp. 128–137).

Gosztonyi-Dovala, M. (1983). Perexodnyj period iz detskogo sada v školu. In P. Furman (Ed.), *Preemnost' obučenija i vospitanija doškol'nikov i mladši škol'nikov* (pp. 14–32). Berlin: Akademie der Pedagogischen Wissenschaften der DDR.

Jakab, R., & Mokuter, I. (Eds.). (1975). *Nemzetiségi iskola—anyanyelvi nevelés* [Nationality school and mother tongue education]. Budapest: Országos Pedagógiai Intézet.

Karsai, E., & Rostás Farkas, G. (1984). *Sityovas te gingavas. Olvasni tanulunk* [We learn to read]. Budapest: Országas Pedagógiai Intézet.

Kökény, I. (Ed.) (1984). *Statisztikai tájékoztató. Óvodai intézmények* [Statistical information on institutions of nursery school education]. Budapest: Müvelődési Minisztérium.

Központi Statisztikai Hivatal [Central Bureau of Statistics]. (1984). *Statisztikai évkönyv 1984* [Statistical yearbook of 1984]. Budapest: Központi Statisztikai Hivatal.

Kurucz, D., & Veres, G. (Eds.) (1975). *Statisztikai tájékoztató. 1974/75. Alsófokú oktatás* [Statistical information on primary education]. Budapest: Müvelődési Minisztérium.

Kuti, G., & Ligeti, R. (1978). Globális olvasási program a korrekciós osztályokban [A global reading program in the remedial classes]. In J. Gosztonyi (Ed.), *Iskolaéretlen tanulók az elsö osztályban* (pp. 157–171). Budapest: Tankönyvkiadó.

Ligeti, R. (1982). *Az írástanítás pszichológiája* [The psychology of writing education]. Budapest: Akadémiai Kiadó.

Losoncz, M. (Ed.). (1981). *Az óvodai anyanyelvi nevelés továbbfejlesztése* [The further development of mother tongue education in the nursery school]. Kecskemét: Kecskeméti Óvónőképző Intézet.

Nagy, J. (1980). *5–6 éves gyermekeink iskolakészültsége* [School maturity of 5–6 year old Hungarian children]. Budapest: Akadémiai Kiadó.

Papp, F. (1982). Írástanítás—a nyelvész szemével [Writing education looked at with the eyes of the linguist]. In K. Fülöp & Z. Lengyel (Eds.), *Az orosz nyelv tanítása az általános iskola 4. osztályában* [The teaching of Russian in the 4th class of the primary school] (pp. 147–163). Szeged: Juhász Gyula Tanárképző Főiskola.

Petriné Feyér, J., & Végh, E. (1984). A olvasástanítás helyzete [The situation of reading education]. *A tanító, 22,* 1–10.

Pirisi, M. (1975). Anyanyelvi nevelés [Mother tongue education]. In L. Faragó (Ed.), *Az iskolára előkészítő foglalkozások vezetése* [Guidance of school preparatory activities] (pp. 43–74).

Réger, Z. (1986). Cigány gyermekek nyelvi szocializációjának vizsgálata [Investigation into the linguistic socialization of gypsy children in Hungary]. Manuscript.

Rét, R. (1978). The Hungarian plan for the school of tomorrow. *Prospects, 8,* 251–262. Paris: UNESCO.

Sugárné Kádár, J. (Ed.) (1985). *Beszéd és kommunikáció az óvodás—és kisiskoláskorban* [Speech and communication at the age of nursery school and the lower level of primary school]. Budapest: Akadémiai Kiadó.

Szende, A., & Szépe, G. (1978). Le développement à long terme de l'enseignement de la langue maternelle à l'école. *Acta Linguistica Hung, 28,* 329–344. Budapest: Akadémiai Kiadó.

Szépe, G. (1978). The issue of mother tongue education and the attempts to rejuvenate mother tongue education in Hungary. In G. Szépe & A. Zampolli (Eds.), *Studies on mother tongue education* (pp. 106–119). Pisa: CNUCE.

Szépe, G. (1984). Mother tongue education, language policy and education. *Prospects, 14,* 63–73. Paris: UNESCO.

Terestyéni, T. (1987). An inquiry into the role of the written word in Hungarian cultural communication. *Prospects, 17,* 39–48. Paris: UNESCO.

Török, G., & Vekerdi, I. (1981). A beszédhangok tudatosításának kifejlesztése az óvodában [The development of conscious use of speech sounds]. In M. Losoncz (Ed.), *Az óvodai anyanyelvi nevelés továbbfejlesztése* [The further development of mother tongue education in the nursery school] (pp. 102–117). Kecskemét: Kecskeméti Óvónőképző Intézet.

UNESCO (1983). *Backgrounder: Literacy education.* Paris: UNESCO.

Veres, S., & Lengyel, M. (1984). *Statisztikai tájékoztató. 1983/84. Alsófokú oktatás* [Statistical information on primary education in Hungary]. Budapest: Művelődési Minisztérium.

Virágh, S. (1982). Olvasástanítás [Reading education]. In K. Fülöp & Z. Lengyel (Eds.), *Az orosz nyelv tanítasa az általános iskol 4. osztályában* [The teaching of Russian in the 4th class of the primary school] (pp. 43–53). Szeged: Juhász Gyula Tanárképző Főiskola.

Virágvölgyi, P. (1980). Handwriting in Hungary. *The Journal for Italic Handwriting, 103,* 17–21.

Virágvölgyi, P. (1981). A kézírásról [On handwriting]. Budapest: MTA Nyelvtudományi Intézet.

Zsolnai, J. (1982). *Nyelvi-irodalmi-kommunikációs nevelési kísérlet* [Experiment in education of language, literature, and communication]. Veszprém: Országos Oktatástechnikai Központ.

CHAPTER 10

Multilingual Education in Britain
The State of the Art

SAFDER ALLADINA

1. LANGUAGE SURVEYS

A multilingual education program in schools needs information on the linguistic repertoire of school children and information on levels of literacy and competence in those languages. There is no comprehensive survey of languages spoken in Britain. Information on language use among British school children is either area specific or is contained in sample surveys from various parts of Britain. Even these linguistic sketches have a great degree of statistical unreliability due to weaknesses in methodology and language classification (Alladina, 1982, 1985a,b). The Department of Education and Science estimates that the number of pupils aged between 5 and 16 years whose first language is not English is somewhere between 375,000 and 500,000 (Commission of the European Communities, 1984). In the absence of a comprehensive language survey of school children in Britain, the Inner London Education Authority's 1983 Language Census (ILEA, 1983) can be used to illustrate the language situation in the inner-city schools in Britain. Of the 147 languages recorded, 12 had more than 1,000 speakers each and among them accounted for 83% of pupils speaking a language other than or in addition to English. These languages were: Bengali (9,089 speakers), Turkish (4,316), Gujrati (3,632), Spanish (3,466), Greek (3,410), Urdu (3,326), Panjabi (3,022), Chinese (2,825), Italian (2,421), Arabic (2,345), French (2,167), and Portuguese (1,861). The census did not collect information on the levels of literacy of these pupils in their home lan-

---

SAFDER ALLADINA • School of Teaching Studies, The Polytechnic of North London, London NW5 3LB, England.

guages. Language surveys in Britain that give information on literacy have relied on self-reports in data collection and not on statistically or pedagogically sound methods of eliciting information on levels of literacy.

2. THE QUESTION OF LANGUAGE DEFINITION

In addition to the fact that the language-use surveys contain only superficial information on literacy in the home languages, figures for languages like Gujrati include speakers of Kachchi. Speakers of the Hindu, Muslim, and Sikh varieties of Panjabi, each with its own tradition of separate scripts, are subsumed under the category of Panjabi speakers. Similarly, the category "speakers of Chinese" incorporates speakers of Putung-hua, Hakka, Wu, and other dialects of Kwantung. The majority of the 2,167 speakers of French in the ILEA schools, one could assume, are speakers of African–French Creoles. Speakers of the African–English Creoles are not included in these surveys because these languages are considered to be varieties of English. The terms African–English and African–French Creoles were advocated by the author (Alladina, 1984) to indicate the partnership of African and European languages in the creation of these Creoles. The tradition so far has been to refer to these languages either as varieties of English and French or as "English-based" and "French-based" Creoles—terms of reference that reveal a Eurocentric view of world languages. It has also to be noted that in Britain, speakers of Italian include a large number of speakers of the Sicilian variety. Similarly, Turkish and Greek include speakers of the Cypriot varieties of those languages; Bengali includes a larger proportion of Sylhetti speakers; and the term Arabic obscures speakers of the Middle East, Maghreb, and Koranic varieties of Arabic. This lack of clarity in the definition and description of languages, coupled with vague estimates of the numbers of speakers of those languages, indicates the lack of a serious approach to language teaching in Britain.

3. THE LINGUISTIC REPERTOIRE OF SCHOOL CHILDREN IN BRITAIN

The multilingual situation in the British schools may be summarized as follows:

A. Speakers of English and/or indigenous languages of Britain
    1. Speakers of Welsh or Gaelic
    2. Speakers of regional/class variety of English
    3. Speakers of Standard School English

B. Speakers of Afro-Caribbean languages
   1. Speakers of African–English Creoles
   2. Speakers of African–French Creoles
   3. Speakers of British black English
   4. Speakers of regional/class variety of English
   5. Speakers of Standard School English
C. Speakers of African, Asian, European, and other languages
   1. Speakers of a variety of a dialect of a language
   2. Speakers of the standard form of that language
   3. Speakers of a related language
   4. Speakers of regional/class variety of English
   5. Speakers of Standard School English

The term Standard School English has been used to describe that variety of English, in its spoken and written forms, which all school children need to have to succeed in the British school system. In each of the above groups, a student may speak one or a combination of languages. Some speakers may even have an unrelated or a foreign language in the repertoire. Literacy in these languages cannot always be taken for granted. Each of these students has his or her linguistic strength and educational needs. An assessment of the linguistic repertoire and levels of literacy of each learner has to be made before any educational recommendations can be made for the language development of these children. Lawton (1968), Bernstein (1970), Rosen (1972), the Bullock Committee Report (1975), the Rampton Committee Report (1981), the Hargreaves Report (1984), and the Swann Committee Report (1985) have discussed the language needs of school children in British schools. Specific comments have been made in these studies on the poor performance of speakers of languages other than English. However, in practice, speakers in Group C have been identified as those needing English as a second language, in which no use is made of the child's home language. Speakers in Group B get identified as those needing remedial English or as educationally subnormal. The net result is that the educational development of these children has been retarded. The Swann Committee Report, the latest in the series, goes as far as to advocate that the teaching of home languages should not be part of the British school curriculum and should be conducted outside school hours.

The multilingual resource of the British school children can be made use of by the teaching and strengthening of literacy, exploiting the home language resource of the learners, and teaching elaborate codes involving different styles, registers, and standards. Children who speak African–French Creole, for example, could be taught Standard French using the home language, and that Standard French could be used in the teaching of Standard School English. Similarly, the multilingual resource of the South Asian school children could be made use of by building bridges between the language used in the homes and the standard form of that language which could be used in the teaching of the Standard School English. It makes pedagogical sense to teach literacy to a child through a language most familiar to him or her instead of expecting that child to make a formidable conceptual leap in tackling literacy in a language which is less familiar and which the child is still in the process of learning and acquiring.

4. THE HISTORY OF AFRICAN AND ASIAN LANGUAGES IN BRITAIN

The history of the presence in Britain of the languages of African and Asian people and, indeed, other languages of the world is not recent (Alladina, 1984).

In the third century A.D., the Roman imperial army in Britain had a division of Moors in it. In 1555, John Lock, a London-based merchant, brought a group of West Africans to Britain with the intention of teaching them English and sending them back to Africa as interpreters and "public relations men" (Fryer, 1984). The imperial administrators who returned home from the colonies brought back with them servants from Asia, Africa, and the Caribbean. By the end of the nineteenth century, there were well-established groups of people in Britain who spoke languages other than English. At an academic level, the chair of Arabic had been established at Cambridge in 1632 and at Oxford in 1636. In 1897, the Indian Institute was set up in the University of Oxford. The Oriental School was established at the Imperical Institute in London in 1889. King's College in London had a lecturer in Kiswahili in 1895, and Cambridge initiated a lecturership in Hausa in 1896. University College in London had appointed a professor of Gujrati in 1885. In 1866 the Honour School of Oriental Studies in the University of Oxford offered Sanskrit, Persian, Arabic, Hindustani, Hindi, Marathi, Bengali, Tamil, and Telegu. Language was an important component in the examinations for the recruitment of personnel for the Empire. The London School of Oriental and African Studies serviced that need. There had been courses at Oxford, Cambridge, and London to prepare candidates for the rigors of the Indian Civil Service Examinations. Urdu was a compulsory language for those wishing to join the Indian Civil Service. A "language allowance" was awarded to those who had acquired the rudiments of a language of the subject nations they were going to administer. Hailbury College in Hertfordshire, which specialized in preparing English youngsters for the Civil Service Examinations, gave "rudimentary instruction in Oriental languages." The Civil Service Commission Examination of Officers in the Army in Modern Foreign Languages gave tests in Kiswahili, Hausa,

Urdu, Persian, and Arabic. It was after the Second World War that larger numbers of African and Asian people from the British colonies came to the metropolitan centers of Britain to meet the demand for labor in industries. Although the languages of these people were in daily use in the homes, families, and social networks, the British education system disregarded the relevance and the validity of these languages in its schools and in the society at large. The language communities, on the other hand, took it upon themselves to continue with education in the culture and language for their children outside school hours.

5. THE BILINGUAL DEBATE—THE ART OF THE STATE

Although there was a well-established tradition of teaching African and Asian languages to "the Sons of the Empire" in universities and private schools, when it came to teaching these languages in British schools, debates were initiated by educationists to discuss the wisdom of teaching these languages in schools. Languages that were "modern foreign languages," which had established examination standards and departments in universities, began to be referred to as "ethnic minority languages," "new minority languages," "England's newer languages," "community languages," "heritage languages," and so on. This is in spite of the fact that in the last two decades there has been ample evidence from multilingual societies around the world in support of multilingual education. The British educationists seem to have remained oblivious of it. There has been a huge debate in Britain on "mother-tongue teaching," whereas it should be obvious that schools cannot teach the mother tongue, it is mothers who teach the mother tongue. What the schools can do is to take that language of the home and teach the extended forms of that language and then use that to teach the language of education.

The problem with plurilingual education in Britain is that research and educational policy-making still suffer from a strong monolingual bias.

REFERENCES

Alladina, S. (1982). The question of self-image and attitude to language of the speakers of South Asian languages in Britain. Mysore, India: The Third International Conference on South Asian Languages and Linguistics, Central Institute of Indian Languages.

Alladina, S. (1984). Black people's languages in Britain—historical and contemporary perspective. Conference on the History of Black People in London, Centre for Multicultural Education, University of London Institute of Education, 27–29 November 1984. *Journal on Multilingual and Multicultural Development*, 1986, 7(5), 349–359.

Alladina, S. (1985a). Research methodology for language use surveys in Britain—a critical review.

In P. H. Nelde (Ed.), *Methods in contact linguistic research* (pp. 233–240). Brussels: USFAL Research Centre on Multilingualism.

Alladina, S. (1985b). *South Asian languages in Britain: Criteria for description and definition.* London: Centre for Multicultural Education, University of London Institute of Education, Occasional Paper No. 5.

Bernstein, B. (1970). *Social class, language and socialisation in theoretical studies towards a sociology of language.* London: RKP.

Bullock Committee Report. (1975). A language for life. London: HMSO.

Commission of the European Communities. (1984). A Report from the Commission to the Council on the Implementation of Directive 77/486/EEC, COM(84), 54. Brussels.

Fryer, P. (1984). *Staying power. The history of black people in Britain.* London: Pluto Press.

Hargreaves Report. (1984). Report of the committee on the curriculum and organisation of secondary schools, ILEA (70392 3/84). London: Inner London Education Authority.

ILEA. (1983). 1983 language census. RS 916/83, London: Inner London Education Authority.

Lawton, D. (1968). *Social class, language and education.* London: RKP.

Rampton Committee Report. (1981). The West Indian children in our schools. London: HMSO.

Rosen, H. (1972). *Language and class—a critical look at the theories of Basil Bernstein.* England: Falling Wall Press.

Swann Committee Report. (1985). Education for all. The report of the committee of inquiry into the education of children from ethnic minority groups. London: HMSO.

PART II

Psycholinguistic, Linguistic, and Educational Issues and Problems

CHAPTER 11

Psychoeducational Language Awareness Assessment and Early Reading

MARC SPOELDERS AND LUT VAN DAMME

1. INTRODUCTION

The "normal" 6-year-old child who is about to learn to read in the educational setting of the school is already able to comprehend a first language and to use this medium to express orally his or her feelings and ideas more or less adequately. Thus, it would sound somewhat counterintuitive to expect children not to be linguistically equipped to undertake the reading conquest. Reality, however, teaches us that for (too) many there is no *veni, vidi, vici* in this so important domain. And, indeed, traditionally psychoeducationists have paid much attention to perceptual and motor factors for explaining reading failure. However, a not to be neglected portion of reading failure does not seem to be due to malfunctioning in these domains. Thus, some authors advanced the idea that the (psycho-) linguistic makeup of the beginning reader should also contain "metalinguistic awareness": the child should be able to reflect upon language and linguistic behavior. Although the precise nature of the relationship between metalinguistic awareness and the acquisition of the reading skill has not yet been revealed, recent research suggests that metalinguistic ability functions as a facilitator in the beginning stage of learning to read (for a review, see Spoelders, 1982; Spoelders & Van Damme, 1982, 1983; Van Damme & Spoelders, 1983).

Based on these theoretical considerations, we formulated the following hypothesis: *children who have a higher level of metalinguistic awareness at the*

MARC SPOELDERS and LUT VAN DAMME • Seminarie en Laboratorium voor Experimentele, Psychologische en Sociale Pedagogiek, Rijksuniversiteit Gent, 9000 Gent, Belgium.

beginning of learning to read will achieve better in reading than children who manifest a lower level of metalinguistic awareness.

2. ORIGIN: P.I.

In order to measure metalinguistic awareness, we need a valid and reliable instrument. Since no such device (in Dutch) is at the disposal of psychoeducational researchers, we had to construct one of our own.[1] We decided that a first version of it should contain a large pool of items, so that after the tryout a smaller, less time-consuming one could be assembled. Let us here call the larger version Parent-Instrument (P.I.).[2] Its different parts and items have been selected and adapted from the range of materials reported in the already voluminous psycholinguistic literature on metalinguistic awareness.

The P.I. contains three main sections:[3]

I. *Recognizing and understanding literacy behavior:*
Given a drawing the child was asked what a person in the picture is doing (32 items). With the help of 28 other drawings we tried to find out if the child understood the purposes of literacy, for instance, knowing that reading a story can be enjoyable.

II. *Concepts of features of printed language:*
Here the child's knowledge of technical terms describing language, for instance, "word," "letter," was tested (36 items).

III. *Concepts of features of spoken language:*
This section included:
Phoneme Awareness
III.1. Phoneme differentiation: The child had to separate the first phoneme from a given word.
III.2. Rhymes: We asked the child to judge if some given words rhymed with a fixed one.
Word Awareness
III.3. Concept "word": The child was asked if a given item was a word.
III.4. Long/short word: Out of two given words the child had to indicate the longer one.

[1] Downing, Ayers, and Schaefer (s.d.) developed the LARR Test (Linguistic Awareness in Reading Readiness). Apart from the language differences it should also be noted that LARR is centered on the measurement of the extent to which children are able to recognize literacy behavior, understand literacy functions, and have knowledge of some technical terminology. It does not, however, investigate metalinguistic awareness of spoken language in relation to reading acquisition.
[2] This version has also been called M.A.T. (Metalinguistic Awareness Test; see Van Damme & Spoelders, 1985a).
[3] A full description can be found in Van Damme and Spoelders (1985b).

Form Awareness

III.5. Concept "sentence": The child was asked if a given item was a sentence.

III.6. Semantic/grammatical acceptability of sentences: We presented a sentence orally and asked if it was right or wrong. (The sentence could be syntactically or semantically correct or incorrect.)

Each subtest contained 12 items.

Scoring with P.I. was easy: for each correctly solved item the child received one point.

3. STATISTICAL DATA

A sample of 131 kindergarten children was screened with P.I. just before they entered the first grade of elementary school. Because of absenteeism or organizational difficulties, only 104 could be administered the complete P.I. We obtained three reading achievement scores for 100 subjects (50 male, 50 female). Two of them were given by the teacher(s): school marks for reading (after 4 months of instruction) and a score on a Likert-type scale (5-point scale ranging from very weak to very good reading competence). The third score was obtained by means of a standardized reading test *(Enschedese Leeskaart 2)*, which was individually administered to the subjects. In this test the child was asked to read a story which was made up of "regular" one-syllable words and printed without capitals. The score was computed with the correctly read words in one minute. The test was administered after a half year of formal instruction.

Reading achievement and P.I. scores were correlated, using the Bravais–Pearson formula. Table 1 presents the correlation coefficients.

For all correlations, $p < .01$. No significant differences were found between boys and girls. Our initial hypothesis seemed to be confirmed: children who began formal reading instruction with a higher level of metalinguistic

Table 1. Correlation between Language Awareness (P.I.) and Reading

	I	II	III	Total
Enschedese leeskaart	.36	.52	.54	.58
5-point scale	.36	.49	.68	.60
School marks for reading	.28	.44	.49	.51

awareness achieved better after half a year of reading instruction than the children with low metalinguistic awareness. It should be noticed, however, that these findings, given the correlational data on which they are based, do not permit any statement on the possible causal influence of metalinguistic awareness on reading achievement. In order to come to grips with this relation in more detail, we decided to undertake a more sophisticated investigation in which a larger sample is involved and also some possibly interfering factors are "controlled" (see section 5, "Discussion").

In this study-in-progress, we make use of a reduced version of P.I. As a matter of fact, P.I. was too time consuming. Therefore, for each item of P.I. we have determined the index of difficulty (the proportion of subjects that gave a correct answer to the item), as well as the discrimination index (the correlation of each item with the subject's total score on the subtest in which the item figured). Both indexes were computed according to Davis (1965), P.I. items which were either too difficult (passed by fewer than 20% of the subjects) or too easy (passed by more than 80% of the subjects) were deleted. Nondiscriminated items (discrimination indexes below .35) were also eliminated or revised.

The reliability of P.I. has also been determined. We used Cronbach's α executed according to the SPSS program (Nie et al., 1975). With dichotomous items, α is equivalent to Kunder–Richardson's Formula 20 reliability coefficient, a widely used method for determining the reliability of a test. Coefficients of .80 (at least) or .90 (preferably) are desirable when predictions are to be made. As shown in Table 2, the total test obtained a reliability coefficient of .92; one subtest obtained .90, and, four others obtained reliability coeffi-

Table 2. The Reliability of P.I.

	Cronbach's α[a]	σx[b]	k[c]	N[d]
I$_1$	.72	1.76	32	131
I$_2$	.90	2.10	28	131
Total I	.89	2.83	60	131
II	.86	2.47	36	131
III$_1$	.89	1.24	12	104
III$_2$	.75	1.17	12	131
III$_3$	−.21	1.66	12	131
III$_4$	.75	1.39	12	131
III$_5$	.65	1.54	12	131
III$_6$	.48	1.39	12	104
Total III	.83	3.58	72	104
Total	.92	5.20	168	104

[a] Reliability coefficient.
[b] Standard error.
[c] Number of items.
[d] Subjects.

Table 3. Structure of G.T.L.

		Material	Items
I.	1. Recognizing literacy behavior	Drawings	10
	2. Understanding literacy behavior	Drawings	20
II.	Concepts of features of printed language		
	Knowledge of technical terminology	Test-booklet	20
III.	Concepts of features of spoken language		
	Phoneme awareness		
	1. Phoneme differentiation	Two toy frogs	6
	2. Rhymes	Puppet "Jos"	6
	Word awareness		
	3. Word boundaries	Cubes	6
	4. Long/short words		6
	Form awareness		
	5. Morphemes	Puppets	6
	6. Grammatical acceptability of	"Rankie-Pankie"	
	sentences	and "Mies"	6
			86

cients between .80 and .89. The most eye-catching coefficient is in III3 (the concept "word"). Subjects were probably guessing when asked for their implicit criterion to judge what was a word and what was not. The P.I. subtests III3 and III5 (the concept "sentence") as well as III6 (the acceptability of sentences) have been completely changed or reworked. From the other subtests, items with low and/or unproductive indexes of difficulty or of discrimination have been deleted.

4. G.T.L.

The reworked version of P.I. is called G.T.L. (Geindividualiseerd Taalbewustzijnsonderzoek bij het Leesbegin/Individualized Language Awareness Testing at the Beginning of Reading Instruction; Van Damme, 1984). The G.T.L. has the same general structure as P.I. (see Table 3).

4.1. Subtest I

The first part of this instrument concerns the recognition of literacy behavior and the understanding of literacy functions. Recognizing activities such as reading and writing exemplifies a sort of general awareness (I1). In our opin-

Figure 1. Girl writing down her name.

ion, learning to read may be very difficult for a child if he or she has no working definitions of reading and writing. Some investigations conclude that, in fact, many first-grade pupils do not have any specific expectancies of what reading is going to be like, of what it consists of. They also indicate that young beginners have difficulty in understanding the purpose of written language (I2), a kind of pragmatic awareness. The G.T.L. tests the child's knowledge of these aspects by means of some drawings that either do or do not illustrate the reading or writing activities or the purpose of literacy. The following are some examples (see Figures 1, 2, and 3):

Figure 2. Man reading the method of preparation on tinned soup.

Figure 3. Man reading the signpost.

- The child is shown a picture of a girl writing her name down on the plaster of the broken arm of her friend and is asked, "What is this girl doing?"
- The child is shown a picture of a man reading the method of preparation on tinned soup and is asked, "Show me everything that people can read. Rub it with your finger."
- The child is shown a picture of a man sitting in his car reading the signposts and is told, "This man has lost his way. Can he find the right road this way, as on the drawing? How do you know that?"

4.2. Subtest II

The second subtest investigates the child's knowledge of some technical terms often used in reading instruction (a kind of metalanguage belonging to the teacher's Reading Instruction Register). As a matter of fact, the teacher uses these terms from the very beginning, and it can be expected that many children will be confused. It is important for the teacher to have a clear notion of the children's knowledge in this respect. In G.T.L. we use a test-booklet in which the child is asked, for example, to draw a circle around "one word" or "all the letters," given a series of printed stimuli. Two examples are given in Figure 4.

4.3. Subtest III

The last part of G.T.L. tackles phoneme, word, and form awareness. It is generally accepted that in order to learn to read, children have to bring their knowledge of the spoken language to bear upon the written language. This requires the ability to deal explicitly with the structural features of spoken lan-

Figure 4. Example of Subtest II. (a) Task: draw a circle around each word; (b) Task: draw a circle around the first letter.

guage. It is, therefore, justified to suppose that some reflection on spoken language is necessary for the child to be able to discover the properties of spoken language that are central to the correspondences between the written and the spoken mode. The G.T.L. investigates metalinguistic awareness of the spoken language by means of six tasks at three levels:

4.3.1. Phoneme Awareness

III1. *Phoneme differentiation:* In this task the child has to give the first phoneme of a given word. Before this the child is instructed on what is meant by "first sound in a word." Afterwards, two toy frogs are introduced (a little one and an old king frog). The old king frog wants to play a game with the little one. The game consists of pronouncing the first sound in a given word. The children are asked to help the little frog, because it does not know how to perform this task.

III2. *Rhymes:* The children are first asked if they can give a word that sounds like *roos* ('rose'). A few examples are generated. This procedure is repeated with the word *beer* ('bear'). Then the child is acquainted with a hand puppet called "Jos" who likes words that sound like his name. Six test words are presented in random order (three rhyme, three don't). For each word presented the child answers the question "Does . . . sound like Jos?"

4.3.2. Word Awareness

III3. *Word boundaries:* A sentence is read aloud to the child, and for each word spoken, the child lays down a cube. Six sentences are presented, differing in length and types of words used. A justification for the inclusion of this test can be found in the often reported correlation between this sort of activity and reading achievement.

III4. *Long/short words:* In this task we first present (orally) the child with two words and tell which word is the longer one and which is the shorter. Then we present six pairs of words (in randomized order as to length). No feedback is given.

4.3.3. Form Awareness

III5. *Morphemes:* The child has to make judgments on the morphemic endings of words. Therefore, he or she is acquainted with two puppets: one, called "Rankie-Pankie" (a character played by the experimenter), is still learning how to talk properly; the other, called "Mies" (a character to be played by the child), is helping. The child is told that now and then Rankie-Pankie says words the wrong way and that Mies' job consists of helping him to pronounce them appropriately. An example is given. For each item a picture is shown together with a verbal context for the test word. For example: Rankie-Pankie is shown a large dog and a small dog. At the same time the experimenter asks: *"Een kleine hond is een. . . ?"* ('a small dog is called. . . ?'). The correct answer would be: *hondje* ('doggie'). If Rankie-Pankie gives the wrong answer, Mies (the child) should correct him. If the child answers: "wrong," he or she is asked to say it correctly in order to help Rankie-Pankie. There are six items. Morphemic endings tested include third-person simple present tense, plural, and diminutive. For each of these a correct and an incorrect item are given (at random).

III6. *Grammatical acceptability of sentences:* This subtest concentrates on word order. For this form judgment task, the two puppets are used again. Mies (the child) has to judge if the sentences, uttered by Rankie-Pankie (the experimenter), sound good or funny. There are six items, three correct and three incorrect sentences (at random).

The scoring for G.T.L. remains easy: for each correctly solved item, the child receives one point (total score: 86).

5. DISCUSSION

The motivation for the investigation reported in this chapter can be found in our belief that metalinguistic awareness plays an important role in learning to read and probably in other learning tasks as well. The preliminary findings are encouraging.

In a longitudinal study in progress, metalinguistic awareness is measured by means of G.T.L. We believe that besides the predictive validity, there are

solid psycholinguistic grounds for ascribing construct validity to our operation-
alization of metalinguistic awareness.

In this study we also control for some other variables: school readiness,
(traditionally tested) reading readiness, readiness for arithmetic, intelligence,
social background, birth order, auditory and visual perception, language development, motivation for reading.

As to the latter variable, a reading motivation scale is administered at the
beginning of the process of learning to read and after a period of 7 months of
reading instruction. Motivation for reading may have important predictive qualities. It is also worth studying, however, in order to investigate whether and to
what extent difficulties in learning to read reflect on attitudes toward reading.

We measured reading achievement in the preliminary study by means of a
standardized reading test which centered on the decoding capacity. Since reading cannot be equated with merely decoding, we also test for understanding in
the study-in-progress.

We hope we shall be able to report elsewhere at length on this research.
For the time being and as a conclusion of this chapter we would like to suggest
two related research topics that will be tackled by our team in the near future.
One is linked to the observation that exposure to a second language has been
considered to be a factor in promoting metalinguistic awareness (because it may
lead to an earlier separation of word sound from word meaning). Some research
findings, indeed, seem to indicate that bilingual children show a slightly superior performance in tasks which require focusing on formal aspects of language.
We would like to set up a study—given the multilingual character of our society—which examines the relation between bilingualism (or diglossia), metalinguistic awareness, and reading acquisition. The other topic is based on an
exploratory fieldwork in the framework of our involvement in a total communication project with deaf toddlers which seems to suggest that it would be
worth investigating the development of metalinguistic awareness in relation to
reading in this kind of "atypical" population. We believe that the linguistic
behavior of those children, deprived from "parole," may also lead in a unique
way to some fundamental theorizing about metalinguistic awareness in general.

REFERENCES

Davis, F. (1965). *Item-analyse*. Leuven/Amsterdam: Nauwelaerts/Swets & Zeitlinger.
Downing, J., Ayers, D., & Schaefer, B. (s.d.). *Manual for the Linguistic Awareness in Reading
Readiness test—LARR*, s.1.
Nie, N. H. *et al.* (1975). *Statistical package for the social sciences*. 2nd edition and updates.
Spoelders, M. (1982). Psychopedagogische verkenning van (leren) lezen via case-study. In *Han-
delingen van het 2de internationaal IRA- symposium, Belgische sectie over leesstoornissen*.
Antwerpen, 1981.

Spoelders, M., & Van Damme, L. (1982). Early metalinguistic awareness and reading. *Scientia Paedagogica Experimentalis, 19,* 117–129.

Spoelders, M., & Van Damme, L. (1983). En de leeuw? Hij las voort. Het leesonderwijs in Vlaanderen. *En nu over jeugdliteratuur, 10,* 220–222.

Van Damme, L. (1984). *Geïndividualiseerd Taalbewustzijnsonderzoek bij het Leesbegin. G.T.L.* RUG: Laboratorium voor Pedagogiek (experimental version).

Van Damme, L., & Spoelders, M. (1983). Luisteren en blijven luisteren. *Moer, 6,* 8–13.

Van Damme, L., & Spoelders, M. (1985a). Reflections on a metalinguistic awareness test for pre-readers. In M. Spoelders, F. Van Besien, F. Lowenthal, & F. Vandamme (Eds.), *Language acquisition and learning. Essays in educational pragmatics 2* (pp. 67–68). Leuven/Gent: ACCO:C & C.

Van Damme, L., & Spoelders, M. (1985b). Individualized language awareness testing and early reading. *Scientia Paedagogica Experimentalis, 22,* 127–134.

CHAPTER 12

The Development of Metalinguistic Awareness and the Acquisition of Formal Speech in Mother-Tongue Education

GILLES GAGNÉ AND LUC OSTIGUY

1. INTRODUCTION

This chapter is about the development of oral language in primary school children whose native language is part of the school curriculum as both a subject of study and a medium of teaching and learning. It is concerned with the development of a component of communicative competence: the ability to choose the linguistic forms appropriate to the register asked for by the communicative situation in which one is producing speech. More specifically, it deals with the ability of children to use, in formal situations, the linguistic forms required.

2. THEORETICAL FRAMEWORK

Linguistic variation can be defined as the possibility to use two or more variants to convey the same contextual denotative meaning. It is known that the use of a variant, apart from the linguistic constraints, depends on two main categories of factors: firstly, the geographical, sociocultural, and socioeconomic background of the speaker and, secondly, the pragmatic and topical aspects of the communicative situation. Characteristics of the speaker being con-

GILLES GAGNÉ • Faculté des sciences de l'education, Université de Montréal, Montréal H3C 3J7, Québec, Canada.   LUC OSTIGUY • Département de français, Université du Québec à Trois-Rivières, Trois-Rivières G9A 5H7, Québec, Canada.

sidered invariant, a speech register is defined as the set of linguistic forms which would be more probably used in such and such a communicative setting. Among the variety of identified components of communicative situations that would command variation of register, one can name topic, medium of transmission, social function of the speech, relations between participants, their numbers, and so on (Ervin-Tripp, 1964; Gumperz, 1964; Halliday, McIntosh, & Strevens, 1972; Hymes, 1972). Authors seem to agree on at least two registers: formal and informal.

Children entering primary school are normally quite fluent in the informal register, but do not seem to be as competent with the formal register. It seems obvious that children of any region or socioeconomic background, who have access to radio and television, do understand formal speech in messages that are semantically and discursively at their cognitive level. Their lack of competence would rather be in producing formal speech.

There are theoretical and pedagogical reasons for school not to condemn but to accept the informal speech used spontaneously by children. There is also sound justification for school to develop mastery of formal oral speech, a kind of "oral literacy." A lengthy discussion of the basis of such a pedagogical dual orientation is to be found in Gagné (1983). This chapter is precisely concerned with the development of formal register in primary school children, development promoted by the children's observation of their own speech variations.

It is known that children, even before entering school, are capable of using different variants depending on whether they are speaking to children or to adults (Berko-Gleason, 1973; Andersen, 1978). Research done on linguistic variation among primary school children has also shown classroom variation in the use of a more formal or a more informal register according to whether they are speaking with other children or not and depending on the communicative task (Borders-Simmons & Lucas, 1982; Houston, 1970; Jensen, 1973; Reid, 1978; Gambell, 1981). However, research does not yet seem to have answered the question of children's awareness or, more precisely, of their conscious awareness of such variations. It is postulated that they have at least an "unconscious" awareness, but we do not know if they are able to make such awareness explicit and at what age they show such metalinguistic and metacommunicative conscious awareness.

The utility of conscious metalinguistic awareness on linguistic performance has been challenged by results of research on language development and criticism of the teaching of traditional grammar (Wesdorp, 1983; Wilkinson, 1971). However, if success in spontaneous performance does not seem to depend on metalinguistic consciousness, it does not mean that the development of such consciousness will not have a beneficial effect on the ability to choose verbal forms and on the adaptation of oral performance to the situation, particularly in the case of formal situations.

3. OBJECTS OF THE RESEARCH

Research has been undertaken to see whether the development of metalinguistic consciousness will improve children's spoken ability to use formal variants in formal situations. This chapter presents the results of an exploratory study conducted first to answer two preliminary questions: are children capable of linguistic variations and are they conscious of those variations? Such a verification is needed before one builds pedagogical interventions to develop metalinguistic consciousness. The analysis of the objects of variations and of consciousness can offer the linguistic ground on which to build the classroom interventions.

The second aim of the study consists in the preliminary testing of the hypothesis that the development of metalinguistic conscious awareness is possible through classroom activities and that it will improve the use of formal variants in formal situations. The metalinguistic classroom activities, in conformity with the double pedagogical orientation mentioned above, are based on the observation by the children of their own linguistic variations, with the purpose of developing their use of formal variants without condemning the informal variants they more spontaneously use.

4. METHODOLOGY AND RESULTS

The exploratory experiment has been conducted in a regular primary school classroom of 9- and 10-year-old French-speaking children with their usual teacher. The school is situated in a semirural French area in Québec.

4.1. Are the Children Capable of Linguistic Variation and What Are the Variables Affected?

Children were divided into six groups of four. Each group was put in three different oral communicative situations:

Situation I: Spontaneous explanation of a game to the three other children of the group.

Situation II: Exchange of information in planning a library "research" project.

Situation III: Presentation of the research results in front of the class,
with parents in the audience.

Each situation was videotaped and analyzed as regards pre-identified linguistic variants. The variants that were included were of three types. They
correspond to variables whose existence has been either demonstrated (D) by
previous sociolinguistic research done on adult Quebecers or attested (A) in
descriptive linguistic works or, for a few others, proposed by the researchers
who intuitively (I) believed that they were present in the community.

Because of the nature of the corpus, which was not prescriptive, and the
resulting small number of occurrences of the expected linguistic variables in
each child's speech, the figures that were compiled are those of the whole
class. Table 1 presents only the variables that were present more than 10 times
in each situation. The numbers in the table express the percentage of occur-

Table 1. Frequency of Use of Formal Variants according to Situations

	Formal variants	Informal variants	Situation I	Situation II	Situation III	Situation IV
I[a]	et, puis, et puis	pis, et pis	0	6	39	97
A[b]	[ɑ] in word final position	[ɔ]	0	0	6	92
D[c]	preposition + article uncontracted	contracted	4	69	93	100
D	interrogative structure wh + subject inversion	wh + est-ce que wh + subj. + V.	0	0	—[d]	92
D	personal pronouns il, ils, elle, elles	i, i, a, i	0	4	18	87
A	[wa] in word final position	[we]	15	65	97	100
D	undiphthongized vowel [ɑ:]	[aᵘ]	15	33	61	95
A	[ɛ] in word final position	[æ]	33	67.6	94	100
A	interrogative structure est-ce-que + subj. + V?	subj. + V. + tu?	38	84	80	100
D	final consonant cluster	simplified	0	12	37	60
I	ici [isi]	[isIt]	30	38	82.5	—[d]
D	consonant ℓ of pronouns la and les unelided	[a] and [e]	50	72	86	100
D	consonant ℓ of articles la and les unelided	[a] and [e]	53	92	95	100
D	undiphthongized vowel [ɛ:]	[aⁱ]	3	8	10	11

Note. All numerical values are percentages.
[a] I: intuitively proposed by researchers.
[b] A: attested in descriptive works.
[c] D: demonstrated by previous sociolinguistic research.
[d] No data.

rences of the formal variants. Note also that no inferential statistical test was used.

Results show a notable increase in the frequency of use of formal variants with the increase of situational formality, especially between situations II and III. But even between situations I and II, which differed mainly in the topic of the discourse, variations did occur, some of them in a very neat way. On the whole, between situations I and III, 10 variables showed a difference of use of more than 30%, and four showed a difference of use of between 0% and 18%.

It comes out clearly that the children used variation spontaneously, that is, without their attention being called to it. The second observation is that the variation is mostly on the pre-identified variables, that is, on variables existing within the French language used in Québec.

4.2. Are Children Aware of Such Variation?

Large videotaped excerpts of speech from situations I and III were put together and presented to the class. Children were asked to pay attention to the language used while looking at the excerpts. After the viewing, the teacher asked them to identify differences in their ways of speaking in situations I and III. Children very spontaneously said that there were differences which they themselves labeled as *familier* and *soigné*. They were also able to name easily many communicative situations where one changes one's speech register.

It seems therefore that the children's metacommunicative awareness was already well present, so that there was no need to develop it by classroom activities. However, they were unable to identify precise linguistic variants. Their metalinguistic conscious awareness proved to be global and impressionistic. It was then appropriate to test if classroom activities specially conceived for that purpose could develop such awareness.

4.3. Examination of the Hypothesis That the Development of Metalinguistic Awareness of Precise Linguistic Variables Is Possible

In order to examine the hypothesis, two metalinguistic activities were elaborated.

First, in the same class, one day after the comparison of oral speech excerpts in class, the same children were collectively exposed to excerpts of their own familiar speech and were asked after hearing each statement to say how the statement could have been said more formally. There were 45 short statements extracted from speech produced in situation I, and exceptionally in situation II. The statements were chosen on the ground that they included one or

Table 2. Formal Variants Produced in the First Attempt in the Variation Task

Phonological	
[ɑ]—ex.: "il v*a*, il y *a*, Canad*a*" in variation with [ɔ]	(A)[a]
[wa]—ex.: "m*oi*, v*oi*t" in variation with [we]	(A)
[ɛ]—ex.: "il ét*ai*t, parf*ai*t, l*ai*d" in variation with [a]	(A)
Unelided *R* or *l* inside of word	
Ex.: "que*l*que chose, fi*l*m, par*c*que"	(I)[b]
Unelided *R* in final position of *sur*	(I)
Unelided *ℓ* in articles *la* and *les*	(D)[c]
froid in variation with frette	(I)
ici in variation with icitte	(I)
puis in variation with pis	(I)
n'importe où [nɛ̃pɔrtu] in variation with [nɛ̃pɔrtəju]	(I)
en dessous [ãtsu] in variation with [ãtsu:ʀ]	(I)
Morphophonological	
Uncontracted pronoun *tu*—ex.: *tu* as, *tu* en as in variation with t'as et t'en as	(I)
il, elle, ils, elles in variation with [i], [a]	(D)
Uncontracted preposition + article	
Ex.: *dans la, sur la, dans un, sur une* in variation with [dã:], [sa:], [dœ],	
[sYn]	(D)
Uncontracted pronoun *en* in variation with [n]	(A)
Unelided [*ℓ*] in pronouns *la* and *les*	(D)
Morphological	
Formal variants of verbs	
Ex.: "je *vais*", [ʒvɔ] in variation with [ʒvɔ] et [mɔ]; "il faut que tu *aies*"	
[ɛ] in variation with [ɛ:j]	(A)
Lexical	
pas du tout [padzytu] in variation with [pãtʊt]	(I)

[a] A: attested in descriptive works.
[b] I: intuitively proposed by researchers.
[c] D: demonstrated by previous sociolinguistic research.

more casual variants and, if possible, no formal variant, in order to maintain a certain homogeneity of register.

The viewing and discussion took about two sessions of one hour each. Tables 2, 3, and 4 show the results of the analysis of the transcriptions. At the first attempt, the formal variants of 18 variables were produced by the children. They were almost exclusively at the phonological and morphophonological levels (Table 2). Formal variants of six other variables were produced with more difficulty by the children, that is, the variants were uttered only at the third or fourth attempt. Among these, we found a higher proportion of interrogative structures and lexical items (Table 3). Finally, for 13 variables, the children were not able to produce the formal variants. The number of strictly morphological items increased here (Table 4).

With the centering of their attention on language, the children then seemed to show a certain ability to produce formal variants corresponding to the familiar ones perceived on the hearing of their own statements. Some of the items easily produced could be interpreted as resulting from an activation of implicit knowledge. The second category of items, those produced with more difficulty, could maybe offer indications of new learning. At this point, however, the metalinguistic awareness is not complete: some variants are not identified and not all the children show some awareness.

In order to give the same group of children another occasion to develop their conscious awareness, a second metalinguistic activity was conceived and tried out with them. It consisted of the preparation and presentation by the children of short oral dialogues, in which they had to say the same thing to two different persons, one familiar and the other one unfamiliar and imposing. Six themes were given by the teacher, one for each group of four children. To avoid interference from written language models, children were instructed not to write down their dialogues, but to prepare them orally "in their heads." After two children had performed the familiar version of the dialogue, the other two children of the group had to identify the familiar variants that had been used and vice versa; that is, the first two children had to point out the formal variants used by the latter two in the formal version of the dialogue.

Analysis of the dialogues and of the metalinguistic identifications gives interesting results. Firstly, children mostly produced and identified the variants that came out in the previous activity. They added but a few. Secondly, the casual dialogues contained more appropriate variants than the formal ones; the identifications were also more productive for the variants of the informal register. Thirdly, the variants most often produced and identified are phonological ones, then lexical, and last, syntactical and morphological.

Table 3. Formal Variants Produced in the Third or Fourth Attempt in the Variation Task

Morphophonological	
Mets-*le* [lə] in variation with [le]	$(I)^a$
Liaison between pronoun *ils* and the verb	
Ex.: *ils ont* [ilzɔ̃] in variation with [jɔ̃]	
Il y en a [iljãna] in variation with [jãnɔ]	$(A)^b$
Lexical	
quand in variation with *mais que*	(A)
Complementizer "∅" in variation with *est-ce que, c'est que*	(A)
Ex.: *"je sais où tu veux aller"* in variation with ". . . *où est ce que*/*où c'est que tu* . . ."	(A)
Syntactical	
Interrogative form *est-ce que* . . . ? in variation with . . .-*tu*?	(A)
Ex.: *"est-c'que c'est* à toi? / *c'est-tu* à toi?"	

^{a}I: intuitively proposed by researchers.
^{b}A: attested in descriptive works.

Table 4. Formal Variants Unproduced in the Variants Task

Phonological	
Final consonant cluster "unsimplified"	(D)[a]
Ex.: "table, triste, monstre"	
Undiphthongized long vowels [ɑ:], [ɛ:], [o:], [ɔ:], [œ:]	(D)
"essayer" [ɛsɛje] in variation with [asɛje]	
Morphophonological	
tout or tous [tʊ] in variation with [tʊt]	(A)[b]
fait [fɛ] (past participle of faire) in variation with [fɛt]	(I)[c]
en in variation with [nã]	(D)
j'suis allé in variation with "j'suis-t-allé" [ʃytale]	(D)
Morphological	
Application of the past participle rule	(I)
Ex.: "les fleurs que j'ai prises" in variation with . . . que j'ai pris	
Plural form of the verb être: "ce sont les . . ." in variation with "C'est	
les . . ."	(I)
"Si j'avais" in variation with "si j'aurais"	(I)
Formal variant of verb jouer (third person plural form)—	(A)
Ex.: "ils jouent" in variation with [ʒu:z]	
Lexical	
Complementizer quand in variation with quand que	(I)
Complementizer quel in indirect question in variation with quoi	(A)
Ex.: "j'sais pas quel est / c'est quoi son âge"	

[a]D: demonstrated by previous sociolinguistic research.
[b]A: attested in descriptive works.
[c]I: intuitively proposed by researchers.

It seems then that awareness of informal variants is greater than awareness of formal variants. This suggests the existence of a relation between children's use of a variant and their awareness of it, since informal variants are more frequently used than formal ones. The results also give indications about an order of facility in the linguistic nature of the variables perceived: phonological ones, then lexical, and last, morphological and syntactical.

It appears that the hypothesis was confirmed. The children were able to produce and identify precise linguistic variants, and therefore their metalinguistic awareness was developed in the activities they were involved in.

4.4. Examination of the Hypothesis That Metalinguistic Development Will Produce a Greater Use of Formal Variants in Formal Situations

In order to see if, following such activities, children would use more formal variants in an appropriate situation, an activity involving communication in a formal situation was proposed to the children 2 weeks later.

It consisted of a role-playing situation involving pairs of children in a dialogue between two fir trees, complete strangers to each other, who express their feelings about approaching Christmas. Before preparing the dialogues, the class talked about the feelings that could be expressed and the formal register of speech needed. The presentation took place in front of the class.

After the metalinguistic activities in which the children were involved, one would normally expect them to use more formal variants than before in the dialogues. To test this hypothesis, we compared for each variable the proportion of occurrences of formal variants in the dialogues (situation IV) with the proportion already observed in formal situation III. Situation III took place before the metalinguistic activities and consisted in the presentation of the results of research to the whole class with parents also being present.

Results are presented in Table 1. They clearly indicate an increase in the number and proportion of uses of formal variants compared to casual ones. As a matter of fact, there was an increase for all variants except one. Even those variants whose use was higher than 90% in situation III showed an increase: they all went up to 100% of use. All variants that were in the 80% bracket also got up to 100% in situation IV. Of the six variants whose use in situation III was 61% or less, four got up to 87% and more, one of them passing from 6% to 92%. Only one, undiphthongized vowel $[\epsilon :]$, did not show any increase.

The experimental design was not controlled enough to demonstrate that such increase in the use of formal variants is a consequence of the metalinguistic activities undertaken by the children. For example, there was no control group, and the comparability of situations III and IV was not perfect. Other possible biases have not been controlled either.

The apparent results nevertheless seem to indicate that the increase in the use of formal variants can be related to the metalinguistic activities undertaken by the children. The fact that the only variant that did not show an increase (undiphthongized $[\epsilon :]$: .10 in situation III and .11 in situation IV) was also the only one in the list that had not been identified in previous metalinguistic activities lends credence to the hypothesis that metalinguistic activities seem to improve the oral ability of children to use formal variants of speech in proper situations.

5. CONCLUSION

From this experience, some preliminary observations can be drawn:

- Nine- and 10-year-old children do vary their speech spontaneously, according to formality of situation in classroom settings.
- They are well aware of the situations that command variation, but, linguistically, their spontaneous awareness is global and impressionistic.

- Classroom metalinguistic activities on their own speech develop their consciousness of linguistic variables.
- It seems that such activities can develop the use by children of formal variants in appropriate situations.

We intend to undertake a new experiment, more controlled and centered exclusively on the development of metalinguistic awareness and its results on the development of children's use of formal variants.

From the preliminary observations obtained, suggestions can be inferred for two other aspects of literacy. First, metalinguistic activities on oral language could be used, after adaptation, in the cases of dialects which are linguistically close to each other and in situations asking for some kind of code switching. Second, metalinguistic awareness, if fruitful at the oral level, could probably serve, with at least equal efficiency, for the development of the formal aspects of writing, a part of literacy which is considered socially important.

REFERENCES

Andersen, E. S. (1978). *Learning to speak with style: A study of the sociolinguistic skills of children.* Unpublished doctoral dissertation, Stanford University.

Berko-Gleason, J. (1973). Code switching in children's language. In T. E. Moore (Ed.), *Cognitive development and the acquisition of language* (pp. 157–167). Academic Press.

Borders-Simmons, D., & Lucas, C. (1982, March). Language diversity and classroom discourse. Paper presented at the annual meeting of the American Educational Research Association, New York.

Ervin-Tripp, S. (1964). An analysis of the interaction of language, topic and listener. In J. Gumperz & D. Hymes (Eds.), *The ethnography of communication. American Anthropologist, 66,* (Part 2), 86–102.

Gagné, G. (1983). Norme et enseignement de la langue maternelle. In E. Bédard & J. Maurais (Eds.), *La norme linguistique* (pp. 463–509). Québec: Conseil de la langue française/Paris: Le Robert.

Gambell, T. J. (1981). Sociolinguistic research of children's language: The culture of the classroom. Paper presented at the annual meeting of the Canadian Society for the Study of Education held in Halifax.

Gumperz, J. J. (1964). Introduction: Toward ethnography of communication. In J. J. Gumperz & D. Hymes, *The ethnography of communication. American Anthropologist, 66* (Part 2), 1–35.

Halliday, M. A. K., McIntosh, A., & Strevens, P. (1972). The users and uses of language. In J. A. Fishman (Ed.), *Readings in the sociology of language* (pp. 139–170). La Haye: Mouton.

Houston, S. H. (1970). A re-examination of some assumptions about the language of the disadvantaged child. *Child Development, 41,* 947–963.

Hymes, D. (1972). Models of the interaction of language and social life. In J. J. Gumperz & D. Hymes (Eds.), *Directions in sociolinguistics: The ethnography of communication* (pp. 35–71). New York: Holt, Rinehart & Winston.

Jensen, J. M. (1973). A comparative investigation of the casual and careful oral language styles of average and superior fifth grade boys and girls. *Research in the Teaching of English, 7,* 339–350.

Reid, E. (1978). Social and stylistic variation in the speech of children: Some evidence from Edinburgh. In P. Trudgill (Ed.), *Sociolinguistic patterns in British English* (pp. 159–171). London: Arnold.

Wesdorp, H. (1983). *Research vs. tradition: The unequal fight; the evaluation of the traditional grammar curriculum in the Netherlands.* Amsterdam: University of Amsterdam, Center for Educational Research.

Wilkinson, A. (1971). *The foundations of language.* London: Oxford University Press.

CHAPTER 13

Evaluation of Text Reading Comprehension
Results of a Research at the End of Primary School and in Junior High School

MICHEL PAGÉ

1. INTRODUCTION

The research presented in this chapter aims at evaluating the text reading comprehension abilities of students at the end of primary school and in junior high school in the city of Montreal. This evaluation is performed by means of a test developed according to the standard procedure of test construction (Anastasi, 1976). First it is important to state explicitly the objectives to be attained by the research, because they strongly contribute to determine the nature of the test developed. The version of the test experimented is then presented. The general results obtained from the analysis made of the experimental data constitute the third part. The conclusions reveal what this first phase of the research permitted us to learn about the development of a test to evaluate reading comprehension, and they emphasize the most significant observations on the comprehension abilities of the students.

2. RESEARCH OBJECTIVES

The reading evaluation test developed for this research aims at three objectives:

MICHEL PAGÉ • Department of Psychology, University of Montréal, Montréal H3C 3J7, Québec, Canada.

1. To evaluate the *ability* of students to *comprehend informative texts* at the end of primary school (grades 5 and 6) and in junior high school (grades 7 and 8).
2. To discriminate between students with high and low ability in text comprehension by diagnosing what difficulties the low-ability students have in comprehending informative texts.
3. To be practical to use, especially with regard to the following characteristics:
   (a) being group administered.
   (b) having lower correction expenses due to the automatic coding of responses.

The ministerial programs for the teaching of French in Québec schools make comprehension skills of different types of current texts the main objective of the teaching of reading. Among the different types of texts considered as current, the informative text occupies a very important place. It is also the main resource for transmitting knowledge in the natural and social sciences. Therefore, the first objective is that the test evaluating the ability to read texts should place the emphasis upon the reading of informative texts.

Two implications of the first objective are discussed: first of all, the choice of the particular text from which the test aims to evaluate comprehension, and then the establishing of a success level of the ability evaluated.

The text used in the test was written by French teaching specialists within the school system. It is consistent with the informative texts currently used in teaching at the end of primary school and in junior high school concerning fundamental characteristics such as length, maximum amount of words per sentence, syntactic constructions, length of paragraphs, and use of titles and subtitles. The choice of a text is of paramount importance in the development of a test that is to be used to give a fair evaluation of the ability of the students involved. It should be accessible to students in the fifth grade of primary school, and it should also be able to captivate the interest of students in the eighth grade of junior high school. The particular text designated by the school system to be the subject of evaluation satisfies these conditions.

To determine a success level is a necessity inherent in all performance evaluations. What about text comprehension?

According to the first objective, the test must evaluate the ability to encode in semantic memory the information given by the text. Does this mean that a complete level of success is the encoding of all information given by the text? Research accomplished up to now on the process of comprehension would tend to invalidate such a criterion. The process of text comprehension as it presents itself in research that compares text recall to texts read by the authors of those recalls appears as an interaction in which the reader always transforms, in different ways, the text he or she reads. The inferential activity of a reader modifies a greater or lesser proportion of elements of information given by the text. An analysis of the representation that the reader gets of the whole text always reveals that some parts of the text are completely missing, that some have changed place and are integrated with others, and the like.

This is how research describes the activity of the reader, even in cases where the reading instructions or the objective assigned to the task prevent the reader from favoring certain information from the text at the expense of other information or from processing this information through cognitive operations such as comparison or generalization.

Since the maximum success in text comprehension does not imply the encoding of all the information as given by the text, a maximal success level can only be taken from a performance table of students of different abilities, among whom the best students of the school population are found. A maximal success level established this way is related to the condition in which the development of the abilities of this school population is found in order to read the specific text used in the test. It is also related to the reading task in which the students receive the instruction to decode the greatest amount of information possible given by the text.

The second objective creates an interesting challenge for research in text comprehension. In fact it enforces the use of knowledge available in this area in order to separate a global process into its components. The advantage expected is that the test may succeed in identifying specific difficulties in text reading by low-ability students. Students that have insufficient knowledge of the French language or a different ethnocultural origin are a part of the population that is particularly taken into consideration because the school system where the research was conducted includes a large percentage of this type of student.

Concerning the third objective, it is very clearly stated. It establishes a clear difference between academic research and research that must produce results that can be used in well-defined practical situations.

Taking these three objectives into account, the recall methodology currently used in research on text comprehension has been proven to be useless. This methodology consists of obtaining from the reader a connected discourse of all the information he or she understood and retained after reading the text. This methodology permits the best analysis of the structure of information that the reader retained. By doing this, it will satisfy the first objective but not the second. Recall analysis, in fact, does not permit the specific evaluation of the comprehension of text elements which could be a source of difficulty, nor does it show the reason why we do not find traces of certain information in the recall, which reduces its diagnostic potential. Since recall is a methodology that demands long analysis which, in turn, requires a long training period, it could not satisfy the third objective either.

The second objective is forced to look for a model of text comprehension which can be used to guide the development of a test that evaluates the comprehension of isolated elements of the text as well as the integrated comprehension of large chunks of information. To satisfy the third objective, the model must be used to plan out the construction of a test employing the conventional method of test construction. The test described below meets these requirements.

3. PRESENTATION OF THE TEST

Van Dijk and Kintsch's model (1983) includes a series of strategies that contribute to the comprehension of texts. It has been proven to be useful in helping to design a test that has the diagnostic potential required by the second objective. The main quality of this recent contribution of Van Dijk and Kintsch in the area of text comprehension is to bring together, in a coherent model, the components of the comprehension processes studied separately elsewhere. Although the model is not an integrated one, their contribution permits us to see the role of each component while considering its relation with each one of the others in a unique model. Table 1 presents, in the left column, the list of components involved in the comprehension process according to this model. The model proposed by Van Dijk and Kintsch resumes two fundamental arguments from the cognitive sciences:

1. The comprehension of a text is a process that proceeds at several interdependent levels. At certain of these levels, units of elementary information are processed, and at other levels the comprehension of relationships between these elements is achieved;
2. At the different levels, the process of comprehension depends on textual indicators that the reader should know how to process and on the knowledge that the reader should have in memory.

It ensues from these two fundamental ideas that we can evaluate the ability of the reader at different processing levels by evaluating his or her capacity to process the different textual indicators. It follows that an evaluation of the reader's ability must also consider whether he or she possesses the required knowledge at each level of cognitive activity.

Let's clarify the idea of level being used to separate the comprehension process. The model uses the concept of cognitive strategy to define the different levels of the process by presenting comprehension as the result of the activity of several cognitive strategies, each one producing a partial result that contributes to the comprehension of the text as an organized set of information. The cognitive sciences have taken the concept of strategy from the action theory. In this theory, achieving an objective always requires a sequence of moves, each move being accomplished with the purpose of producing situations that

Table 1. Strategies of Text Comprehension Evaluated by This Instrument[a]

Component	Evaluated by the instrument	
	Yes	No
Letter and word identification		Not relevant in grades concerned
Strategic understanding of clauses and sentences	Parts 1, 2, and 4	
Accessibility of lexical knowledge implied in parts 1, 2, and 4	Part 3	
Strategic understanding of the meaning and function of cohesion markers	Part 5	
Strategic understanding of the coherence relations between clauses and sentences	Part 6	
Accessibility of world knowledge implied in part 6	Part 7	
Strategic understanding of whole parts of the text and of the whole text	Elaboration of this part is in progress.	
Schematic strategy		Not included
Stylistic strategy		Not included

[a]Strategies are from the Van Dijk and Kintsch (1983) model.

establish a step in the pursuit of the objective. Strategy is what controls the choice one makes in the development of a sequence of moves in order to ensure, in the best way possible, the achievement of the objective.

Applied to the comprehension of a text, the concept of strategy is defined as follows. The cognitive strategy guides the mental moves in the efficient achievement of an objective which, in the present case, is a fast and coherent comprehension of a text. More specifically, this objective is defined as the development of a representation in memory, including the establishment of links between this representation and other representations that are kept in memory. The attainment of such an objective requires the performance of two types of strategies which are mentioned in Table 1:

- Local strategies that establish the meaning of clauses and sentences, on the one hand, and the meaning of relations between these sentences and clauses, on the other hand.
- Global strategies that determine the global meaning of parts of the text or of the whole text.

Even though the test evaluates the different strategies of one or the other type separately, it is important to watch out for possible signs of interdependence between them. Above all one must see if the efficiency of one type of strategy seems to ensure the efficiency of the other type.

Not all the strategies gathered in Van Dijk and Kintsch's model are evaluated by the test developed. Table 1 indicates which are not and states the main reason why it is so.

Three parts of the test, the first, second, and fourth, evaluate the efficiency of the local strategy that guides the construction of semantic propositions, that is, the process that results in the comprehension of sentences in the text (Pagé, 1985). Semantic propositions are made up of concepts representing people, objects, places, time, and so on, that help to specify these events, actions, and consequences. The textual indicators from which the reader constructs the semantic propositions are words from the text placed in syntactic structures and the morphological markers.

It is not possible for an English translation of items taken from these three parts to reproduce in this language the French cases of which comprehension is measured. We do not present translated examples for these three parts since it is not really necessary.

The *first part* measures the comprehension of the particular meaning of words that in the dictionary have several possible meanings. This success supposes the comprehension of the semantic function of the word with an ambiguous meaning in the proposition to which it belongs, as well as in the total number of propositions denoted by a sentence.

The *second part* measures the comprehension of rare words whose meaning is given in the text, usually in the sentence where the rare word is used. The reader does not arrive at this meaning unless he or she is capable of constructing the semantic relation that links this rare word with other words in the text that give its meaning.

In the *fourth part,* the comprehension of semantic propositions is directly measured by asking the student to indicate the concept that, in a sentence, has a definite case relation with the concept that indicates an action, event, or circumstance.

The *fifth part* of the instrument evaluates the local strategy from which results the comprehension of cohesion markers that are the textual markers of the thematic continuity (Charolles, 1983). The first case of cohesion markers evaluated in the test is lexical recurrence, which consists of repeating words from one sentence to the other, or the use of synonymous terms or words joined by a subordinate clause.

The second cohesion marker is coreference, which is the use, in successive sentences, of several expressions that designate the same referent. Only anaphoric coreference is evaluated by the test because it is the sole coreference marker used in the text. In this case, an expression activating a certain referent in a sentence is followed in the next sentence by a substitute form indicating the same reference. It is the pronoun that most often fills this function, as in the next example, where one of the items of this part is translated into English. The anaphoric coreference marker "it" is substituted for "one of the three lakes":

> Loch Ness is one of the three lakes forming a chain in the Scottish Highlands. *It* is a narrow lake 39 km long and 300 m deep.

Junction is the third cohesion marker from which comprehension is evaluated in the fifth part. It consists of the connection between units of the text, sentences, and clauses by connectors of conjunction (and), of disjunction (or), and of subordination, such as causality (because) or temporality (then).

The comprehension of coherence relations evaluated in the *sixth part* of the test constitutes the key aspect of text comprehension as an organized set of information. It is the comprehension of coherence relations between the successive sentences of a paragraph that constitutes the ability evaluated.

In the following example, where a paragraph of the text is translated, the coherence relations between the clauses are indicated on the left. We can see there in what way these relations link together all the sentences of that paragraph. Two arguments (sentences 25 and 26) constitute an explanation of the sentence with which the paragraph begins. These two arguments are in a parallelistic relation. The second of the two arguments (26) needs the elaboration which is given by clauses 27 and 28, between which a contrast relation is established. Definitions of this variety of coherence relation are given by Hobbs (1979).

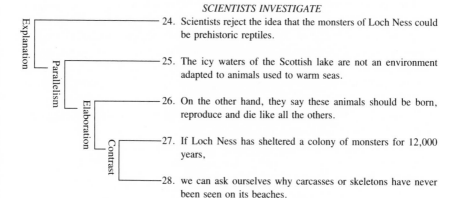

SCIENTISTS INVESTIGATE

24. Scientists reject the idea that the monsters of Loch Ness could be prehistoric reptiles.

25. The icy waters of the Scottish lake are not an environment adapted to animals used to warm seas.

26. On the other hand, they say these animals should be born, reproduce and die like all the others.

27. If Loch Ness has sheltered a colony of monsters for 12,000 years,

28. we can ask ourselves why carcasses or skeletons have never been seen on its beaches.

The comprehension of coherence relations of each paragraph of the text is evaluated separately, one paragraph after the other. The subjects reread the paragraph just before reading and answering the question asked. Loss of information due to passage of time is greatly reduced this way. Asking a question rather than asking for a free recall is a procedure that helps the subject, because students are more used to writing answers to questions than to writing out free recalls of texts read. Therefore, the procedure calls for skills that are well developed in the students, and the performance obtained is used to evaluate their ability to construct a coherent representation of the information given in a whole paragraph.

Two parts of the test, the third and the seventh, evaluate the knowledge that could play a role in the efficiency of strategies evaluated. The *third part* evaluates lexical knowledge, following a procedure in which rare words used in the text are paired with the proper definition. The *seventh part* verifies how much knowledge the subjects possess about phenomena that are implicitly evoked by the text. Therefore, items 4 and 5 of this part verify if the subjects know that the carcasses of animals that die in the water can be found. The knowledge of this phenomenon is involved in the comprehension of coherence relations between sentences 24, 25, and 26 in the example presented above.

4. PRESENTATION OF RESULTS

The testing procedure described helped to evaluate the comprehension of a text on the monsters of Loch Ness, from which the examples mentioned are taken, as well as the comprehension of another text on the disappearance of dinosaurs. The student sample first passed the Dinosaur test and subsequently the Loch Ness test. The analysis of data presented in this area represents the performance of students in the Loch Ness test, for which a multivariate analysis proved impossible, due to the lack of participation of two groups of students in the second phase of the experiment. The teachers responsible for underprivileged students in the fifth and sixth grades decided it would be better not to continue their participation in the experiment until the end, because they feared that their students would find forbidding a type of exam that required a written task they were not used to. The additional information provided by the multivariate analysis of data from the Dinosaur test, where the sample is complete, is added to the presentation of these results.

The analyses are presented from two standpoints. The first refers to metrological characteristics of the test, and the second presents the results of a comparison between groups of students from different academic levels and from three socioeconomic levels.

4.1. Metrological Characteristics of the Test

The total number of students to whom the Loch Ness test was administered is 242. Table 2 shows the distribution of these students at the four academic levels and the three socioeconomic levels represented in the sample.

The results of 121 students, randomly taken over the whole sample, helped to achieve the internal consistency analysis for the first five parts of the test. The`coding response method used in the sixth part, which is presented further on, and the small number of items in the seventh part do not permit the internal consistency analysis to be applied to those two parts. The method used is the Biserial r.

The application of a criterion .50 (this index r is significant at a threshold of .05 at .40) leads to the rejection of 7 among the 50 items that constitute the first five parts. Seven items have an index lower than .60 and six other items have an index higher than .80. Therefore, this means that 30 items have an index of internal consistency located between .60 and .80. Among the items maintained after the application of the criterion .50 for internal consistency, 14 have a success rate exceeding 80% and have to be eliminated from a subsequent version of the test. It is necessary to eliminate a certain number of items in the first five parts in order to shorten the presentation time of the test. Analyses clearly demonstrate that an evaluation of strategy efficiency can be done with only four or five items for each part, without losing important information concerning the abilities of the students. An analysis of the consistency by another method, the Guttman Scalogram (Green, 1956), makes certain that no student fails the totality of items in one part of the test, which means that all the students possess a minimum efficiency in each one of the strategies. If the differences between the subjects that have a low-success rate and those that have a high rate do not depend on the inability of the weak student to perform

Table 2. Number of Students in Each Subgroup of
the Sample

	Socioeconomic level		
Subgroup	Upper	Middle	Lower
Primary			
5th grade	28	22	—
6th grade	24	26	—
Junior high			
7th grade	28	22	20
8th grade	30	24	18

Note. N = 242.

certain strategies, we can suppose that they depend above all on knowledge of the language and text structures that only the best students possess. If this is the case, a version of the test that limited itself to four or five items in each of the first five parts would be enough to disclose such differences. It should be enough to choose among the items having the best indexes of internal consistency, some of them covering the whole extent of the variation levels of success.

Based on the data obtained from this first experiment, we can develop a version of the test that would include four items for each one of the first parts, whose success rate is between .50 and .75, and whose indexes of internal consistency range from .60 to .85, the greatest number of indexes being situated between .70 and .80. It is also possible to disclose a wide variation in the strategy evaluated in the sixth part by using three paragraphs only.

Since the first half of the sample was used for the internal consistency analysis, the analyses presented from now on apply to scores obtained from the other half of the students ($N = 122$). These scores were the ones that were established after the seven items whose index of consistency was below .50 were withdrawn.

The correlation between the seven parts of the test composes the first part of these analyses. The index calculated (Pearson's r) reveals a positive and significant intercorrelation at a threshold of at least .05 between each one of the parts of the instrument. Therefore, the scores match each other in their distribution; the students who reveal themselves more skilled in a given strategy are also the most skilled in all the others. A multiple regression index rising to .625 demonstrates that the degree of correspondence between the score distribution in the first five parts and this distribution in the sixth part is quite high ($F < .01$). Therefore, the score distribution in the strategy of paragraph comprehension (sixth part) as a structured set of information is highly predictable from score distributions in the comprehension of sentences and cohesion markers. No theoretical interpretation of the interrelation between strategies is possible from data of this nature. But the results are interesting when they are considered from the perspective of a diagnosis of comprehension ability. They eliminate the possibility that the subjects may reveal themselves weak in one strategy and strong in another. The ability development of weak readers places them in a lower position in all the strategies. Therefore, remedial education for such students should aim at increasing their efficiency in all the strategies.

The comparison of success levels of the sample in each part of the test adds a supplementary dimension. Because of the inequality in the number of items from one part to the other, a statistical comparison of the mean scores of each one of the parts is not possible. Table 3 shows that the mean scores obtained at each one of the parts by the second half of the sample have a tendency to decrease from the first part to the seventh.

Table 3. Mean Scores and Standard Deviations of the Sample for
Each Part of the Test

Part of test	Mean	Standard deviation
First part: comprehension of ambiguous words	82.72	16.95
Second part: comprehension of unknown words	82.23	20.71
Third part: lexical knowledge	70.60	23.16
Fourth part: comprehension of case relations	70.44	22.26
Fifth part: comprehension of cohesion markers	66.87	21.39
Sixth part: comprehension of coherence relations	37.42	14.51
Seventh part: knowledge of the world	23.31	20.71

Note. $N = 122$. All numbers are percentages.

The examination of these data reveals that the mean score obtained in the sixth part is distinctly inferior to the scores obtained in the first five. The same can be said about the seventh part, but it is not necessary to spend time discussing this result because the score dispersion is too big $(SD = 20.71)$, due to the very small number of items in this part.

This important drop in the scores obtained in the sixth part in relation to the intercorrelation indexes demonstrates that, if the high- and low-ability students are the same in all the strategies, their success level is not the same in each one.

A high degree of success in the strategy of proposition construction, comprehension of cohesion markers, and lexical knowledge does not assure a high degree of success in the ability to comprehend the information in a paragraph as a coherent whole. By stating how the responses are evaluated in this sixth part of the test, we demonstrate how this part evaluates the efficiency of a strategy that is specifically responsible for the comprehension of chunks of information as large as the paragraph. Figure 1 presents the network of semantic propositions that constitute a complete answer to the question asked by item 55. This network is composed of the information coming from the three sentences of this paragraph. The comprehension of each one of these sentences supposes the construction of a set of propositions; therefore, we already know that it is a strategy successfully used at a high level by the students. In order to obtain a high score in the sixth part, the student must necessarily produce an answer containing propositions coming from the three sentences. He or she should succeed in comprehending the coherence relations that link these sen-

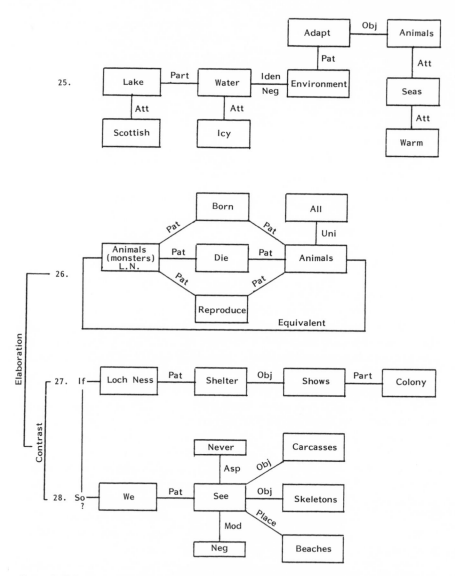

Figure 1. Coherence structure of a complete response to item 55—semantic relations and logic of propositions. Key: UNI = universal; IDEN = identity; MOD = modality; PART = part; ATT = attribute; OBJ = object; ASP = aspect; PAT = patient.

tences in order to be able to construct in his or her response a coherent network composed of elements taken from these three sentences. Here is the most literal translation possible of these three sentences:

- The icy waters of the Scottish lake are not an environment adapted for animals used to warm seas.
- On the other hand, they say that these animals should be born, reproduce, and die like all the others.
- If Loch Ness has sheltered a colony of monsters for 12,000 years, we can ask ourselves why carcasses and skeletons have never been seen on its beaches.

Success in such a case depends in part on success in the preceding parts, as the multiple regression index points out. But it is clear that success in the strategies evaluated in parts one to five is not enough to assure efficiency in the strategy evaluated in part six, which in addition involves the capacity to construct the coherence relations indicated.

4.2. Group Comparison

The results presented from this aspect come from two analyses of variance (factorial schema $A \times B$); the first comparing students from four academic levels coming from upper and middle socioeconomic levels, the second comparing students from three socioeconomic levels in only the seventh and eight grades of junior high. These analyses are completed by an analysis of variance on the group variable, which through the Newman-Keuls method (Winer, 1962) permits the identification of groups that by significant mean differences are separated from the others.

These analyses show that significant differences in the efficiency of strategies are attributable to factors such as grade level and socioeconomic environment.

Among the first four parts where the success rate is higher, it is in the first three that significant differences are found between the upper and lower socioeconomic level groups, hence the extreme groups of the sample on this variable.

The influence of grade level begins to appear in the score comparison at the fifth part, concerning the comprehension of cohesion markers. This influence presents itself by way of an interaction between this variable and the socioeconomic environment.

In the sixth part, which evaluates the ability to construct a network based on the coherence relations between the sentences of the paragraphs, the differences between the groups are most noticeable. They can be seen between the extreme groups only (fifth grade versus eighth grade and upper socioeconomic level versus lower socioeconomic level). This part of the test, like the others, differentiates little between the groups that are closer by grade level or socio-economic level. More precisely, it is the fifth and sixth grade groups that are significantly inferior to the eighth grade groups. In the same way, the lower socioeconomic level subjects also have significantly lower scores than those of the upper socioeconomic level students.

It is convenient at this time to point out that the mean score of the best group at the sixth part is only 52.07%, which leads us to ascertain that the performance of students who are significantly inferior to them is very low. Since this is the part of the test in the present version that evaluates the comprehension of chunks of information of an absolute textual dimension, these results establish that in the sample, on the whole, the ability to understand the text is not entirely developed yet.

These observations on the comparative performance of groups are globally confirmed by the multivariate analysis accomplished on the students' results in the Dinosaur test. There are two important pieces of information that are added by multivariate analysis; the first is that the test as a whole measures the same function and the second is that two parts of the test contribute more definitely than the others to discrimination between groups. It is the third part that measures the knowledge of nondefined rare words in the text and the sixth part that refers to the comprehension of coherence relations that compose the coherence structure of the paragraphs; these results tend to give more importance to information made possible by the sixth part. The result concerning the third part was largely expected.

5. CONCLUSION

In the description of this research, a predominant place was given to methodological aspects, with the intention of giving a precise idea of the procedure by which we seek to evaluate text reading comprehension. The presentation of results also indicates the degree of scientific precision that it was possible to achieve in this first experiment. The instrument developed for this first experiment can be improved considerably; this is the objective of a research in progress at the moment.

Particular insistence is placed on the methodological aspects of the research because, in this area, the most useful contribution is the one that presents a procedure of test construction that can evaluate text reading comprehension rather than one that proposes a test already made for a particular text. The reason why a test already developed on a particular text is less useful is due to the fact that it is limited to the evaluation of the comprehension of a particular text and that the choice of this text always has specific characteristics adapted to the particular context at hand. Due to other specific constraints, it is highly probable that an eventual user of the test should use another text. No test developed to evaluate the comprehension of a specific text will ever be able to satisfy the very diversified needs of potential users. That is why our research work concentrates on the development of a procedure rather than perfecting the best possible test on a particular text. Therefore, our work leads us to apply the testing procedure to different texts, which, so far, are all informative texts.

These standardized procedures for the evaluation of text reading comprehension will permit research on the development of language abilities to go beyond the comprehension of sentences in or out of context. The data that we have presented on the development of paragraph comprehension strategies clearly demonstrate the importance of taking this aspect into consideration, because it has been proven to be the most discriminating factor between the groups of diverse grade levels and different environments. Research must also focus its attention on the development of procedures which evaluate the efficiency of strategies involved in the comprehension of relations between the paragraphs and the textual macrostructure, because this aspect is without doubt as important.

Among the set of procedures we intend to develop, those which permit us to express semantically the information in a text and in that way free it from its particular linguistic formulation can constitute an important contribution to research done in the plurilingual education context. These procedures permit the construction of semantically equivalent texts written in different languages and the comparison of the comprehension of these texts. When such procedures are used, text comprehension can become a criterion taken into consideration in the comparison of readers' performances while reading in their mother tongue and in a second language.

REFERENCES

Anastasi, A. (1976). *Psychological testing.* New York: Macmillan.

Charolles, M. (1983). Coherence as a principle in the interpretation of discourse. *Text, 1*, 71–97.

Green, B. F. (1956). A method of scalogram analysis using summary statistics. *Psychometrika, 21*, 79–88.

Hobbs, J. R. (1979). *Why is discourse coherent?* Menlo Park, CA: Stanford Research Institute.

Pagé, M. (1985). Lecture et interaction lecteur/texte. In M. Thérien & G. Fortier (Eds.), *Didactique de la lecture au secondaire* (pp. 31–74). Montreal: Ville-Marie.

Van Dijk, T. A., & Kintsch, W. (1983). *Strategies of discourse comprehension.* New York: Academic Press.

Winer, B. J. (1962). *Statistical principles in experimental design.* New York: McGraw-Hill.

CHAPTER 14

Problems of Written Comprehension and Production in Children
A Textual-Pragmatic Study

ELISABETTA ZUANELLI SONINO

1. INTRODUCTION

This chapter presents data concerning written comprehension and production in children.

The first part discusses problems of reading comprehension through the analysis of the results of "informal" tests administered to elementary school pupils.

The second part elaborates on the results of comprehension problems through a qualitative analysis of "spontaneous" written production of children.

The research study was carried out during winter 1984 through spring 1985, and it is part of a wider research project[1] aiming at a threefold objective:

1. To improve mother-tongue teaching through the application of textual-pragmatic methods to literacy programs.
2. To collect a corpus of data which will deepen understanding of diverse problems concerning written comprehension and production, in particular as regards primary school pupils.

---

[1] It is part of the research section of the project on "plurilingual education": *"Educazione linguistica: italiano, dialetto, lingue straniere,"* which has been underway in the elementary and high schools of the Veneto area, in Italy, since 1980. For the organizational, methodological, and scientific structure of the project see Zuanelli Sonino, 1982, 1983, 1987.

ELISABETTA ZUANELLI SONINO • Seminar of Linguistics and Language Teaching, University of Venice, Ca' Garzoni e Moro, San Marco 3417, 30124 Venice, Italy.

3. To elaborate, with time, homogeneous and objective criteria for the evaluation of levels of literacy effectively achieved by children, by comparing them also with levels of achievement in older pupils.

2. PROBLEMS OF WRITTEN COMPREHENSION: TESTS, SAMPLES, RESULTS

What I report first is the result of a few informal tests administered to a number of second-grade pupils (aged 7–8 years) and a first evaluation of the kind of reading problems which seem to appear from these tests.

There were two basic assumptions for this study:

1. That different types of texts are responsible for different problems of written comprehension and production.
2. That problems in written performances can be partially analyzed as the counterpart of reading performances.

Accordingly, three types of comprehension tests were administered: (1) questions requiring open and closed answers; (2) written paraphrase; and (3) an adaptation of the cloze procedure concerning two types of texts: *narrative* and *informative*.

The first test consisted of the silent reading of a story by a class of 14 pupils. The reading was immediately followed by eight questions, requiring open and closed answers, on the key situations and events in the story. Out of 14 children only one replied successfully to all questions, three replied with two negative answers, three replied with one negative answer, and four replied to less than four questions. All in all, global comprehension for about half the class covered about 75% of the text; for the other half of the class comprehension ranged from about 50% to even lower.

By analyzing the questions which scored worst, it appeared that a possible reason for this was that the questions, which allowed two alternative answers, were badly formulated. The other negative answers seemed to follow a random distribution.

The second test was administered to seven second-grade classes with a total of 121 pupils. It consisted of the silent reading of a story followed by 13 closed questions.

Of the total number of pupils, 19 did not understand 50% of the story, and 18 understood all of it; 43 pupils understood the story with one or two mistakes. All in all, about half the class understood all the story or almost all of it.

The largest number of wrong answers concerned questions implying the *identification* of expressions coreferent with the characters of the story, that is, the use of appellatives correlated with features of form and behavior of the characters, namely, *pettegolo* (gossiper) and *bestione* (great beast), with reference to the *monkey* and the *elephant* of the story.

These characteristics and their linguistic denomination, being recoverable only through an *inference mechanism,* appeared to be a possible explanation for the problems of comprehension.

A third test concerned four second-grade classes with a total of 75 pupils. It consisted of the reading of a story and the written paraphrase of it. Even acknowledging the difficulty of evaluating comprehension on the basis of written performance, such an evaluation was made possible nevertheless by verifying only the presence of the key concepts which had been deemed essential to the comprehension of the story, whatever their linguistic formulation.

About 18% of the pupils did not understand anything. Almost 43% did not understand the conclusion of the story. About 40% did not understand the key event for the development of the story.

The search for difficulties connected with the linguistic formulations in the text, at least in the case of the key event, revealed that the linguistic element *coreferent* with the main character (that is, a possessive adjective referring to "fox") was not immediately preceded by the explicit *referent* ("the fox"). It was recalled only by the morphological connectors of *number* and *gender*. It also appeared in a new paragraph of the story. This observation may hint at the existence of a qualitative relevance of the linguistic means of cohesion, especially in connection with coreference, which might in turn imply a difficulty in retaining referents in short-term memory, unless they are explicit.

The fourth test concerned three second-grade classes; it was based on the written paraphrase of an *informative* text. In this case also, the evaluation of the paraphrase took place on the basis of four key concepts.

Out of 73 pupils a very high percentage, 52%, did not understand the key information; 89% did not understand the explanation of this information. Several explanations of the difficulty may be advanced: first, the use in the passage of linguistic items requiring *inference* operations; second, the use of coreference mechanisms based on synonyms (*scia odorosa* 'waft', *traccia* 'track' 'trail', *messaggio odoroso* 'scent message'). The coreferent nouns, in fact, required for their interpretation the activation of a chain of inference operations: the *scia odorosa* 'waft' is a "message"; the *scia odorosa* 'waft' is a "track trail," and so on; these operations require the existence of an encyclopedic and world knowledge. This holds true also for the interpretation of other words contained in the text, such as *operaie,* with reference to "ants." In this case, one must know that (1) working ants are called *operaie* workers and (2) that their basic work consists in the search for food. Other difficulties seem generally connected with lexicon (words such as *persistent, graded, fade away*). These considerations may explain why a high school class also showed an identical high percentage of incomprehension.

A last test concerned only one second-grade class whose written productions were also analyzed as a second part of our study. It was a test which consisted of filling in the blanks of a story. The blanks concerned different linguistic items implying lexico-semantic, morphosyntactic, and textual competence.

Out of the eight missing items, the one that created most difficulty was the insertion of the past participle in a present perfect, the auxiliary having been left in the text. This difficulty seemed to have more to do with a semantic than with a morphosyntactic problem. No past participle nor any other substitution was inserted by 9 out of 14 children. The semantic explanation may be found in the redundancy of the word and in the information which had already been expressed in the immediately preceding text. This might confirm the existence of context-dependent previsional skills in children too.

The "incidental clause" also caused perplexities: five pupils could not find a solution, others inserted substitutions implying the use of *explicit verbal forms* which were correctly coordinated with the addition of the conjunction *and*.

As for the other blanks, the ones that created most difficulty for half the pupils appeared to be verbs of introduction and comment to direct speech, such as *rispose* '(he) answered' and *chiese* '(she) asked'.

The results of these first observations served as a basis for confrontation with problems of written production by the same group of children. The idea was that from the type of textual elements used in written productions we might reach confirmation of the difficulties of comprehension already hypothesized. In addition, we believed that problems of written production might implicitly highlight other problems of comprehension, besides supplying specific information on the features characterizing children's written productions.

3. WRITTEN PRODUCTIONS OF CHILDREN AND TYPOLOGICAL CONSTRAINTS: A QUALITATIVE ANALYSIS

The second part of the research was therefore conducted on the written work of a class of school children aged 7–8; it has attained preliminary conclusions as regards the following topics:

1. "Textual" features characterizing children's written production.
2. Problems and difficulties in written production to be analyzed or explained in a textual-linguistic perspective.
3. Psycholinguistic strategies apparently used by children to be correlated with a textual typology.

A first assumption was that the written work produced by children might be analyzed through an attempt at "typologization" of texts that might explain or make evident different kinds of difficulty.

A second assumption was that these written productions might be analyzed not only through strictly linguistic-grammatical parameters but in light of the global planning possibly required by the text as well as of the textual-pragmatic "cues" offered by the productions, confirming this planning.

From this viewpoint I have examined the written work of a single class, a second grade, concerning three different types of written productions: (1) the *creation* of a story; (2) the *description* of a job; (3) the *recounting* of a TV show.

The first basic difference I had assumed was that type (2), that is, the description of a job, might require a linguistic-textual planning and development different either from (1), the creation of a story, or from (3), the recounting of a show.[2]

Diverse types of conceptual planning seem to have a direct counterpart in the different "connections" between units in a text.[3] This implies the use of linguistic means that differ as a function of the diverse patterns of planning, namely, the diverse textual patterns.[4]

The difference between the diverse types of texts was supposed to be of a twofold nature: as regards the *contents* to be presented, the description of a job seems to imply "general" world knowledge, with a sort of "linear" planning without temporal-sequential linkage or relations of cause–effect that might be required for (1) and (3).

Moreover, whereas the description of a job and the recounting of a show seems to require a reference to a specific, typical, or accidental knowledge,[5] the creation of a story seems to require an *ex novo* elaboration of the textual knowledge, based both on the *episodic* and the *semantic memory*.

Finally, whereas in the description of a "job" the textual knowledge (and

---

[2] As for the different models of textual planning and the related linguistic features, see the synthesis by Beaugrande and Dressler, 1983 (chaps. V and IX).

[3] Stein and Glenn, 1979, stress that a model of the processing of texts should take into account different types of elaborated prose and different types of conceptual relations between units in the text as specific in the diverse types of prose.

[4] As for textual models see Beaugrande and Dressler, 1983, pp. 184–185; on the types of "narrative" texts, see also van Dijk, 1972.

[5] According to Beaugrande and Dressler, 1983, the coherence of a text, namely, the continuity of meaning, corresponds to a configuration of concepts and relations among concepts underlying the text and defined as *textual world*. The textual world is not made up, however, only of the linguistic units of a text, because it also implies a "commonsense knowledge" (pp. 83–87). "Determinate" and "typical" knowledge allowing for the definition of concepts are distinguished from "accidental" knowledge, which is connected with one's personal experience. These types of knowledge correspond to the distinction between *semantic memory* and *episodic memory*.

the *semantic knowledge*) may be considered of a general type, the textual knowledge required for the creation of a story or in the telling of a show seems to be specific, coinciding with the notion of *episodic knowledge*.

In other words, the memory and consequent written recalling of a TV show are different from the generalized typical knowledge concerning a job and its description, as well as from the process of elaboration of a specific, new, and not-given text required for the creation of a story.

As we see later on, these differences seem to have a direct bearing on the linguistic means used by children, namely, on the way they plan and compose the text both globally and in its sequences, as well as in the linguistic items used to express it.

The first problem I came up against in this approach consisted of the difficulty of applying textual parameters common to the three types of texts produced by the children. In fact, even the assumption of the existence of "different" types of texts implied at least the partial "impossibility" of adopting common grids of analysis. The solution I found was to sort out a certain number of linguistic items of textual relevance and to compare their more or less varied, pertinent, or adequate use in the different written productions. In particular, "comparative" observations include such items as: problems of *reference* and *coreference* ("naming," lexical substitution, lexical repetition, proforms)[6] and the articulation of the text into sequences marked by *punctuation, new paragraphs,* and *transfrastic connectors.* I elaborated analytical grids that single out linguistic features present in each text and in different children. By means of these, I also singled out specific difficulties related to the different types of text.

3.1. The Sample, the Grids, the Analysis

As I have already said, the study was conducted on three different types of written works produced by children aged 7–8 in a primary school in Venice in the school year 1984–1985. I now present the criteria used for their analysis along with the results. A few general conclusions follow.

3.1.1. The Creation of a Story

As regards the creation of a story, I assumed it to be possible that, according to a procedural analysis, such a production represents a narrative type, with control centers such as actions and events, ordered in particular sequences implying conceptual relations of cause, reason, aim, temporal proximity, and

---

[6] For the diverse mechanisms of reference and coreference, I considered, particularly, Halliday and Hasan, 1976. See also Kieras, 1977.

enablement. As to the global pattern, it should represent a "schema."[7] I assumed the following as linguistic parameters of these basic typological data:

1. The explicit linguistic *specification-characterization* of agents, affected entities, and instruments of actions, as referents in the story and, in as much as they are needed, for the development of the story.
2. The specification of the *initial state* or *situation* of the story, in accordance with which the actions and/or the events take place.
3. The specification of its conclusion into a *final state*.

At the linguistic level the following items were analyzed:

1. The explicit introduction of agents/affected entities/instruments as *referents* in the story.
2. The explicit presence of an *introduction* (i.e., the initial state of the story), the *development,* and the *conclusion* of the story.
3. Means of *coreference* as regards referents mentioned in 1: lexical repetition, synonyms, the use of the definite article (the shift from the indefinite to the definite article), paraphrases, and pronominal anaphora and cataphora.
4. The number of sequences according to language expedients such as punctuation, new paragraphs, and transfrastic connectors.
5. The types of subordinate clauses.
6. The types of coordinate clauses.
7. The quality of transfrastic connectors.

As to the explicit presentation of referents in the story, all the children immediately present the character or characters around which the story is to develop. The characters are mostly animals (a little bird, a cat and a mouse, two little pigs, a panda, and so on); in two instances the stories concern children; there is only one cartoon character, Donald Duck, and a "monster." As to the development of the topics of the stories, no fantastic or supernatural elements are present.

Out of 14 stories, six end with an explicit "moral" and five with a coherent conclusion; only two stories do not provide an end. In all the texts, the preliminary state from which the story begins is clear; in other words, there is an explicit presentation of the character(s) plus the initial situation from which the story will develop. The section of the text that presents most of the difficulties encountered in composition is generally the development of the story. All in all, 10 out of 14 children succeed in presenting meaningful and necessary

---

[7] As for textual models and related psycholinguistic planning, see Beaugrande and Dressler, 1983, Van Dijk, 1977, 1980, Kintsch, 1977, and Rumelhart, 1980; on the notions of frame, script, and scheme, see also the critical evaluation by Tannen, 1979.

sequences for the story; four show they had difficulty as regards the articulation of the sequences and their interconnection. The conclusions instead, as we have already seen, are coherent with the general themes of the stories, except for two cases where they are absent.

As to item 3, the use of mechanisms of coreference such as lexical repetition, the definite article, synonyms, paraphrases, pronouns, and the like, we may state as follows. All the children seem to master coreference by means of lexical repetition and the use of the definite article. Moreover, they use possessive adjectives, relative pronouns, and personal pronouns as subjects or in the indirect form and also, though more limitedly, in the clitic form. No coreference by means of synonyms and paraphrases is used. This fact seems to confirm the difficulties of reading comprehension already signalled, as related to the presence of synonyms and appellatives.

Coreference is missing in the following cases:

1. In cases of "extended reference," namely, when coreference to a previous part of the text (i.e., to already mentioned information) is needed. So, Irene writes:

(1)

    Nino andò a dire alla mamma
    "Nino went to tell to mother"

    instead of *dirlo alla mamma,* "to tell *it* to mother."

2. When the coreferent item corresponds to the use of an adverb of place (*dove* 'where'), or a pronoun of place both in the relative form (*nella quale* 'in which') and in its personal indirect weak form *(ci)*:

(2)

    C'era una casa là nel bosco era una casa vecchia e viveva un brutto mostro (Dario)
    "There was a house there in the wood it was an old house and lived an ugly monster"

    instead of "an old house where lived . . ." or "an old house and there lived . . ."; in this example, a rule is apparently working according to which the *proximity* of the element to which the coreference corresponds allows for the cancellation of the coreferent linguistic item.

3. When the coreferent item functions as a subject, it is cancelled even though it is necessary, and the item with which it is coreferent precedes it.

Irene writes:

(3)

> . . . *per alcuni giorni non poté vedere la televisione. Finalmente arrivó*
> *e gli diede la colpa alla televisione.*
> ". . . he could not watch television for a few days. Finally (it, "the
> television") arrived and he put the blame on the TV."

> In this case, *la televisione* was to be repeated or replaced by a pronoun.
> We see another example of this type further on.

As for the use of subordination, at this stage the children could manage
temporal, causal, and relative subordination and objective dependent clauses,
both explicit and implicit. Few are *final* clauses. Totally absent are more complex forms of subordination. Coordination is realized through the conjunction
and and the adversative *but*. There appears also the use of the "polyvalent"
che ('that') in the function of coordinating item, replacing punctuation or different types of connectors.

Other forms of connectors include temporal, temporal-additional, and conclusive connectors: *un giorno* 'one day', *una volta* 'once', *ad un tratto* 'all of
a sudden', *allora* 'then', *e, e poi, e dopo* 'and', 'and then', *finalmente* 'finally',
perciò 'therefore', *così* 'so'.

There is a total lack of connectors of consequence, enumeration, correspondence, contrapposition, demonstration, evaluation, or exposition. Wrong
tenses often characterize subordinate clauses. Table 1 sums up synthetically
some of the data.

3.1.2. The Description of a Job

As for the description of a job, the job of being a dustman in this case, I
supposed the existence of a global pattern such as a *frame*, having as a control
center a *nonspecific* referent object, that requires the activation of conceptual
relations such as attributes, states, examples, and specifications. I also supposed that this text might require the activation of a semantic memory, even
though based on episodic memory, concerning the direct experience of the
children.[8]

For such a text the grid evaluated the following points:

1. The explicit definition of theme-object, the dustman, with its general
   qualification-attribute.
2. A sequence of specifications and/or exemplifications of the theme.

As for the linguistic correlates, they concerned:

[8]On episodic and semantic memory see footnote 5.

Table 1. Synthesis of the Presence of Some Textual
Features in the Creation of Stories

Pupil	Textual feature[a]			
	1.	2.1.	2.2.	2.3.
Andrea	+	+	+	+
Fabio	+	+	+	−
Sara	+	+	±	+
Thierry	+	+	±	+
Dario	+	+	+	+
Irene	+	+	+	±
Elisa	+	+	+	+
Tommaso	+	+	±	+
Alex	+	+	+	+
Serena	+	+	+	+
Lucia	+	+	+	+
Tania	+	+	+	−
Alvise	+	+	±	+
Daniela	+	+	+	+

Note. + = clear; ± = unclear, nonexplicit; − = absent.
[a]1., explicit qualification of agents/patients/instruments of the story; 2.1., presence of the premise; 2.2., presence of the development; 2.3., presence of the conclusion.

1.1. The explicit denomination of the theme-referent with the general qualification of the referent.
1.2. The number of attributes/specifications on the basis of the use of new paragraphs, punctuation, or connectors.
1.3.1. The number and type of coordinate clauses.
1.3.2. The number and type of subordinate clauses.
2. The presence or absence of generalization of the theme.
3. The types of coreference with the main referent (the dustman).
4. The types of transfrastic connectors.

Here are the results. Some of the data are also synthetically summed up in Table 2.

As for the explicit definition of the theme, consisting in the general *qualification* of the object to be described, namely, its general attributions, only half the class succeeded in giving it. Four only partially succeeded (one general attribution plus details), and five did not succeed at all but just described the different operations carried out by the dustman. Eight out of twelve children presented the description in general terms, two gave some specific examples, and two described in an exemplarily specific way.

These modes of presentation can, perhaps, imply a difficulty in using information in a generalized way, as well as a strong dependence on the "episodic memory." This fact becomes relevant at a linguistic level, as we see later on, as regards the expressive means used to recount a show.

As for the procedure of articulation of concepts into sequences of attributes, eight pupils out of 12 used new paragraphs; sometimes the use of the "comma" was extended to cover the function of a marker to delimit a concept. This feature may signal an overlapping of qualifications or concepts due perhaps to a nonhierarchical cognitive organization, namely, to the fact that, as regards the relation to the general theme, each attribution seems to fill the same "conceptual rank" as the others. Only where the ordering of attributes is "consequential" could I find clearly explicit connectors, mainly temporal or additive: *and when, and, then, and then, after, and after, sometimes.*

As to subordinate clauses, their use was meaningfully balanced in this type of text: we found *relative, final,* and *implicit* clauses. In some cases we even found more subordinate than coordinate clauses. Five pupils used no coordinate clauses at all.

As for the type of coordinate clauses, we found the conjunction *and* and the adversative *but,* which are also the usual forms in the free narrative text. I

Table 2. Synthesis of Some Textual Features in the Description of a Job

Pupil	Textual feature[a]				
	1.1.	1.2.	1.3.1.	1.3.2.	2.
Sara	±	3	0	2	+
Irene	±	6	2	3	−
			and		
Tania	−	5	1	4	+
Alex	±	7	4	3	+
Serena	+	3	0	3	+
Alvise	+	3	0	6	+
Fabio	−	8	8	1	−
Dario	±	3	0	0	+
Lucia	+	4	0	1	+
Thierry	−	5	3	3	±
			polyvalent *che*		
Elisa	−	3	3	2	+
Tommaso	−	4	2	1	+
			(e)		

Note. + = correct feature; − = incorrect feature; ± = partially correct feature; 0 = absence of feature.
[a]1.1., definition of the theme and the qualification of the referent; 1.2., number of specifications; 1.3.1., number of coordinate clauses; 1.3.2., number of subordinate clauses; 2., presence of generalization of theme.

also found the typical connector already mentioned, used in "italiano medio," the "polyvalent" *che* ('that').

In almost all written productions I found the use of *final clauses* such as *per scopare* 'to sweep', *a pulire* 'to clean', *a cercare* 'to look for', and the like. These clauses seem to characterize this type of text, requiring the expression of attributes of the referent.

As for mechanisms of coreference, besides the use of morphological connectors, I found the use of *lexical repetition*.

The generalizing function of the definitive article seems to be correctly differentiated from its use as the marker of the shift from indefinite to definite reference, as we noticed in the previous text. Moreover, another feature was present: the shift from the singular referent to the plural *(the dustman, the dustmen)*. The shift may represent a marker of class distinction: "the dustman" in the singular is specific, the one we can see every day; "the dustmen" (plural) represent the job. In other words, a generalizing function seems to be assigned to the use of the plural that includes all the instances of what the word *dustman* may refer to. This feature might confirm the need to deepen the study of the linguistic principles of generalization in children and the difference between episodic and semantic memory.

Finally, in this type of text I also found, even though in a restricted number of cases, a feature that I examine later on in another type of text: the use of a coreference external to the text and to the communicative situation. This coreference concerns an item belonging to what is called a *generalized textual knowledge* (very close to the concept of semantic memory). I have named this type of coreference *exophoric generalized contextual coreference* (EGCC). It is exemplified by utterances such as *lo mettono* 'they put it', *le buttano* 'they throw them' (Dario) or *lo portano* 'they carry it', and *le mette* 'he puts them' (Lucia), where the pronouns *(lo, le)* refer to garbage, which has never been mentioned explicitly in the text.

3.1.3. The Recounting of a Show

This type of text represents a sort of "historical-narrative" (van Dijk, 1972), where the subject/narrator uses a particular textual knowledge of a different type, referring to a show, a movie, or the like. Given the specificity of this type of text, I deemed it interesting to evaluate the following items in the grid:

1. The "collocation" of the narrator as regards the event/show he or she recounted.
2. A thematic definition concerning the type of show and its actors/interactants.

3. The articulation of the theme into an introduction, a development, and a conclusion.

The linguistic-textual parameters for the analysis were the following:

1. The explicit or implicit collocation of the subject/narrator.
    1.1. His or her temporal collocation.
    1.2. His or her spatial collocation.
    1.3. The (explicit or implicit) qualifications of the topic/theme.
2. The explicit introduction of the agents/referents of the theme.
    2.1. The introduction, that is, the presentation of the initial state or situation which influenced actions and/or events that follow.
    2.2. The development of a sequence of actions and events.
    2.3. The conclusion, namely, the attainment of a final state.
3. The mechanism of reference and coreference.
4. Transfrastic connectors, use of punctuation, and new paragraphs necessary for the expression and parsing of the text.

Table 3 gives some of the results concerning points 1 and 2.

As for the explicit presentation of the ego-narrator, the child himself or herself, all the children but one qualified it along with its temporal collocation (*sabato sera ho visto . . .* "Saturday evening I saw"). Only two also gave a spatial collocation. Out of 14 children, nine succeeded in introducing the general theme/topic; 11 were able to present the referents as well as the initial state or event.

Problems became evident as regards the articulation of the topic into an introduction, a development, and a conclusion.

Only five out of 14 children proposed a "clear" introduction coherent with the development of the text. In the texts of six children, the introduction was either confused or not coherent with the rest of the text or not explicit, and three children presented no introduction at all. In the work of 11 out of 14 children, the conclusion was clear in connection with the introduction and/or the development; for two it was not; and one did not write it down, perhaps for lack of time.

As we can see from these first data, the most difficult part seems to be the development of the "recounted" shows. Shows recounted by children were of two types: TV animation movies (10 children) and TV variety shows (four children).

All the texts present a consistent articulation into new paragraphs that seem to delimit the events or actions narrated. Such articulation is also accompanied by the only partially correct use of connectors (problems are evident for Tommaso, Fabio, Thierry, Daniela, Tania, Andrea, and Dario). For instance, Tommaso writes:

Table 3. Synthesis of Some Textual Features in the Recounting of a Show

Pupil	Textual feature[a]							
	1.	1.1.	1.2.	1.3.	2.	2.1.	2.2.	2.3.
Elisa (storia *Lucy me*)	+	−	−	+	+	−	+	+
Tommaso (storia *Carletto*)	+	+	−	−	+	+	+	−
	Not specific							
Alex (storia *WilliFog*)	−	−	−	−	+	±	±	±
Serena (spettacolo quiz)	+	−	−	−	+	+	+	+
Lucia (storia *WilliFog*)	+	+	−	+	+	+	±	+
Alvise (storia *La storia infinita*)	+	+	−	+	+	+	+	+
Tania (storia *Pinocchio*)	+	+	+	+	+	±	±	+
Daniela (spettacolo *Drive-in*)	+	−	−	+	−	±	±	+
Andrea (spettacolo varietà *Buona Domenica*)	+	+	−	+	±	−	±	+
Fabio (storia *Occhi tondi Occhi neri*)	+	+	+	±	+	+	+	+
Sara (spettacolo *Drive-in*)	+	+	−	+	+	±	+	+
Dario (storia *CiarliBrao*)	+	+	−	+	+	−	±	±
Thierry (storia *Jeeg robot*)	+	+	−	±	±	±	+	+
Irene (storia *Carletto*)	+	+	−	+	+	±	±	+

Note. + = clear; ± = unclear; − = absent.
[a] 1., explicit collocation of the subject/narrator; 1.1., temporal collocation of the narrator; 1.2., spatial collocation of the narrator; 1.3., explicit qualification of the topic/theme; 2., introduction of the referents/agents of the theme; 2.1., explicit premise, namely, initial state or situation; 2.2., development of a coherent sequence of actions and events; 2.3., presence of a coherent conclusion or final state.

(4)

> *venne un temporale perché avevano rubato il ventaglio Carletto lo ritrovò.*
> ''A storm came because they had stolen the fan Carletto found it.''

This sentence can be analyzed in two ways. A storm was caused on account of the fact that someone had stolen the fan and later on Carletto found the fan. In this case the second clause in the sentence is in no way coordinate, not even by means of a comma. Or else, it may mean that a storm came. Since someone had stolen the fan, Carletto found it. In this case the connector *perché* 'because' is ambiguous and incorrect as far as a relation of cause and effect is concerned. Tania writes:

(5)

> *Alla fine Pinocchio vide una barca e si accorse subito . . .*
> ''Finally Pinocchio saw a boat and he realized at once . . .''

Tania uses *alla fine* 'finally' several times, not in the sense of a temporal end but in the sense of the end of a partial temporal sequence. Daniela uses an uninterrupted series of *there are, there is, there are,* and so on, in her sequences. Andrea uses a temporal connector:

(6)

> *Nella seconda parte c'era Corrado*
> ''In the second part there was Corrado''

without a previous temporal referent corresponding explicitly to the first part of a show. Dario uses *quando* 'when' to mean the temporal beginning of an action instead of a phrase like, ''one evening,'' ''once,'' or the like.

(7)

> *Quando Ciarli Brao andava ha letto il suo cane va fuori della casa ha bere la birra e quando sente canzoni tristi si mette a piangere e quando sente canzoni allegre si mette a ballare.*
> ''When Ciarli Brao went to bed his dog goes out of the house to drink beer and when he hears sad songs he starts crying and when he hears merry songs he starts dancing.''

All these ''whens'' but the first one seem to refer to specific temporal moments in the story; they are not used in the sense of ''whenever'' but rather in the correlative form ''when . . . something happened.''
Dario also uses *però* 'but' in the function of *perciò* 'therefore':

(8)

> *perché Ciarli Brao ci entra sempre nei guai però finisce sempre che si prende le sgridate.*
> ''because Ciarli Brao always gets into trouble but he always ends up getting scolded.''

Another wrong use of the adversative ''but'' to introduce the development of the story appears in Fabio's work.

(9)

> *Testa tonda era nemico di occhi neri, ma un giorno occhi neri gli disse di fare una sfida con le pistole.*
> ''Round head was an enemy of black eyes, but one day black eyes suggested they fight a duel using guns.''

With regard to the ''appropriate'' use of connectors, I found the already mentioned presence of the polyvalent *that* (in the texts of Thierry, Sara, and Fabio):

(10)

> *con delle palle e con un bastone che le dovevano colpire e buttare* (Sara).
> "with some balls and a bat that they were supposed to hit and throw them."

A second order of problems with regard to connectors concerns the use of connectors coreferring with referents not explicitly mentioned in the text; often these coreferences used as connectors are of temporal type:

(11)

> *Il giorno seguente le capre vennero sgridate e non mangiarono mai più nell'orto.*
> "Next day the goats were scolded and they never again ate in the orchard."

"Next day" does not refer to any specific previous moment/day. Irene writes:

(12)

> *Quella sera c'era un cagnolino*
> "That evening there was a little dog"

without having mentioned any previous evening with which "that" evening might be coreferent. This aspect of the use of connectors implies the existence of a wider and more complex mechanism of reference and coreference present in texts of this type.

More generally, such temporal connectors signal the difficulties of the shift from an atemporal perspective of the action to a specific temporal action.

A second level of difficulty in the development of the text concerns the absence of elements of information necessary for the comprehension of the text. A third difficulty concerns the differentiation between general and specific information, for instance, in the listing and exemplification of "games" proposed in "variety shows."

The use of tenses in correlation is another well-known problem that might also be interpreted as depending on the difficulty concerning the use of connectors, in general, and of the already mentioned temporal connectors, in particular.

The already mentioned phenomenon of "ambiguous coreference" appears as well. In this case, disambiguation is possible if we accept the following hypothesis.

In a sequence of "coreferent" elements performing different grammatical functions, a subject and an indirect pronoun, for instance, if the last coreference is not explicit, it must be reconstructed as having the same coreference as the immediately preceding one.

(13)

La principessa Rhomi era rimasta con Fog allora Rigodonh decise di ritornare da lui allora decise di sposare la principessa . . . (Alex)
"Princess Rhomi had stayed with Fog then Rigodonh decided to go back to him then (he) decided to marry the princess . . .":

lui   refers to Fog

Fog   ————————>   lui   ————————>   0

The nonexplicit 0, and the ambiguous subject in the sentence "then (he) decided to marry princess Rhomi," must be understood as coreferent with the same referent as the preceding coreferent, that is *lui* (him), namely, Fog.

Still regarding problems of reference and coreference, let us deal with one problem which is responsible for the development of the theme in this type of text. Seven children (Alex, Elisa, Andrea, Lucia, Sara, Thierry, Irene), that is, half the class, present this textual feature. According to an accepted distinction, an *endophore* is the reference to a piece of information contained in the text, namely, in the co-text, whereas an *exophore* is a reference to an element of the communicative situation.[9] According to this distinction, children frequently use exophoric reference in oral speech, that is, reference to the speech situation. This context-bound speech, also called "neighborhood speech," is present in adults too, as Bernstein's studies have pinpointed. Its presence in children has been verified through pictorial tests in which children had to reconstruct orally a story through a series of picture stimuli. In these cases, however, we must observe that this context-bound speech always refers to a directly copresent referent, be it part of a game or a visual stimulus. In writing, though, the referent is not "materially," so to speak, present. As our corpus suggests, it would be useful to distinguish between the *situational context,* with the amount of situational information it may offer, and a *contextual knowledge,* referring to a stock of information already memorized by children, be it of a generalized or specific type.

Situational information allows for the use of a linguistic item for reference and coreference in a precise context of situation; in other words, this is the case for the so-called exophoric reference that I prefer to call *exophoric situational reference.* Different from this is an exophoric reference which is external both to the text and to the communicative situation. This reference depends on *contextual knowledge.* Such contextual knowledge is of two types: generalized, meaning the system of *world knowledge;* and specific, meaning a block of specific *episodic knowledge,* interacting with the generalized knowledge. The

---

[9] Halliday and Hasan (1976) introduce the concept of *exophore* with reference to the situational context. The concept of *homophoric reference* is proposed to designate the exophoric reference that does not depend on the communicative situation. Homophoric reference, however, comprises referents that stand for a whole "class" or a general phenomenon (the *sun,* the *moon,* etc.).

reference and coreference to this contextual knowledge, generalized and specific, allows for four different types of textual mechanisms in children:

1. Exophoric generalized contextual reference (EGCR).
2. The exophoric specific contextual reference (ESCR).
3. The exophoric generalized contextual coreference (EGCC).
4. The exophoric specific contextual coreference (ESCC).

Now, let us try to illustrate the four types of contextual reference or coreference
and to correlate their numerical presence with the different types of texts produced by the children.

Most of these types of contextual reference or coreference seem to appear,
not by chance, in the recounting of the show or the story. Alex told the story
of "Jolly Fog," an adaptation of "Round the World in Eighty Days." He
introduced the characters correctly, but the premise was not very clear: he did
not mention the "bet" made by Jolly Fog that he could complete the journey
around the world in 80 days nor other events which are important for the development of the story and which belong to his specific textual knowledge. In
Alex's text, therefore several instances of ESCC appeared:

(14)

> *credeva di aver perso la scommessa*
> "he believed he had lost the bet"

where *the* bet has never been mentioned before;

(15)

> *Gli amici di Jolly Fog lasciarono la casa*
> "Jolly Fog's friends left the house"

a house which had not been introduced before;

(16)

> *La principessa Rhomi era rimasta con Fog.*
> "Princess Rhomi had stayed with Fog"

where this princess appears for the first time, even though Alex writes about
the fact that the princess had stayed.

In sentences (14), (15), and (16), the use of the definite article, together
with the preceding verb, implies reference to a situation (the bet), to an object
(the house), and to a character of the story (Princess Rhomi) that are meant to
be already known, given, and "acting" in the story. The definite article, therefore, works as a mechanism of coreference as regards a referent (object, character, situation) external to the text and to the communicative situation, although well present in the specific textual knowledge of the child.

Another example of ESCC is the use of demonstrative adjectives:

(17)

    Quella sera c'era un cagnolino carino (Irene)
    "That evening there was a pretty little dog."

The demonstrative adjective is coreferent with an evening specified only in the exophoric reference, but not explicit in the text.

    A similar mechanism appears in the use of a particular type of "comparative" coreference based on the use of ordinal adjectives (*first, second,* etc.) or temporal expressions such as *next,* or *following.* Elisa writes:

(18)

    Il giorno seguente le capre vennero sgridate
    "Next day the goats were scolded"

without having ever mentioned in the text the specific day when the goats did the thing for which they were to be scolded the next day. A twofold case of ESCC and EGCR appears in the following sentence:

(19)

    Nella seconda parte c'era Corrado che faceva . . .
    "In the second part there was Corrado who did . . ." (Andrea)

"In the second part" is an example of ESCC coreferring to a first part of the show not mentioned before. Besides, *Corrado* is a case of EGCR: indeed, notwithstanding the fact that Corrado, a TV quizmaster, has never been mentioned before, Andrea supposes that everybody knows him and also that everybody knows that he presents the show in question. Another case of EGCC is the following:

(20)

    Loro dovevano rispondere
    "They were supposed to answer"

where "they" refers to the competitors/audience never mentioned before. The generalized coreference is based on the presupposition that everybody knows that in the show "the audience" (*loro* 'they') is supposed to participate in the games by answering questions.

    Let us consider a few examples of ESCR: Tania retells the story of Pinocchio. At a certain point she writes that Pinocchio and Geppetto could save themselves:

(21)

    . . . con l'aiuto del tonno.
    . . . "with the help of the tuna fish."

The tuna fish appears for the first time in the story; it is a specific exophoric reference which is dealt with as though it were a generalized ("homophoric") reference. Through the same mechanism Thierry writes:

(22)

    . . . *poi arriva il mostro che combatte contro l'amico della terra*
    . . . "then comes the monster who fights against the friend of the earth"

taking for granted the identification of the new character, the monster, in the story.

In general, these mechanisms of exophoric reference and coreference appear *noncohesive* and determine to a large extent the degree of obscurity and nonintelligibility of the text. Out of 14 children, seven use these mechanisms of exophoric generalized/specific contextual reference and coreference. A limited use of these mechanisms can be seen in the description of a job. They are practically absent in the invention of a story, unless the story is a retelling of something.

We may, perhaps, conclude that this way of referring to a specific world knowledge, not generalizable though as used as if it were, together with the use of a generalized knowledge not made explicit, causes the use of noncohesive linguistic items requiring one or more inference operations on the part of the reader which may sometimes prove useless. These mechanisms appear:

1. In the "naming" of a character, situation, or object in a direct way as though it were a generalized knowledge.
2. In the coreference with this generalized and specific knowledge that is manifest in the use of various linguistic expedients: proforms, adverbs, adverbial phrases, and general common nouns.

It is obvious that the reader's understanding of these expedients depends on his or her degree of shared knowledge with the child–writer. These mechanisms also seem to depend on the types of texts being produced by children and appear:

1. With less frequency in descriptions because references are often generalized categories introduced explicitly in the theme being dealt with (however, we find instances such as *le mete* 'they put it' or *lo portano* 'they carry it' as referring to *garbage*).
2. With the maximum frequency in the retelling of a story or in recounting a show or event where the textual world is already built up.
3. With limited frequency in the creation of stories where references and coreferences are explicit and where, perhaps, the construction of the text demands a constant choice of the means of expression of the con-

tents, which implies, in turn, a constant check on the referents and coreferents being used in the texts.

A further proof of this may be signalled in the invention of stories in the case where the pupil is actually summing up something he or she has read or seen. In a text which is a clear summary of a story of famous cartoon characters such as Tweety, Sylvester, or the like, Tommaso writes:

(23)

> *prese la gabbia dell'uccellino morto*
> "he took the cage of the little dead bird"

referring to a little bird never mentioned before.

An interesting feature found in the creation of stories, which also appeared in the description of a job, was a clear articulation of sequences through mechanisms such as new paragraphs, temporal, adversative, or causal transfrastic connectors: *once, once upon a time, finally, but, because*. Only in one case did I find sequences connected by the conjunction *and* and the dominance of a paratactic style.

As for the relation between subordinate and coordinate clauses, we may observe a greater variety in the use of subordination in the creation of stories: final, consecutive, hypothetical, relative, causal, and objective clauses and a limited use of them in the description of a job and the recounting of a TV show.

From a quantitative viewpoint, subordinate clauses are more abundant than coordinate clauses, in general, and coordination is mainly assigned to the use of the conjunctions *and* and *but*.

4. CONCLUSION

We may sum up the results of our analysis in a scheme (see Table 4), comparing a few textual features present in the different types of text. It is possible to notice that the third text, T3, namely, the recounting of the show, appears the most problematic production by children: it reveals faulty coordination, subordination, and connectors; difficulties in the use of punctuation and new paragraphs; abundance of exophoric contextual reference and coreference. T1 and T2, on the contrary, seem to be balanced as regards "communicative" acceptability, presenting differences in relation to just a few features, such as the type of coordinate clauses and the linguistic items used for coreference.

We may, therefore, conclude for the moment with the observation that the

Table 4. Comparative Synthesis of the Presence of Different
Textual Features in the Production of Three Types of Texts

Textual feature	Type of text[a]		
	T1	T2	T3
Coreference			
Lexical repetition	+	+	+
Synonyms	0	0	0
Definite article (singular/plural)	+	0	+
Periphrasis	0	0	0
Anaphora	+	0	+
Cataphora	0	0	0
Subordinate clauses			
Temporal	+	0	−
Causal	+	0	−
Final	0	+	+
Relative	+	+	+
Coordinate clauses			
And	+	+	−
But	+	+	−
(Che) that	0	0	+
Transfrastic connectors			
Temporal	+	+	−
Additive	+	+	−
Causal	+	+	−
Contextual reference[b]			
EGCR	0	0	+
EGCC	0	+	+
ESCR	0	0	+
ESCC	0	0	+

Note. + = correct feature; − = incorrect feature; 0 = absence of the feature.
[a]T1, creation of a story; T2, description of a job; T3, recounting of a show.
[b]EGCR, EGCC, exophoric generalized contextual reference/coreference; ESCR, ESCC,
exophoric specific contextual reference/coreference.

recounting of the story is probably the most difficult type of written production
for the child.

As regards the explanation, we may dare to put forward a hypothesis. It
is possible that the creation of a story requires a global plan[10] which may be
realized through a *breadth-first search* aiming at a series of proximate subgoals
and organized into different sequences of actions and events. This planning
seems to be signalled by explicit coreferences and transfrastic connectors. The
linguistic means, in other words, seem to control the different phases of idea-

[10]For procedural analysis, see Beaugrande and Dressler, 1983, pp. 37–38.

tion, development, and expression of the story and allow a clearer expression of an introduction, the development, and the conclusion of the story itself.

Quite different is the case of "summing up," where the child may be planning through a *means–ends analysis,* corresponding to a previously existing textual world which has to be recalled.

In this case, the type of global planning would not allow him or her to check, step by step, the different subgoals in a coherent sequence, up to the end of the story. This would result in the nonexplicitness of units of information necessary for the development of the "recounted," and the correlated abundance of exophoric contextual reference and coreference, as well as the overlapping of actions and events signaled by a less precise use of graphic articulation and transfrastic connectors.

If we accept this hypothesis, recounting would make evident both problems of comprehension of the story and emotional accentuations which correspond to the presentation and expansion of minor "details," reproduced in an emphatic or disconnected way.

Finally, the description of a job seems to call for the linear ordering of concepts, not necessarily subordinated hierarchically. This planning might require a *depth-first search,* which does not imply the search for linguistic alternatives but does imply the constant control of referents and of articulation.[11]

If these first conclusions are correct, educational implications of a serious type would derive from them as regards the choice of materials and the definition of procedures to be used to approach reading and writing in early literacy.

REFERENCES

Beaugrande, R. de, & Dressler, W. (1983). *Introduction to text linguistics.* London and New York: Longman.

Dressler, W. (1974). *Introduzione alla linguistica del testo.* Roma: Officina.

Freedle, R. O. (Ed.) (1979). *New directions in discourse processing.* Worwood, N.J.: ABLEX Publishing.

Halliday, M. A. K., & Hasan, R. (1976). *Cohesion in English.* London and New York: Longman.

Just, M. A., & Carpenter, P. A. (Eds.). (1977). *Cognitive process in comprehension.* Hillsdale, NJ: Lawrence Erlbaum.

Kieras, D. (1977). Problems of reference in text comprehension. In M. A. Just & P. A. Carpenter (Eds.), *Cognitive process in comprehension* (pp. 249–269). Hillsdale, NJ: Lawrence Erlbaum.

Kintsch, W. (1977). On comprehending stories. In M. A. Just & P. A. Carpenter (Eds.), *Cognitive process in comprehension* (pp. 36–62). Hillsdale, NJ: Lawrence Erlbaum.

Rumelhart, D. (1980). Schemata: The building blocks of cognition. In R. J. Spiro, B. C. Bruce, & W. F. Brewer (Eds.), *Theoretical issues in reading comprehension* (pp. 33–58). Hillsdale, NJ: Lawrence Erlbaum.

[11] On textual "markers" in descriptive informative text productions, seen in a developmental perspective, cf. Schneuwly and Rosat, 1985.

Schneuwly, B., & Rosat, M. C. (1985, June). *Les organisateurs textuels comme trace de certaines opérations impliquées dans la production de textes écrites: étude développementale*. Paper presented at the 1st International Congress of the International Society of Applied Psycholinguistics (ISAPL), Barcelone.

Stein, N. L. & Glenn, C. G. (1979). An analysis of story comprehension in elementary school children. In R. O. Freedle (Ed.), *New directions in discourse processing* (pp. 53–120). Worwood, NJ: ABLEX Publishing.

Tannen, D. (1979). What's in a frame? Surface evidence for underlying expectations. In R. O. Freedle (Ed.), *New directions in discourse processing* (pp. 137–181). Worwood, NJ: ABLEX Publishing.

Van Dijk, T. (1972). Foundations for typologies of texts. *Semiotica, 7*, 297–323.

Van Dijk, T. (1977). Semantic macro-structures and knowledge frames in discourse comprehension. In M. A. Just & P.A. Carpenter (Eds.), *Cognitive process in comprehension* (pp. 3–32). Hillsdale, NJ: Lawrence Erlbaum.

Van Dijk, T. (1980). *Testo e contesto*. (Trans. from English). Bologna: Il Mulino.

Zuanelli Sonino, E. (Ed.). (1982). *Italiano, dialetto, lingue straniere alle elementari*. Venice: Arsenale.

Zuanelli Sonino, E. (1983). *Plurilinguismo, lingue materne, educazione plurilingue*. Venice: ITE.

Zuanelli Sonino, E. (1987). Planificacion de la enseñanza de primeras, segundas y terceras lenguas: el proyecto Venecia. In M. Siguan (Ed.), *Lenguas y educacion en Europa* (pp. 83–100). Barcelona: ICE, PPU.

CHAPTER 15

Standard Language Acquisition by the Swiss–German Dialect-Speaking Child

OTTO STERN

1. INTRODUCTION

This chapter investigates the first steps of the acquisition of Standard German (StG) by Swiss–German (SG) dialect-speaking children.[1] The aim of the research is a better understanding of children's knowledge of StG when entering school in order to get a base for mother-tongue instruction. The study is based on data of 6- to 7-year-old children in kindergarten and first grade. The data have been gathered in a number of pilot studies carried out by students of the Deutsches Seminar of Zurich University,[2] a *Lizentiatsarbeit* (licentiate paper) by Erny (1984) comparing text comprehension in SG and StG, and a corpus compiled by Stern (1978).

For a better understanding of the following analysis of acquisition processes it is necessary to know some general facts about the specific linguistic situation of the Swiss–German dialect-speaking part of Switzerland. More details about the linguistic situation are found in the recent publications by Lötscher (1983) and by Sieber and Sitta (1984).

The linguistic community of Swiss–Germans comprises about three-fourths of the Swiss population, that is, about 5 million speakers, the remaining 2 million speaking French, Italian, or Romansch. The SG dialect is spoken in all

[1] A different version of this chapter has been published in J. C. P. Auer & A. Di Luzio (Eds.). (1986). *Interpretative socioluistics variation and convergence*. Berlin: de Gruyter.
[2] See references: *Seminar Papers*.

OTTO STERN • Deutsches Seminar, Abteilung Linguistik, Universität Zürich, Rämistrasse 74, CH-8001 Zürich, Switzerland.

domains of private and public life. The written language is Standard German, often called *Schriftdeutsch* (writing-German); it is used almost exclusively for written communication, whereas the use of SG dialect in writing is marginal. StG is spoken only when quoting or reading from written notes, for example, news broadcast, lectures, some public talks, and when communicating with speakers of other languages.

The two varieties, that is, SG and StG, are clearly distinct, divergence being greatest in phonology and morphology, smaller in syntax and the lexicon. Switching from SG to StG demands an effort on the speaker. Whereas most Germans are able to move continuously between a standard and a dialect pole, for Swiss–Germans this means a considerable change that is experienced like switching from one language to another, especially by the less trained, non-academic speakers.

> Whereas in other parts of the German speaking territory a colloquial variety has developed between dialect and standard, it is missing in German speaking Switzerland. For the understanding of the specific situation it is important to note that, in general, speakers of different dialects have no problems of understanding each other, or, if there are major differences between two dialects, the speakers are able to modify their speech for successful communication. Since the dialects are the only means of communication across different regions as well as across different social groups, dialects have a high prestige, i.e., they are evaluated positively and accepted in every situation of public life. (Schwarzenbach & Sitta, 1983, p. 64)

Since dialect is spoken in all domains of public life, there is almost no situation of oral language use where StG enters in competition with the dialect. This poses serious problems to schooling where, following the curriculum, StG should be spoken in order to build up an oral base for the teaching of literacy. But it is not easy to teach or learn a linguistic variety in school, when there is no outside societal reward for doing so (cf. Chapter 3, by J. A. Fishman, this volume). Note, however, that there is never any question about the use of StG for the purposes of writing.

Swiss–Germans do not like to speak StG. It seems that a negative attitude to the speaking of StG develops during the school years, where skills in StG form the base of qualification and assessment. Furthermore, the speaking of StG is difficult, because it is the written variety of StG (*Schriftdeutsch*) that is spoken in Switzerland, acquired at school through reading and writing. Thus, written norms of syntax, lexicon, and style are used in speaking.

The speaking of StG among Swiss–Germans is "unnatural" in everyday life situations. In the traditional classroom favoring teacher-centered instruction, naturalness of the communication situation was not an important factor. However, in a student-centered, communicative approach to teaching, the quality of the speech situation becomes a central issue. Thus, although the curriculum requires the speaking of StG in the classroom, more and more teachers from the elementary to the university level are using dialect for oral instruction.

Table 1. Transcription Conventions

The transcription of the SG examples and the children's attempts to speak StG follow the convention of Dieth's (1938) *Schweizerdeutsche Dialektschrift*. The familiar aspect of StG writing is largely maintained, especially concerning the representation of consonants. All voiced consonants, however, are pronounced voiceless. Continuous StG discourse is transcribed in standard orthography.

gg   Double consonants = geminate articulation, e.g., *ggangę* (*gegangen;* gone).

h   Glottal constrictive; it does not indicate vowel lengthening in Dieth's transcription.

Special conventions for vowels:

:   Marks long vowels, e.g., *ęr ga:t* (*geht;* goes).

ˋ   Open articulation, especially of long vowels, which otherwise would be close, e.g., *ich wè:r* (*wäre;* would). Short vowels always have an open articulation.

ų   In the children's attempts to speak StG there is sometimes exaggerated closing of short vowels; this is indicated by a period under the vowel, e.g., *hụnd* (dog).

ä   very open *e*-sound, e.g., *s gält* (*das Geld;* the money); also used for the very low diphthong /äi/, e.g., *wäisch* (*weisst;* you know).

ę   *schwa.*

Let us now return to the topic of this chapter, that is, the acquisition of StG by children in kindergarten, before having gotten any formal instruction in StG.

2. SPONTANEOUS PRODUCTION OF STANDARD GERMAN

Despite the fact that the kindergarten is a sacred domain of dialect—a kindergarten teacher would never read a story to the children in StG, but always retell it in SG dialect—at play children very often use single expressions or entire utterances in StG, especially in situations of spontaneous role-playing (see Table 1). The following are examples (Stern, 1978, p. 17):

(1) When calling the spaceship by radio:[3]

ALLES BERÄIT ZUM ABFLÜ:GEN!
everything ready for taking off

(2) When playing cowboys:

HENDE HO:CH ODER IÇ SCHI:SSE
hands up   or   I'll shoot

---

[3] Examples in SG and in StG are italicized. StG expressions within SG discourse are printed in small capitals. The English translation of the examples does not attempt to be idiomatic, but follows closely the structure of German, resulting in unacceptable English sentences in some places.

(3) When playing mother and children:

1. *chindè, gönd i s bett*
   children, go to bed
2. *wän èr ggässè händ, gönd èr ès mittagsschlä:fli go machè/*
   after you've eaten go and take a (afternoon) nap
3. *zwar marsch! (. . .) machèd rasch, marsch!*
   hurry up! do it quickly, hurry up!
4. SONST BÄIST ÖIÇ DER HUND!—ALL DAS IST ES SIÇER.
   otherwise the dog 'll bite you! all that is sure
5. *jo, isch würklich, gällèd.*
   yes, it's true, really.

The spontaneous production of StG is an integral part of role-playing. For the children the roles of queens, cowboys, spaceship crews, and reporters are firmly connected with StG. Evidently, these roles are directly copied from TV which, for most of the preschool children, is the only source of StG.

The linguistic forms of the StG acquired from TV, however, are not part of the standard variety spoken in Switzerland. It is a register of standard spoken in central and northern Germany, which is evident from articulation, intonation, and idiomatic expressions. This is not surprising, since Swiss TV for children is only cast in dialect (see Burger, 1984, p. 221), and the movies children watch (on German channels) are all produced or synchronized in Germany.

The role dependency of the use of StG appears clearly in the following example (4) (Stern, 1978, p. 20). All the discussions about the roles are in SG. There is code switching as soon as the speakers go back to their roles. Commands, exclamations, and arguing, that is, authoritative speech acts, are most likely to be pronounced in StG. As a matter of fact, StG words and expressions are used by adults, too, to add authority to an utterance.

(4) Two girls are playing scenes at the king's court: (M = Monika, Q = the Queen)

20. M: NÄIN, LASS DAS, DAS KIND!
    no, leave that child alone!
21. Q: NÄIN!
    no!
22. M: *wänn—wänn* DAS IMMER MI:R WILL NAGE:N
    if—if she always wants to follow me
23.   DAS IST DOCH WÄIL—WENN DAS KIND MICH LI:B HAT.
    this is because—if that child loves me.
24. Q: *ja, si söt mi:r au hälfè.* JETZT TU:T ÄINMAL WAS,
    yes, she should help me too. now start doing something,

25. *schüsch hau der äis uf d-finger*
or I'll hit you on your fingers

26. M: *ja, chum Marlen* (the queen's name)
come on Marlen

27. *du we:rsch nüd so bö:s gsi: zu de chinde.*
you wouldn't have been so angry with the children.

As soon as the children try to produce more than single words or more or less formulaic expressions in StG, we observe instances of code fluctuation; that is, single parameters, such as phonological, morphological, or lexical, vary in a nonsystematic way between standard and dialect, making it difficult to distinguish the two codes and the point of switching (see Auer, 1984, p. 65). Typically, lack of proficiency in the standard appears in example (4) line 22 (4:22) and in the following example (5) (Stern, 1978, p. 20), where StG is used for explaining and narrating, respectively.

(5) Two boys (P and R) are playing reporters; they speak directly into the mike of the recorder:

1. P: JA:, JETZT SE:EN SI: DEN ROGER UND—JAUSLIN.
yes, now you see Roger and—Jauslin.

2. DER THO:MAS UND ÖI ROGER HABEN ZU:GLU:GT
Thomas and Roger have watched

3. AN DEM BAUM, KASCHTANIENBAUM.
at the tree, chestnut tree.

4. PATRICK IST ZU SCHPE:T GEKOMMEN.
Patrick has arrived too late.

5. R: *ä:*HI:R—HAB IK ⟨*mit*⟩ MÄINEM MOTO GERÖSSLET,
here I have on my moped rattled,

6. *ä:* UND HA-HAT DER ROGER JAUSLIN ÄIN
and has Roger Jauslin a

7. *em* PATRICK SÄIN WELO GENOMM(EN),
Patrick's bike taken

8. IS ABEN, AB DEM *bürzlibaum—i bin i vorne abe gheit*
is down from the somersault—I am I in front fallen

9. *ab ds* WELO HAT ÄIN PÜRZELBAUM GENOMME,
from the bike has a somersault taken,

10. *un nachär* HAB ICH ÄIN LOCH IM KOPF *gha:,*
and then I have had a hole in the head,

11. *noch(er) sim-me mitenander häi,*
then we went home together,

12. *u(n) noch(er) is de Patrick mit mi:r häi,*
and Patrick went home with me,

13.   *un nochèr—un nochèr,* SCHLUSS.
        and then—and then, the end.

In this example, Roger is narrating a personal experience in StG. This type of speech cannot be produced by ready-made expressions but has to be generated step by step from the semantic base. The difficulties, especially in lines 6–9, are induced by this genuine production process.

3. COMPREHENSION AND LEXICAL ACQUISITION PROCESSES

At the age of 6, a child has acquired a relatively large vocabulary for everyday life situations, although individual differences, due to varying socio-cultural environments, are considerable. The study of the natural acquisition of StG shows that for production and comprehension, 6- to 7-year-old children rely strongly on the SG lexical base, transforming the phonological and morphological surface structure of SG into StG.

A study by Weber and Arter-Lamprecht (1983, 1984) of the acquisition of antonymous expressions with SG and StG stimulus words shows very little differences in the responses to the two varieties; that is, acquisition of a lexical item in one variety makes it available in the other too, as soon as surface correspondence can be established.

Comprehension of SG and StG at the kindergarten level (age 6) has also been investigated by Erny (1984). Two groups of children heard the same story either in SG or in StG. Comprehension was tested by retelling and questioning and evaluated by means of a detailed propositional analysis. The results confirm the hypothesis that the linguistic form of the input, that is, SG or StG, has only a minimal impact on comprehension.

The comprehension of narratives depends much more on other variables of text processing than the linguistic variety used (see Stern, 1984, pp. 141–143). Comprehension is the result of the hearer's active generating of the meaning of the text, based on a number of simultaneous processes, which in turn are based on previous knowledge (world knowledge) and on expectations built up during text reception. These hearer-directed comprehension processes work in interdependence with text-directed processes such as comprehending single words or the morpholo-syntactic structure. The hearer-directed processes enable him or her to bridge momentary comprehension gaps on the text level and to close them later. It is exactly this capability of bridging that helps children to understand StG texts. Thus, the general degree of development of text comprehension is important for the acquisition of StG.

Let us now look at specific phenomena of StG text processing by children. It is known that the attention of the listener of a story is greatest at the beginning. Much more details are stored, and later available, at the beginning of a story, whereas toward the end, attention is mainly directed to the understanding of the point. Erny (1984) found that the children who listened to the SG version of the story conformed much more to this general law of text comprehension than those who heard the StG version: until about the middle of the text the SG hearers had stored more details than their StG partners. However, from the middle to the end the result was quite the opposite: StG hearers—against the general findings of comprehension testing—stored more details than their SG partners.

These findings indicate that for the comprehension of StG texts, a part of the attention is not available for normal meaning processing. It seems that the children listening to the StG version use part of the available attention span, at least at the beginning, to perform the phonological transformations (see section 4 below). This allows them to discover SG words behind StG forms and to test whether the meaning found fits into the whole of the story. The problems they are facing have to do directly with the degree of divergence between SG and StG: How far may a StG phonological form differ from SG in order to remain recognizable to the child?

The following example, in which the phonological divergence exceeds the bandwidth of understandability, stems from a study on the acquisition of the StG preterite (see the study by Koch-Niederer, 1983/1984, discussed in section 5). Note that SG has no preterite tense; the only past tense being the perfect formed by the means of the auxiliaries *sein* and *haben*. In the sentence *(sie) trug den Zwerg zum See* (she carried the dwarf to the lake), most children at the age of 6 translated the StG preterite form *trug* in SG present *truckt,* meaning to push (underwater). This shows how flexibly the children adapt the meaning of single words, looking for morphophonological correspondence between StG and SG. In the case of *trug,* however, the divergence was too great to find the correct form, the SG verb being *trä:gè.*

Similar processes are observed in second-language learners, who often have to proceed with a lesser amount of information than Swiss StG learners. A good example is given by Erny (1984, pp. 59–61): the only two children in her sample of foreign L1 retold the story of the *Schne:glöggli* (snowdrop) as the story of the *Schne:flöckli* (snowflake). A Turkish boy transformed the SG verb *verscho:nt* (the snowdrop has been spared) into *gschunè,* in the context of the sun shone.

The capacity to cover a large bandwidth of phonological variation distinguishes the fast learner from the slow one. It is noticed that children with a foreign language background, who learned SG as their L2, differ from Swiss

children exactly in the capacity of using the full bandwidth of morphophonological variation for the semantic interpretation of StG.

This difference, which is also found among Swiss children, has to do with
the differing degree of differentiation of the SG lexicon. A child who for the
first time hears, for example, the StG preterite *sang* will immediately be able
to identify this form as being part of the paradigm of *singen* (to sing), if he or
she already knows at least one of the SG words *gsang* (the singing), *gsangvèr-
äin* (choral society), or *chilègsangbuèch* (hymn-book), which in SG are the
only forms in the semantic field of the verb *singe* containing the ablaut radical
vowel /a/. Note, however, that these words are part of a rather elaborated
vocabulary.

The capability to learn StG forms for SG words already acquired is considerable. This is shown by a longitudinal investigation (see Künzler, Loher,
& Hegglin, 1983/1984) on the possibilities of teaching StG in kindergarten. In
a single lesson the children learned in a playful way 60 StG forms for words
they already knew in SG. The degree of divergence of the two linguistic forms
varied from great to none. (Compare, e.g., StG: *Kamm* vs. SG: *Schtre:l* 'comb',
Zwiebel vs. *zwiblè* 'onion', *Auto* vs. *auto*.) One week later the children were
able to reproduce all the words learned in StG—by naming pictures and translating—without any difficulty.

The study of the acquisition of the StG lexicon and the comprehension of
StG texts shows that—despite the considerable phonological and lexical differences—most children have easy access to the StG variety. They rapidly acquire
the capability to discover familiar words under a divergent phonological form.
We think that this capability develops naturally in contact with the varying SG
dialects during first-language acquisition. Erny (1984, p. 102) observed that
her children were used to hearing stories told in a dialect differing considerably
from their own Toggenburg/St. Gallen variety, since the teacher spoke *Zürich-
deutsch*. Listening to different SG dialects obviously prepares children for the
understanding of the phonological variation of StG.

The capacity to deal with dialect variation also develops early in production. As a matter of fact, in kindergartens of bigger city agglomerations, mixed
groups of children with very different dialectal backgrounds speak among
themselves a relatively homogeneous local dialect, even though their teacher
speaks still another, sometimes a markedly different one (see Stern, 1978).

Summarizing the findings on the comprehension capacity in StG, we can
say that there is full transfer of this capacity from SG. The children acquire
phonological and morphological transformation rules, making it possible for
them to understand StG forms on the basis of the SG lexicon. We are now
going to look at the children's production capacity of StG, in order to explain
what these transformations are.

4. PHONOLOGICAL ACQUISITION PROCESSES

At about the age of 6, children are becoming aware of the linguistic characteristics of StG, but they need the help of the inquiring adult to make the awareness explicit. At kindergarten during an experiment in which a "visitor" spoke only StG, the children realized that his speaking was different only when they were questioned about it (see Künzler *et al.*, 1983/1984, p. 18). To the question of which language the visitor was speaking they answered with *tü:tsch* (German), *schwi:zertü:tsch* (Swiss–German), or *ho:chtü:tsch* (high German).

To the question about their experiences with StG, asked at different points of the longitudinal study, they answered with

- *ęs isch nüd änglisch* (it's not English).
- *das isch wię chine:sisch* (it's like Chinese).
- *hä, tänk vom fernse:* (of course from TV).
- *wię męr i dę schuęl ret* (like you speak at school).
- *ich bin ęmol z tü:tschland gsi:, und döt han i au öppis verschtandę.* (Once I was in Germany, and there I understood something too.)
- HOCHDEUTSCH, *wriladuli:aliduli . . . !* (high German, . . .).

These anecdotal observations illustrate the rather casual knowledge about StG that children have at this age. The analysis of their spontaneous production of StG, however, shows how much more accurate their unconscious knowledge of StG is. Koch-Niederer (1983/1984) reports that during the experiment with kindergarteners, one child, who had refused to speak StG for a long time, suddenly started speaking "fluently" a sort of StG having the following phonological characteristics:

- Raising and unrounding of vowels.
- Transformation of SG diphthongs into monophthongs and vice versa.
- Suffixing of /n/ to SG words.

The following is a closer analysis of these observations, illustrated by examples from the studies of Künzler *et al.* (1983/1984), Stoll and Kunz (1983/1984), and the corpus by Stern (1978).

4.1. Change of Vowels

4.1.1. Raising and Unrounding

The following examples show that the children discover spontaneously some essential phonological rules of correspondence between SG and StG by raising and unrounding the SG vowels, which in general are articulated very open and in back.

(6)

	SG:		StG:	English
(a)	*hùnd*[4]	>	*hu̧nd*[7] (3)	(dog)
(b)	*sìchęr*[5]	>	*siçer* (3)	(sure)
(c)	*Tòmas*[6]	>	*Tho:mas* (5)	
(d)	*händę ho:ch odęr*	>	*hende ho:ch*	(hands up or
	ich schü:ssę	>	*iç schi:sse* (2)	I shoot)
(e)	*z schpo:t*	>	*zu schpe:t* (5)	(too late)
(f)	*mänggmal scho:*	>	*mengmol scho:*	(sometimes yes)

In (a)–(c) the transformations meet the target language, although there is a tendency to exaggerate the raising. That these transformations are rule guided is evident from the frequent overgeneralizations exemplified in (f), the StG target being *manchmal*.

How true these phonological transformation rules are for idiomatic expressions, like (d), cannot be determined on the basis of our data. Since formulaic expressions are acquired in a holistic way (see Fillmore, 1979), holistic learning probably also includes the phonological form. Therefore, phonological transformation rules would not affect single phonemes of these expressions (cf. also the discussion of *schü:ssę > schäisse* below).

Evidently, similar phonological transformations are also characteristic for the transition from one SG dialect to another. In (f), the raising and unrounding of /ä/ to /e/, produced as a StG form, is typical also for eastern Swiss dialects, like St-Gall and Appenzell, using the word *mengmo:l*.

Changes of manner and place of articulation from SG to StG are also found in the acquisition of consonants. In (5:5) R. is trying to change the articulation of *ich*—in SG always pronounced with the velar fricative /x/—resulting in *ik*. In this example, the place of articulation is changed in the right direction (velar > palatal); the manner of articulation, however, is incorrect (occlusive instead of fricative). The acquisition of the StG allophone /ç/ is very difficult to learn for all Swiss children, and many never master it perfectly. At school the overgeneralization of /ç/ is very frequent, for example, *bewaçen* or *maçen* (see Stoll & Kunz, 1983/1984). In the early stage of acquisition, the

[4] The transcription ì, ò, ù stresses the very open articulation of the SG vowels, e.g., the /u/ in SG *und* is almost pronounced /o/, whereas the StG articulation is quite close.

[5] *ch* stands for the velar fricative /x/, ç for the palatal allophone. Note that in SG there exists only the velar fricative, whereas in StG, /x/ and /ç/ occur in complementary distribution before back and front vowels, respectively.

[6] In SG, /t/ is not aspirated, and short /o/ is also much lower than in StG; long /o:/ is close in both varieties.

[7] The numbers in parenthesis refer to previously listed examples the displayed item belongs to; a second digit after a colon, for example, (5:5), refers to the line number of the example.

allophone /ç/ is produced correctly in StG words that don't have the phoneme /x/ in the corresponding SG form. Compare, for example, the queen in (4):

	niçt	<	SG:	*nid*	(not)	(4:6)*
but:	*ich*	<		*ich*	(I)	(4:19)*
and:	*mich*	<		*mi:ch*	(me)	(4:23)

*Not provided in the example.

An exception is found in (3:4), where the girl role-playing a mother produces *siçer* (sure), pronounced with /x/ in SG. However, since her mother is Austrian, this girl has probably already acquired the distinction between /c/ and /x/ and its complementary distribution.

4.1.2. Transformation of Diphthongs into Monophthongs and Vice Versa

Very quickly the children are going to comprehend the systematic relation between monophthongs and diphthongs of the two varieties. In (3) through (5) we find a number of—mostly correct—transformations of this type:

(7)

SG monophthongs		StG diphthongs		
bi:st	>	*bäist*	(to bite)	(3:4)
ɇm P. si:s welo	>	*säin*	(his)	(5:7)
het ɇn p. gmacht	>	*äin*	(a)	(5:9)
wil	>	*wäil*	(because)	(4:23)

SG diphthongs		StG monophthongs		
zuɇgluɇgt	>	*zu:glu:gt* (ZUGESCHAUT)	(watched)	(5:2)
niɇ	>	*ni:*	(never)	(4:18)*
liɇb	>	*li:b*	(nice)	(4:23)
tüɇnd	>	*tu:t*	(do)	(4:24)

*Not provided in the example.

Because SG and StG words very often differ only in phonological form, the phonological transformations lead mostly to correct StG words. Only in the case of *zuɇluɇgɇ* > *zu:glu:gt* does the transformation result in a word not existing in StG.

A special case is the word *hi:r* (5:5). Although there exists a SG word *hiɇ*, it is only used in the expression *hiɇ und da:;* it never stands alone (at least not in the eastern dialects). In free occurrences, as a local adverb, it is always replaced by *da:*. The use of *hi:r* in (5:5) is formulaic, that is, it is part of the reporter's formula: *Here speaks X in Y.*

Although the rules for the monophthong–diphthong transformation are correctly learned quite fast, errors caused by overgeneralization of the rule always occur:

(8)

umflü:gt (falls down)	*umflöigt* (UMFLIEGT, UMFÄLLT)
	(Stoll & Kunz, 1983/1984)
sunębrülę (sunglasses)	*sonnenbräile* (SONNENBRILLE)
	(Künzler *et al.*, 1983/1984, p. 30)
gogę schi:fa:rę (to ski)	*gogen schäi—schi:fa:ren*
	(SKIFAHREN GEHEN) (Stoll & Kunz, 1983/1984)

The treating of /ü/ seems to be especially difficult. There are many cases of Sg /ü:/ leading to StG /öi/ (written *eu* or *äu*); for example, *ü:lę* (owl) > *Eule*, and *hü:lę* (howl) > *heulen*. But there are also some cases of SG /ü:/ corresponding to StG /i:/ (written *ie*); for example, *bü:gę* (to bend) > *biegen*, and *flü:gę* (to fly) > *fliegen*. It is difficult to determine when the children perform the monophthong–diphthong transformation for /ü:/ and when they do not. In (1) there is an example of unchanged use in the StG form: SG *abflü:gę* becomes StG *abflü:gen*.

Note that this rule operates only on long SG /ü:/. Therefore, in (8) its use in *sunebrülę* is erroneous. Overgeneralizations of the diphthongization rule are recognized as erroneous very early, which is confirmed by frequent self-corrections, as in (8): *schäi—schi:fahren*.

Anecdotal evidence of the difficulties children often have with monophthongs/diphthongs is given by the following dilemmatic situation that occurred to my 6-year-old nephew when visiting friends in Germany. When playing cops-and-robbers with his StG-speaking friends, he repeated several times the expression *hende ho:ch oder ich schäisse*. To the playmates correcting him—"It doesn't say *schäisse* (to shit), it says *schi:sse* (to shoot)!"—he answered: "I'm not allowed to say this word at home." When playing at home (in Switzerland) he used to pronounce correctly *ich schi:sse*. To him, however, this was part of his SG repertoire, which needed translation, that is, diphthongization, when used in the actual StG situation. This example shows also that single words and phonemes of a holistically acquired idiomatic expression are not immediately processable as isolated elements (see Fillmore, 1979). The ambiguity of SG *schi:sse* was recognized by the child only when the word was isolated by the playmate's correction.

4.2. N-Suffixing

A striking phenomenon of early StG production is the frequent use of /n/ as an ending of SG words. The following transcription of a discussion between the experimenter and a 6-year-old boy illustrates this procedure (Koch-Niederer, 1983/1984, p. 32):

(9)

> E: *Was machtest du mit der Sonnenblume?*
> what did you do with the sunflower?
>
> B: *Der Vögel ge:n* (SG: *dė vögel ge:*)
> give (it) to the birds
>
> E: *Was machten die Vögel?*
> what did the birds do?
>
> B: *Die picken Kernen usen.* (SG: *diė pickėd chernė-n-usė*)
> *they pick out the kernels*

Evidently, we are witnessing the first attempts to deal with StG morphology. The suffix -*n* is very frequent in StG. For the children this must be a very striking difference between the two varieties, since in SG, due to historical change, very few words have kept the ending -*n*.

This acquisitional process confirms Slobin's (1979, p. 108) statement that ''for various reasons of attention and memory, children find ends of words and utterances more salient than beginnings and middles.'' Searching for meaningful grammatical items children are following the ''operation principle A: Pay attention to the ends of words'' (Slobin, 1979, p. 108). Although this procedure very quickly leads to the acquisition of the noun and verb inflection, it seems that in the early stage of *n*-suffixing, we are dealing with a merely phonological process, allowing the learner to come immediately very close to the phonological gestalt of StG (see also MacWhinney, 1978). This is confirmed by the relatively unsystematic distribution of the *n*-suffixes over the different word classes (Koch-Niederer, 1983/1984, p. 28):

(10)

Verbs

gogen schi:fa:ren (SG: *gogė schi:fa:rė*)
going to ski
hät ghäien la:n (SG: *hät gheiė la:*)
he let it fall down

Nouns: the following are examples of words repeated by the children, after the experimenter's (correct) pronunciation for a drawing dictation in kindergarten (see Künzler *et al.*, 1983/1984, p. 26):

Experimenter:		Child:	
eine Feder	(a feather)	*eine Federn*	(*ė fädėrė*)
eine Zwiebel	(an onion)	*eine Zwiebeln*	(*ė zwiblė*)
eine Schüssel	(a bowl)	*ein Schüsslen*	(*ė schüsslė*)
ein Kran	(a crane)	*ein Kranen*	(*ėn kra:nė*)

Adverbs

usen	(out)	SG:	*usé*	StG:	*raus*
de:ten	(there)		*de:té*		*dort*
aben	(down)		*abé*		*runter*

Of course, SG words ending on *-e* are priviledged to get a *n*-suffix, whereas occurrences like *pischama:n* (pajama) or *Schu:löffen* (shoehorn), from SG *schuelöffel,* are rather exceptional. Thus, most *n*-suffixes occur on nouns and verbs, very often ending on *-e,* and the step to meaningful grammatical marking is only a small one.

As the acquisition of the morphological system of StG progresses, the unsystematic use of the *n*-suffix decreases rapidly. In our investigations, 7-year-old first graders, contrary to the 6-year-old kindergarteners, produced only very few misplaced *n*-suffixes (see Koch-Niederer, 1983/1984, pp. 37–39, and recordings by Stern, 1978).

5. THE ACQUISITION OF THE STG PRETERITE

The discussion of the acquisition of StG on the lexical and phonological level showed typical acquisition processes for the dialect–standard situation which, however, are not typical in situations of greater divergence between L1 and L2, that is, in actual second-language acquisition. The great degree of convergence between SG and StG in the lexicon, and the systematic relation between the two varieties at the phonological level, induces the learner to continue first-language acquisition, that is, to develop new linguistic registers in his or her first language. The new register (StG) is modeled on the SG base by means of adaptations and transformations.

This procedure, however, is not adopted for the acquisition of the StG preterite. The preterite does not exist in SG; there is only a perfect past tense formed by an auxiliary verb + perfect participle (see Haas, 1982, p. 95). Thus, for the preterite we observe participle (see Haas, 1982, p. 95). Thus, for the preterite we observe typical second-language acquisition processes, such as gradual approximation to the target form, simplification and regularization of irregular target structures, and slow progress with large individual variation (see Wode, 1983, pp. 191–193). We assume that in the domains of morphology, in which StG and SG differ rather greatly, typical second-language acquisition occurs, although, up to now, only the preterite has been studied in a more systematic way.

The investigation by Koch-Niederer (1983/1984) documents, by means of *ad hoc* experiments, the process of acquisition of the StG preterite of a small group of 6-year-old kindergarteners (five children) and 7-year-old first graders (six children). The investigation took place during several weeks. The data gathered by the experiments are completed by unsystematic observations and recordings.

Since the preterite occurs mainly in written StG, the investigation of Koch-Niederer is based on a short rhyme, written especially for the purpose of testing. The rhyme contains nine verbs in the preterite, six strong–irregular and three weak–regular forms:

(11)

Test-rhyme:

Es WAR *einmal ein Zwerg,*	There was once a dwarf,
der GING *auf einen Berg,*	he went on a mountain,
dort SETZTE *er sich in das Gras*	there he sat in the grass
und PUTZTE *seine lange Nas.*	and cleaned his long nose.
Dann ASS *er zwei Melonen*	Then he ate two melons
und SCHLECKTE *zwei Zitronen.*	and licked two lemons. Then
Da KAM *die gute Fee*	came the good fairy and
und TRUG *den Zwerg zum See.*	carried him to the lake.
Der Zwerg SCHWAMM *schnell nach*	The dwarf swam quickly
Haus.	home.
Jetzt ist das Märchen aus.	Now the story is finished.

The children learned the rhyme by heart, repeating it together with the experimenter and the teacher on several consecutive days. The children's rehearsals were tape-recorded at all stages. In addition, the experimenter organized play activities (pantomime, puppets) and discussions, in order to provide opportunities for spontaneous reproductions of the heard preterite forms. It was assumed that during rehearsal the children would not be able to reproduce preterite forms they had not yet acquired (Slobin, 1979, p. 104) or that they would change the forms following the actual stage of acquisition. Note that when talking about acquisitional stages, we do not assume that these are necessary actual stages of the individual child but rather reconstructions of observable stages on the basis of our data.

At the beginning the children concentrated on the meaning of the verb stems. They understood the meaning of a verb in StG, if they were able to establish identity—by means of phonological transformation—with a SG verb they already knew. During the first rehearsal of the rhyme, the 6-year-olds reproduced the verbs as follows:[8]

(12)

GING	*gehe, gangt, ging*	(went)
SETZTE	*setzt, sitzt, setzte*	(sat)

[8]The list contains all forms produced by different children of the sample, neglecting the frequency of occurrence.

PUTZTE	*putzt, putzten, putzte*	(cleaned)
ASS	*esst, isst, asst*	(ate)
SCHLECKTE	*schleckt, schleckte*	(licked)
KAM	*kommt, kummt, kunnt, kam*	(came)
TRUG	*truckt, truck, trug sich, trug*	(carried)
SCHWAMM	*springte, schwamm*	(swam)

There is a strong tendency to reproduce StG preterite as SG present. This is confirmed by the reading of 7-year-olds, who tended to omit the seemingly meaningless ending *-e* of the regular preterite form. In (12) the forms *sitzt/setzt*, *putzt*, and *schleckt* are also SG present. The same transformation (StG preterite > SG present) occurs also with the irregular verbs, if the meaning is detected: *kummt/kunnt* and *springt* are SG present.

For the children's reproductions of the rhyme, what is important is the meaning, and not the form. The event the rhyme tells about is temporally situated by the introductory formula *es war einmal* (once upon a time), which was reproduced correctly by all children; in their view there seems to be no need to mark past tense (redundantly) on the following verbs. As a matter of fact, their focus on meaning leads them to very forced interpretations (see comment on p. 409 about *trug* 'carried' understood as *truckt* 'to push down').

For a 6-year-old, past tense—which during the linguistic development of the child emerges from perfective aspect—is expressed by the means of the perfect. It is the auxiliary that carries temporal information in the first place. MacWhinney (1978, p. 53), who studied first language acquisition of the perfect tense in German, states that although the auxiliary enters only after age 3, it is the first form to express perfectivity. Therefore, lack of the auxiliary in the StG text will be interpreted by the child as present tense.

There is some evidence that for his or her first expressions of past tense in StG, the SG child uses the auxiliary verb *tun* (to do) + infinitive. In an experiment with pictures showing what grown-up Anna liked to do when she was a child, that is, representing past events, the experimenter asked the children to comment on the pictures, beginning with the phrase *als Anna klein war.* . . . Many of the answers were of the type *tun* + infinitive (Koch-Niederer, 1983/1984, p. 29):

(13)

> Experimenter: *Als Anna klein war* . . .
> Child: *tut sie flüschteren* (she does whisper)
> *tut sie turnen* (she does gymnastics)
> *tun sie gern be:bi spi:len* (she does like to play dolls)

The introductory clause in past tense did not prevent the children from continuing in present tense; though it is also possible that the actual situation of describing pictures here and now in the present does influence the actual speech situation much more than the verbal stimulus of asking the children to tell the story of Anna's experiences in the past.

Still, they also produced past tense forms in the perfect. The comparison between 6- and 7-year-olds shows a remarkable increase in the use of these forms with age (Koch-Niederer, 1983/1984, p. 46):

| age 6: | 12 present | 4 preterite | 2 perfect |
| age 7: | 19 | 12 | 9 |

The expression *tun* + infinitive is frequently used also by the older children. It is produced simultaneously with present and past tense forms (perfect and preterite) in the same text by several children. When asking a 6-year-old to say the expression *tut spielen* (do play) with other words, it was replaced spontaneously by *spielte* (played). To what extent for these children *tun* + infinitive contains temporal information cannot be determined on the basis of our data. Evidently, it is a typical simplification strategy appearing early also in first-language acquisition of German and SG, as well as in motherese and in foreigner-talk. Typically, this simplification strategy reappears during the acquisition of the StG past tense system revealing second-language processes, long after these children had stopped using this form in their first language (SG) in similar contexts.

In spontaneous production of StG, for example in (5), or when asked to tell personal past experiences, all children use exclusively perfect past tense, as they are used to in SG. Difficulties arise only in the production of the past participle, which very often is phonologically and/or lexically adapted from SG by means of (overregularized) transformations. The following is an example of a 7½-year-old girl after 8 months in first grade. (The StG production is transcribed in regular StG orthography; if the form is incorrect, the corrected form is given in parenthesis: first form, correct StG form; second form, SG lexical base. The English translation is close to literal.)

(14)

1. *wir haben Fernseh gelu:gt (GESCHAUT; gluègt)*
   we have TV   watched
2. *dann ist ein Film gekommen von einem Delphin*
   then has a movie come of a dolphin
3. *und der Delphin ist ganz stark gsein (GEWESEN; gsi:)*
   and the dolphin has been very strong
4. *und ein Bub noch, der ist auch stark gsein (GEWESEN; gsi:)*
   and a boy also, who has been strong too
5. *und dann hat 's Räuber gehabt, die sind ganz böse gsein*
   and then there have been robbers who were very wicked

6. *und denn ist ein Messer im Meer gsi:n* (GEWESEN; *gsi:*)
   and then there has been a knife in the sea

7. *irgendwie angri:ffen go gangen* (ANGREIFEN GEGANGEN; *go a:gri:ffę*)
   somehow (he) went to attack

8. *und da hat er einen Schnitt überkommen* (BEKOMMEN; *übęrcho:*)
   and then he got a cut

9. *ist am Meer gele:gt* (GELEGEN; *glägę*)
   was laying at the sea (the knife)

10. *und der Bub ist auf dem Schiff gsi:n* (GEWESEN; *gsi:*)
    and the boy has been on the ship

11. *und de het es de Bub gesi:n* (GESEHEN; *gse:*)
    and then the boy saw it (the knife)

12. *und ist zum Delphin ⟨gegangen⟩*
    and went to the dolphin

13. *und da hat er s gsi:n* (GESEHEN; *gse:*)
    and then he saw it

14. *das er ein Schnitt gehabt hat.*
    that he (the dolphin) had a cut.

This is a typical example of direct transformation of SG into StG. Evidently, the perfect participles expressed by different words in StG and SG are difficult to translate. What is striking is the coinciding of the two words *gsi:* (been) and *gse:* (seen) in the child's StG expression *gsi:n* (lines 6, 10, and 11), standing twice for *been* and once for *seen*. The phonological adaptation follows the rules described in section 4. The coincidence is caused by omitting the diphthongization leading from *gsein* (in lines 3, 4, and 5) to *gsi:n* (in lines 6 and 10).

These examples show that the StG participle is not acquired in a holistic way but is generated anew, starting from the SG base each time it is used. By doing this, the children do not take the easiest way, that is, they do not simply translate a StG participle into a SG one by means of phonological (surface) transformations. From the early stages of acquisition it is evident that the system of participle formation is reconstructed radically. The following examples were produced by children who are one year younger than the child in (14), that is, 6½ years old (Künzler *et al.*, 1983/1984, pp. 17, 34, and 40):

(15)

StG		SG
wo mir aben gloft sind	<	*abę gloffę sind*
(*als wir hinunter* GELAUFEN *sind*; as we went down)		
dann ist er hinauf gegangt	<	*ufę ggangę*
(GEGANGEN; then he went up)		

wir sind dort eingebrocht	<	*i:bbrochę*
(EINGEBROCHEN; there we broke in)		
wir haben ganz viel gestohlt	<	*gschtolę*
(GESTOHLEN; we stole a lot)		

Although all these children master the distinction between weak/regular and strong/irregular in the SG dialect, they overgeneralize the weak form when producing a StG participle. Since SG and StG have virtually the same forms, it would be easy to translate a SG participle into correct StG by simply adding an *-n* to the SG base (see section 4.2 on *n*-suffixing):

(16)

SG		Stg	
ggangę	>	*gegangen*	(gone)
gschtolę	>	*gestohlen*	(stolen)

Nevertheless, the learners fall back on earlier acquisitional stages and reconstruct the entire system from the beginning.

Summarizing our findings of the acquisition of the StG past tense system more systematically, we distinguish four stages:

Stage I: StG preterite is replaced by present tense forms.

Stage II: Frequent strong–irregular preterite forms are acquired in a holistic way as new words, for example, *war* (was), *hatte* (had), *ging* (went), *kam* (came). At this point we observe an interesting combination of SG perfect and StG preterite: as soon as the preterite forms of the auxiliary verbs *sein* (to be) and *haben* (to have) are acquired, they are immediately used to express StG past tense. The following narrative by a 7½-year-old girl (eighth month in first grade) illustrates this procedure:

(17)

> *Mir waren zuerst auf dem Flughafen gewesen, und da* HATTEN *wir so*
> first, we had been at the airport,   and then we had
> *lang müssen warten, wil unser Auto* WAR *kaputt gewesen, und dann*
> waited for a long time, 'cause our car had been broken, and then
> HATTEN *wir müssen zum Automechaniker gehn, und* HATTEN *müssen das*
> we had had to go to the mechanic   and had had to have
> *Auto la flicken, und dann* HATTEN *wir gewiss noch können gehn . . .*
> the car repaired, and then, sure, we could have gone . . (she is search-
> 7   ing for words and finishes after a long pause).

Although all the verb forms are clearly pluperfect, it is evident that the child doesn't mean to use this tense but simply tries to express past tense in

StG. By doing so, she tries to integrate the dual past tense system of StG in the simple one of SG.

Pluperfect is acquired only much later, and many SG speakers never really master it. In an investigation of the syntax of written reproductions by 13-year-old pupils (sixth grade) of a previously heard narrative, Guyer (1985) states that the use of pluperfect is generally avoided. As a consequence, in subordinate temporal clauses expressing anteriority, the same tense is used as in the main clause.

Stage III: The proper ending *-te* of the regular preterite tense appears first with strong–irregular verbs; that is, it is immediately overgeneralized: *gangte* (*ging;* went), *esste* (*ass;* ate), *stiegte* (*stieg;* climbed). Often the stem of the SG perfect participle is used to form the StG preterite: *gangte* ⟨SG: *ggangé* (gone).

This procedure puts the preterite form closer to the perfect, thus confirming the above statement that learners try to construct a simple past tense system—similar to SG—by merging perfect and preterite.

Stage IV: Finally, the correct target forms of StG preterite and perfect and the correct use of regular and irregular verbs are acquired by most children at age 8 to 10, but at individually greatly varying pace. Exceptionally, as in the example below, even a 7½-year-old first grader is able to produce correct preterite and perfect tense forms:

(18) A girl's narrative about St. Nicolas Day (6th of December):

Mit mir war er ganz zurfrieden. Ich hatte—und wo ich am
With me he was rather pleased. I had—and when I was
Abend daheim war, da hatte ich vergessen, den Stiefel heraus zu tun.
at home in the evening, I had forgotten to put out the stocking.
Und dann, am Morgen, hatte ich doch den Stiefel voll mit
And then, in the morning, nevertheless, I had the stocking full of
Schokoladen. Und dann kam er nochmal in den Wald hinein, und dort
chocolates. And then he came again into the forest, and there
hat er uns noch ein Päckli gegeben, und dort waren noch
he gave us another present, and there was again
ganz viele Sachen drin.
lots of stuff in it.

6. CLOSING REMARKS

The spontaneous use of StG in role-play shows that children integrate StG elements quite easily and rapidly into their SG repertoire, as if it were part of their L1. Evidently, it would be easy for them to acquire a conversational register of StG (see also Stern, 1984, p. 142). However, since TV is almost the only source of input of colloquial StG, opportunities to get sufficient input and practice are very limited. This leads to an interruption of the natural acquisition process at the beginning of school, when children start hearing and using StG for the language-learning purpose in a Swiss context and with a Swiss accent. In phonology, for example, especially concerning raising of vowels, it is evident that in the early phase of "TV-StG" the pronunciation is very similar to German standards. Under the influence of schooling, the pronunciation changes very quickly to a backened and lowered Swiss accent. But not only is the phonological quality changing, the children are also losing the other typical characteristics of (northern) TV-StG, that is, idiomatic terms, interjections, modal particles, and fast-speech forms.

The analysis of acquisition processes on different levels of the linguistic system (phonology, morphology, lexicon) shows clearly that there is not a straightforward additive development of linguistic registers in L1. Although this might be true for the lexicon, on other levels we observe a genuine L2 acquisition process.

At school, where the use of StG becomes crucial for successful language learning, the particular mixture of first-language development and second-language learning leads to a wide gap between passive and active linguistic competence. The ability to express oneself in StG does not correspond to the level of linguistic development reached in SG. This becomes evident when comparing narratives (14), (17), and (18) to narratives in SG of children of the same age or even younger (see Stern, 1984). The narratives in StG are pronounced very slowly, and the intonational shaping is very limited. A good example of these difficulties is given at the end of (17), where the modal particle *gewiss*— being part of a much more elaborated and flexible performance—plays a false note within the rigid and awkward narration.

REFERENCES

Auer, J. C. P. (1984). *Code-shifting: Phonologische und konversationelle Aspekte von Standard/ Dialect Kontinua*. Arbeitspapier, Sonderforschungsbereich 99, vol. 88. Universität Konstanz.

Burger, H. (1984). *Sprache der Massenmedien*. Berlin: de Gruyter.

Erny, M. (1984). *Textverstehen in Mundart und Standardsprache im kindergarten*. Universität Zürich: Lizentiatsarbeit, mimeo.

Fillmore, L. W. (1979). Individual differences in second-language acquisition. In C. J. Fillmore, D. Kempler, & W. Wang (Eds.), *Individual differences in language ability and language behavior* (pp. 203–228). New York: Academic Press.

Guyer, G. (1985). *Syntaktische Untersuchungen von Nacherzählungen nach Mundart und Standard Textvorlagen*. Universität Zürich: Lizentiatsarbeit, mimeo.

Haas, W. (1982). Die deutschsprachige Schweiz. In R. Schläpfer (Ed.), *Die viersprachige Schweiz* (pp. 71–160). Zürich: Benziger.

Lötscher, A. (1983). *Schweizerdeutsch. Geschichte, Dialekt, Gebrauch.* Frauenfeld: Huber.

MacWhinney, B. (1978). The acquisition of morphophonology. *Monographs of the Society for Research in Child Development,* vol. 43/1–2. University of Chicago Press.

Schwarzenbach, R., & Sitta, H. (1983). Mundart und Standardsprache in der deutschen Schweiz. *Bulletin CILA, 38,* 62–71.

Sieber, P., & Sitta, H. (1984). Schweizerdeutsch zwischen Dialekt und Sprake. *Kwartalnik Neofilologiczny,* 31/1, 3–40.

Slobin, D. I. (1979). *Psycholinguistics* (2nd ed.) Glenview, IL: Scott, Foresman.

Stern, O. (1978). *Schweizerdeutsch im Kindergarten: Korpuserstellung, linguistische Analyse, Computer-Verarbeitungssystem.* Zürich: Diss. mimeo.

Stern, O. (1984). Developing decontextualized language in children's narratives. In J. C. P. Auer & A. Di Luzio (Eds.), *Interpretative sociolinguistics* (pp. 129–149). Tübingen: Narr.

Wode, H. (1983). An integrated view of language learning. In H. Wode (Ed.), *Papers on language acquisition, language learning and language teaching* (pp. 175–223). Heidelberg: Groos.

SEMINAR PAPERS

Seminar: *Der Aufbau der Wrotbedeutung bei Kindern,* directed by Prof. H. Burger, Deutsches Seminar der Universität Zürich, 1983/1984.

Koch-Niederer, A. Der Erwerb des Imperfekts bei Kinder mit Schweizerdeutscher Muttersprache. Längsschnittuntersuchung an 6- bis 7-jährigen Kindern.

Künzler, A., Loher, F., & Hegglin, S. Hochdeutsch eine grausge Sprooch. Untersuchung über die Langzeitwirkung von hochsprachlichem Sprachgebrauch im Kindergarten.

Stoll, G., & Kunz, J.-P. Linguistische Analyse spontan produzierter Hochsprache von Kindern.

Weber, D., & Arter-Lamprecht, L. Die Entwicklung der Bedeutung von Antonymen bei 3- bis 8-jährigen Kindern.

CHAPTER 16

Oral Reading Practice
An Institutional Constraint on the Development of Functional Literacy

WILLIE VAN PEER

1. INTRODUCTION

For the majority of people in present-day Western societies the following position holds: the process of learning to read occurs predominantly within the
confines of a specialized *social institution,* that is, the school. (Its institutional
nature need not, perhaps, be elaborated here, though reference could be made
to the existence of special administrations and Ministries of Education, to the
fact that its agents form a professional group with specialized forms of knowledge, or to the straightforward fact of education being compulsory.) Like other
social institutions, schools develop their own specific patterns of (inter-) action
and behavior. These institutional patterns, because they serve the needs of the
institution, will differ more or less from patterns in everyday life. This difference creates, at once, possibilities and pitfalls for the institution. That is to say,
institutional patterns may facilitate learning, but—because they differ slightly
or even dramatically from everyday learning processes—they may, on the contrary, raise obstacles for the learner. One area of research where this contradictory nature of school-based action patterns has been demonstrated effectively is
that of classroom communication (for a state of the art, see Redder, 1983;
Regan, 1983). The work of Ehlich and Rehbein (1977, 1983) especially has
succeeded in describing the subtle mechanisms of these institutional patterns on
a number of linguistic, mental, and interactional dimensions. Thus, because of

WILLIE VAN PEER • Department of Literary Theory, University of Utrecht, 3512 EV Utrecht,
The Netherlands.

the influence of institutional factors shaping the learning process, one would expect research to deal with these from time to time. However, with respect to reading education, little or no attention at all is given to such institutional factors (van Peer, 1984). In The Netherlands, for instance, I think it is fair to say that literally *no* research into reading difficulties has taken factors emanating from the institutional context of the school seriously. Could this be an indication that in the acquisition of literacy these institutional patterns do not (or hardly) interfere with the learning process? Alas, I think not.

In what follows, I concentrate on one particular action pattern taking place in reading classes in Dutch schools (one which is quite dominant, although it is difficult to say exactly how frequently it is practiced), namely, that of *oral reading*.[1] In this pattern, pupils take turns in reading part of a text aloud. The teacher sometimes intervenes, corrects, demonstrates, comments, or asks questions, and at the end of the turn, usually gives an appreciation. The general assumption behind the pattern—and one which I wish to question—is that such oral practice develops technical reading skills, which are thought to be a prerequisite for adequate literacy. It is not possible here to go into all the details of the arguments which speak against this assumption. Instead, I present my major points succinctly and in the form of theses, which—although not verbally elaborated here—nevertheless do not rest, I contend, on quicksand.

Concerning the frequency of this practice in classrooms in The Netherlands, no detailed surveys have been made;[2] hence, only rough indications can be given here. In a recent sketch of reading education, Luidinga and de Vries (1983, pp. 161, 165) described oral reading as the classical and most common type of reading lesson in both primary and secondary education. A second indication of its frequency may be derived from guidelines supplied by materials for "technical reading." Although these have by no means an obligatory status, it is to be expected that teachers will interpret them as "norms" for

---

[1] Needless to say, oral reading presents but one type of institutional practice bearing on the reading process. Others may be identified, for instance, asking questions, discussing, dramatizing the text, and so on. It is in the nature of the present argument that institutional analyses of the kind outlined here may greatly help to clarify complex and apparently paradoxical situations confronting reading education.

[2] Note that the absolute frequency of the pattern of oral reading is only one aspect which is of interest. Even more important is its *relative* occurrence vis-à-vis other aspects of reading. Central to the argument of this paper, moreover, is the fact that the pattern *does* occur in reading classes and that wherever it occurs, it shows an internal structure. The objectivity of this structure need not be demonstrated through large-scale empirical investigations but can be arrived at through a careful and detailed analysis of a representative case of the pattern, in the same way as in anatomy, insight into the internal structure of part of the body may—if thoroughly analyzed—be arrived at through a relatively limited number of dissections. With respect to the oral reading pattern, for instance, it may suffice to point out that the mean speed of reading aloud differs markedly from that at which silent reading takes place. As such this is—together with other characteristics—an objective quality, regardless of the pattern's average occurrence.

their own practice. On the basis of approximately five reading sessions, the producers of the materials advise teachers to devote up to four lessons (out of five!) to oral reading in Grade 2. From a recommended three lessons in Grade 3, there is a drop to one and a half in Grade 4, but one hour of oral reading weekly is still recommended in Grades 5 and 6. Some variation is to be expected in teachers' fidelity to these guidelines—but they nevertheless must represent a picture which is not so outlandish as to be totally isolated from real classroom practice.

As to the German Federal Republic, no data on the occurrence of the practice are available. Informants have assured me, though, that the pattern of oral reading is still regularly and widely used, albeit—from what I gathered in these reports—not in as extreme forms as may be witnessed in The Netherlands. The idea, for instance, of having the class take turns in oral reading for a whole lesson (say, of approximately 45 minutes) will be rejected as of little pedagogical value by most teachers and parents.

The most detailed account surveying the frequency of oral reading is to be found in the U.K., where the Bullock Report provides rather accurate figures on the time devoted in class to different types of reading activity. How widespread oral reading (called "reading practice") is may be gathered from Bullock (1975, p. 375):

> Three-quarters of the 6-year-olds were expected to read *daily* from the books used for reading practice, and almost all the rest at least *three or four times a week*. Among the 9-year-olds, 59% were expected to read from these books *daily*, 28% three to four times a week, and the remainder less often. (italics added)

To conclude, then, these figures, together with the more global indications available in other countries, show that oral reading in class is not a merely incidental practice but an interactive pattern which is at once widely established and deeply embedded in the institutional constellation in which reading is to be learned.

2. SOCIAL FUNCTIONS OF ORAL READING

Before going on to analyze this pattern more closely, attention should be given to the functions oral reading *may* fulfill in society at large. At the present stage of knowledge, however, little is known about these social functions— certainly not in any systematic or exhaustive sense. I therefore propose the following provisional overview:

1. The *economic* function: a text is read aloud because of permanent or incidental scarcity of written texts available to (a subpart of) the social group. This practice arose regularly in medieval Europe, and it arises in present-day

society when, for instance, a last-minute letter is communicated to members of a meeting who have not received a copy of it.

2. The *distributional* function: reading aloud is used as a means to easily distribute ideas or messages contained in written or printed texts in a social group. We can see this function at work in the oral reading of the news on television or when one dictates an address over the phone.

3. The *aesthetic* function: a text read aloud is listened to by an audience mainly for the reason of experiencing delight in the performance—often because the reader is able to induce such delight through his oral rendering of the text. This function is the rule in present-day theatre performances and at poetry readings and festivals.

4. The *didactic* function: the reading aloud of a text is used as a means to a better understanding of its meaning. This function may be seen at work when a student is reading a passage from a textbook or when one is reading aloud from an instruction manual when repairing one's car to get a better grasp of the ideas presented in the text. A special form of this didactic function may be found in "chorus" reading: (groups of) pupils read a text aloud "in chorus." Perhaps this practice has become obsolete now in schools, in spite of its particular didactic potential for allowing the individual to overcome both anxiety and skill limitations in oral practice by virtue of being in a group.

5. The *ritual* function: the reading aloud of a text occurs in order to constitute a ritual event, either of a social, cultural, religious, or political nature. Central to this ritual form of reading is its repetitive and patterned nature, as well as its strengthening of shared value systems or ideologies, thereby enhancing group solidarity. This form of oral reading occurs regularly in various religious institutions of the main world religions, in political speeches, or in communal prayers (being read from print).

6. The *monitoring* function: the reading of the text has as its main purpose the concentration on formulation aspects of the text. This function may be witnessed when a person is reading part of a text (e.g., a letter), which is in the course of production, in order to check whether it "sounds" all right.

7. The *institutional* function(s): a number of institutions in Western societies require for their operation the reading aloud of written texts at specific moments. Apart from religious institutions, mention should be made of juridical and commercial institutions prescribing the oral rendering of some (parts of) documents: a verdict, an indictment, a contract of sale, or a mortgage deed.

As is often the case with functional typologies, conglomerate forms, in which various of these functions merge, are found in reality. For instance, within a school context, the didactic, monitoring, and aesthetic functions occur when the teacher is reading a poem aloud to the class in order to develop stylistic sensibility together with a better understanding of the creative process the writer went through, hopefully leading to the pupil's heightened enjoyment of the text. The existence of such conglomerate forms, however, is not to be seen as a weakness of the basic typology. In fact, the contrary is the case, and conglomerate forms are simply a witness to the possibility (and, in fact, to the frequent occurrence) of multiple–goal-oriented human activity.

When one looks at the practice of oral reading in (mainly primary) schools in the Low Countries with this typology in mind, the most surprising fact is that hardly any of these functions but the institutional one (as will be demonstrated later) occur with any regular frequency. This must be taken as an indication that the potential of the pattern is not in any sense exploited. Instead, it is narrowed down to one highly peculiar institutional practice.

3. SOCIAL ROOTS OF ORAL READING AT SCHOOL

The pattern of reading aloud as practiced in schools nowadays has historical roots taking it back (at least as far as Western Europe is concerned) to the Middle Ages when, because of its scarcity—both in terms of manuscripts and of literate people—reading aloud to others was an optimal form of transmitting knowledge and values in society, hence fulfilling mainly the economic and distributional functions. The pattern continued after the invention of the printing press, for instance, in the family or church practice of reading passages from the Bible, or the practice of a father reading stories to his children—a practice quite common in German middle-class homes until the late eighteenth century, as demonstrated by Hurrelmann (1985). It is likely (though further historical evidence is necessary) that these practices of reading aloud have been subsumed by the educational institution with the introduction of compulsory education.

At present, however, because of the constant availability of multiple copies of one and the same text at reasonable economic costs, such a current practice of oral reading has become dysfunctional. By and large, it has become a relic of the past. The educational institution has not yet found out what to do with it.

The basic assumption on which the "relic" rests is, as pointed out before, one which is aimed at the so-called mechanics, or technique of reading.[3] In other words, current practice takes as its point of departure the assumption that oral reading gives an indication of the pupil's "technical" skill in reading. However, what exactly the status of such a technical skill is remains notably

[3]The distinction between "technical" aspects of reading, on the one hand, and "comprehension," on the other, is one which also generally divides researchers in reading (cf. Stubbs, 1980, p. 5).

vague. Some seem to accept a "window" relationship between oral reading and reading with comprehension. By having the pupil read aloud, the teacher is allowed a window into the pupil's cognitive processing and understanding of the text. Others are somewhat more cautious and maintain that oral reading is but a precondition for content reading: unless the pupil manages to efficiently handle the technical aspects of reading, he or she is not going to be able to understand the meaning of the printed words.

Seen in this light, oral reading would—one could say—be comparable to practicing multiplication tables at the primary education level. Fluent mastery of this skill, even in a mechanical way, must necessarily be a precondition for the pupil's being able to carry out everyday calculations with a sufficiently developed automatism. The comparison is presumably not too farfetched: both the development of reading and of calculating are geared toward high fluency and automatism, presupposing the ability to flexibly handle formal skills. In this sense—and while still acknowledging the differences between the two skills— the comparison may be instructive. For, while drilling the mechanics of multiplication is rather limited in time and is—from an early stage onwards—geared to the application of these skills to tasks of a growing sophistication, the mechanics of reading, as witnessed by the widespread and long practice of oral reading, goes on for about approximately *ten* years! Why are the training programs for these skills so utterly different? Is learning to calculate so much easier than learning to read? Perhaps globally speaking this may be the case, but the difference can hardly be so great as to account for the gigantic difference in time invested. Two factors may be responsible for this situation:

1. Institutional practice of mathematics has been successful in developing action patterns that allow and facilitate an easy and functional integration of the basic mechanical skills, e.g., the pattern of problem solving which is currently put to use in mathematics classes. The pattern, moreover, may be functionalized in the eyes of the pupil by making the problems resemble situations known to the child from everyday experience. Reading instruction generally has not been successful in developing similar action patterns in which the technical skills may be functionally integrated, allowing for further growth of reading skills in general.

2. The teaching of mathematics may profit from the inspired work of Piaget on the development of numerical concepts in the child (Piaget & Inhelder, 1960; Piaget, Inhelder, & Szeminska, 1960). Without denying the importance and earnestness of current and past reading research, I think one cannot really say that our theoretical knowledge of reading development is as well grounded and as solid as that pertaining to math.

4. PROCESSES IN ORAL VERSUS SILENT READING

The opinion that oral and silent reading with understanding are very similar or close processes may be simply disproved by the following dual observation:

1. Children (or, for that matter, grown-ups) performing poorly at oral reading may nevertheless adequately understand what they are trying to read—and cases like this have been documented.
2. It is perfectly possible for a child (or grown-up) to read orally in a perfectly acceptable way and yet hardly understand anything of what has been read. If you do not believe this, have some youngsters read aloud to you some passages from Kant's *Critique of Pure Reason* or from Descartes' *Discourse on Method*.

Consider, however, a current reading test used in Dutch primary schools, the so-called Brus-test. This test consists of a list of unrelated words, printed one below the other, all corresponding to particular criteria such as word length, syllable structure, the occurrence of consonant clusters, and the like. The child is then invited to read for one minute as many words as possible from this list. While the child rattles through this, the teacher scores the number of mistakes made. On the basis of the number of words read and the number of mistakes made, the child is given a mark, allocating him or her to a specific level of "reading." Apart from serious methodological problems connected with the fact that only unrelated words are presented—which I am not going into here—it must be fundamentally clear that the results of such a test can yield but highly questionable indications of any natural reading process. This may be appreciated clearly when one imagines oneself doing a similar test in a foreign language. Providing that one has mastered the basic phoneme–grapheme correspondence rules of a language—but note that this is indeed the case with intermediate readers submitted to the Brus-test—a good number of people will perform pretty well on the test, even if they cannot make very much of the meaning of what they are reading. So, I think one would be able to do well on the test if it were administered in Turkish, Swedish, Roumanian, or Esperanto, even if one did not understand a word of these languages.

The reason for this is simple, I think, and lies in the nature of the oral reading process. For languages rendered with the help of an alphabetic script, the process essentially consists of relating graphic symbols to phonological form, which is subsequently vocalized. Access to meaning in this process is possible, but not necessary. This explains why the interpretative process of relating phonological form to *semantic* content may be bypassed in oral reading. Clearly, this is essentially different in motivated silent content reading: in this form, access to meaning aspects of what is read is inescapable, while it is at least imaginable—and the idea has been proposed by reading theorists—that in this reading practice the intermediate stage of *phonological* representation (in its fully realized form) may be bypassed. For silent content reading, a good command of the language is indispensable, as well as well-developed interpretative skills vis-à-vis conventional cultural meaning as it is presented in writing or in print. As such it is a process rich in social and cultural meaning exploration. In oral reading, on the contrary, concentration on the *utterance* aspects of the text, that is, its phonological realization, suffices to carry out the task successfully. Note that differences in comprehension skills for oral and for silent reading are attested in research literature (Mosenthal, 1976; Pugh, 1978).

In this connection I should like to conjecture that people display considerable individual differences: some are extremely good at reading orally without understanding, while others are good content readers often performing badly at oral reading; still others may be good at reading orally and simultaneously understanding what they read; and finally, some may be weak both at oral and at content reading. Furthermore, it is my contention that reading for meaning may be taught, while proficient oral reading is much more difficult, both to teach and to learn. In this sense I think it is more appropriate to speak of oral reading in terms of a special gift or talent, just as when we say that a pupil has a gift for music, or acting, or painting, a gift which may be further developed if it is there but which, when lacking, is rather useless to exercise endlessly. In the present educational context, absolutely no attention is given to these interindividual differences between pupils, for the straightforward reason that the differences existing between the processes of reading for meaning and of oral reading are simply ignored.

5. ORAL READING AND THE PROCESS OF LEARNING TO READ

Concerning the learning process, oral reading, at least in its extreme forms, is in reality an institutional pattern which obstructs learning. Four major reasons may be cited in this connection:

1. Oral reading occurs at an average speed approximately half the speed of silent reading. Its frequent practice, therefore, impedes the development of an adequate reading speed, while exactly this reading speed is a precondition for functional literacy. Moreover, oral reading practice encourages pupils to continue subvocalization while reading, a phenomenon known to be totally absent in young fluent readers.
2. Frequent oral reading pushes the pupil's conceptualization of the reading act in a highly questionable direction: that is, as occurring in one

standard form under all circumstances, thereby seriously hampering the development of a variety of reading strategies which may be flexibly adapted to the reading purpose.

3. Comprehension of the content is continuously under pressure in the act of oral reading, partly because the information in short-term memory does not get fed into long-term memory fast enough, and partly because the act of vocalization requires attention too. Hence, it is not surprising to see empirical research reporting considerably poorer comprehension scores for oral compared to silent reading.

4. As a result of this, the experience of humor and wit, of tension and emotional involvement, or the experience of and the identification with persons and events in a story are all seriously frustrated—if not altogether thwarted—when oral classroom reading is practiced. As a consequence, general reading motivation may decrease, or in any case, its enhancement is not to be expected as a result of such classroom activities.

Moreover, it may be pointed out that it is not in any way clear how the pupil can improve his or her performance. In general, the feedback of the teacher remains rather vague, and—what is more important, because it shows the underlying mechanism at work—makes heavy use of demonstrating a delivery to the pupil and then having him or her imitate it. For any pupil experiencing difficulties in oral reading, it may remain a dark and mysterious issue how to acquire the necessary skill demanded by the teacher. Or, to use a comparison, if you are bad at singing, does it help to listen to Caruso and then try yourself?

At the same time, one may wonder what the other pupils, that is, those *not* reading aloud, are doing meanwhile. They are forced into a constant frustration of all the efficient reading strategies they have already acquired. Indeed, they are forbidden to "read on" and must pay continuous attention to the progression of one pupil after another taking turns, which often means listening to someone ploughing his or her way through the text in anything but a fluent rendering of it. For the pupil listening to all this, who is able to read silently, hence, at an average speed which is more than twice as fast as that of the pupil reading orally, this must be deadly. In any case, sitting through hours and days of reading in which one is strictly forbidden to read in a natural and meaning-acquiring way is nothing but a perversion of the reading activity. Wherever such perversion is practiced regularly, only perverted results of reading instruction should be expected from the majority of pupils.

To sum up, then, oral reading practice is, in purely educational terms, a highly undesirable method for teaching children to read. This, by the way, has been noticed time and again by educationists. At least one mention of the problem was made in Holland as early as the 1920s! And yet current school practice of oral reading continues as before. This in itself is a clear indication that the pattern belongs to the deeply engrained action forms of the institution, virtually immune to influence from outside, since stability is a central characteristic of social institutions generally. It takes more than the arguments of a couple of academics to change institutional patterns.

Moreover, to mention the fact only briefly, present-day practice gains considerable consolidation from the fact that the bulk of reading research in The Netherlands similarly accepts the assumption that oral reading is directly related to general reading skills. As such, this research is a clear illustration of Ehlich and Rehbein's (1977) concept of second-order reflection on the institution. Reading education research in The Netherlands generally ignores the institutional presuppositions on which it is itself based. It is therefore also somewhat alarming (though sociologically quite understandable) that it is exactly the representatives of this research tradition who are made responsible for in-service training of teachers.

6. THE CREATION OF AN INSTITUTIONAL "NICHE"

Insofar as this situation has consolidated current institutional practice, one must point to an interesting phenomenon that has accompanied it over the last decade or so. The phenomenon may be termed *niche creation:* the institution carves out for itself a social space defended from influences which may endanger its niche-like character. Thus, reading education becoming a "niche" refers to the fact that anything which is straightforward, or simple,[4] or linked to everyday practice or conceptions should be avoided, if not eradicated altogether from thinking. The phenomenon may be characterized sociologically as consisting of two simultaneous movements:

1. The introduction of technocratic and pseudoscientific jargon and paraphernalia into the institutional discourse bearing on the reading process, together with heavy emphasis on the "scientific" foundation of teaching methods

---

[4] Note that in psychological terms reading is not a simple activity. In fact, nobody knows exactly what goes on in the mind of someone reading. Yet in social terms reading must be said to be "simple," that is, attainable by virtually all members of society. The comparison with learning to drive a car may be instructive in this respect. In fact, the finely tuned and highly coordinated perceptual and motor skills which are essential to driving are of a staggering psychological complexity. Yet as a social phenomenon, one is bound to acknowledge that the process must be relatively simple to learn. Similarly, the high literacy rates achieved by some nations demonstrate the relatively easy mastery of reading skills. My own judgment is that a concentration on matters concerning the psychological *complexity* are far less helpful (in educational terms) than a concentration on the social *simplicity* of the learning process.

and materials—the latter produced by specialized teams of "experts" and distributed by commercial firms. An interesting side effect of this movement in Holland, which should not go unnoticed in this connection, is the free borrowing from another social institution, namely, *medical* science, in the discourse on reading. It can hardly be accidental that so many terms in this discourse are importations from medicine: thus, one frequently talks of *prevention* of reading difficulties, of early *diagnosis* of them, and the like. In this way the process of learning to read becomes heavily loaded with metaphorical terms derived from the domain of disease and endangered health. Reading, by implication, is a process constantly threatened by inherent destructive forces, comparable to a viral infection or to dental decay. The task of the teacher then is to be constantly on his or her guard against all kinds of bacterial attacks and to counterattack, essentially, by putting the patient in quarantine or into an intensive care unit—usually called remedial teaching or orthodidactic treatment. Concerning this medical metaphor, which now regularly overshadows reading education in The Netherlands, one can only be glad that wherever serious problems arise, appropriate professional help should be readily available. However, in so far as the use of this metaphor suffuses the reading atmosphere with medical overtones, I am inclined to think that its effect on general reading attitudes cannot but be detrimental. (For a further treatment of the medical metaphor in education, see Illich, 1972, p. 31.)

2. As a second movement in the creation of a niche, the general notions held by teachers on matters of reading must be disqualified. Teachers are led to believe that their own (or other people's) intuitions concerning reading, and also their professionally gained insights, are to be distrusted. (Do not forget that this movement goes hand in hand with loud emphasis on the so-called scientific insights on which teaching should base itself.) The net result of this movement has been that teachers:

a. Become doubtful of the legitimacy of their own teaching methods (this is something which in itself might also have a beneficial effect, for it is doubtful that these teaching methods are in all cases of optimal efficiency).

b. Have now become extremely dependent on commercially developed teaching materials, the diffusion of which has never been subject to reasonable requirements but instead is subject to market mechanisms. I think it is no exaggeration to say that in present-day Holland, any change in reading education at this moment is not very likely, precisely because a considerable majority of schools have become dependent on these materials, while the commercial firms producing them have vested interests in them. (In this respect, certainly, the situation in socialist countries may be much simpler.)

7. ORAL READING AS INSTITUTIONAL CONTROL

A central issue remains: if oral reading is apparently so intrinsically linked to the needs of the institution school, the question must be asked why this is so. I cannot do more here than point out the direction in which we can look for an answer. My conjecture is that oral reading—contrary to institutional claims—takes its place among the *control mechanisms* to which the school must have recourse. Such control mechanisms are part and parcel of any institutional practice, since they are a constitutive characteristic of institutions *per se,* a fact that has long been known in sociology. Because reading, by its very nature (at least from an intermediate level onwards), is an *internal* (or mental) activity, the educational institution is presented with a problem to be solved: how can control be exerted over the internal reading process? Oral reading practice does, I venture to say, meet this demand. It is a historical solution to a historically evolved institutional problem intrinsically tied to the psycholinguistics of the reading process. Whether the solution is one suited to the needs of the institution depends largely on the importance attached by the institution to the mechanisms of control. I have demonstrated that in The Netherlands the mechanism of control over reading is highly valued. One should not be blind, however, to the fact that *other* institutions, that is, similar educational institutions in different nations or at different historical periods, may have made different choices and may have put different values on procedures for exerting control. It is here that I see an important task for comparative and sociological-historical studies. To mention one example only, the practice of oral reading hardly occurs in the intermediate reading curriculum of primary schools in Denmark. Yet statistics do not show an average reading proficiency of the Danish population lower than that of the Dutch population. If any different features are discernible from the respective statistics, they rather point in the opposite direction. This demonstrates, if anything, the relatively minor contribution to overall reading skill of oral reading as practiced in current reading education in Holland, in spite of what educationists are saying.[5] Rather, it seems to be the case that the practice generates its own internal contradictions: although pretending to help both the teacher and the child by ordering and controlling learning experiences, it discredits the teacher's intuitive and professional knowledge

---

[5] I have sometimes been struck by researchers' unwillingness to believe descriptive reports on types of school events which do not match their own theoretical projections on to the educational field and by their tendency to subsequently declare such reports as exaggerated or caricatural.

It would in itself be an interesting project to examine the discrepancies between convictions concerning educational practice as held by researchers in the field, on the one hand, and the reality of classroom practice, on the other hand. One must concede that such a type of self-reflection has not, as yet, been the object of investigation, contrary to other disciplines; for a demonstration in the field of psychology, see Lindauer (1968).

by making him or her dependent on externally produced methods and materials, while it is exactly these methods that pose a major obstacle for the child on his/her way to functional literacy.

REFERENCES

Bullock, A. (1975). *A language for life.* London: HMSO.

Ehlich, K., & Rehbein, J. (1977). Wissen, kommunikatives Handeln und die Schule (Knowledge, communicative action and the school). In H. Goeppert (Ed.), *Sprachverhalten im Unterricht* (Language in Education) (pp. 36–114). München: UTB.

Ehlich, K., & Rehbein, J. (Eds.). (1983). *Kommunikation in Schule und Hochschule (Communication in school and higher education).* Tübingen: Narr.

Hurrelmann, B. (1985). *Lesepädagogik zwischen Dialog und Kontrolle. Kinderliteratur und Lesekindheit im 18. Jahrhundert (Reading pedagogy between dialogue and control).* Bielefeld: mimeo.

Illich, I. (1972). *Deschooling society.* London: Calder & Boyars.

Lindauer, M. S. (1968). Pleasant and unpleasant emotions in literature. A comparison with the affective tone of psychology. *Journal of Psychology, 70,* 55–67.

Luidinga, G., & de Vries, J. (1983). Het lezen van fictionele teksten in B.O. en V.O. (The reading of fictional texts in primary and secondary education). *Moer, 3, 4, 5,* 160–167.

Mosenthal, P. (1976). Psycholinguistic properties of aural and visual comprehension as determined by children's abilities to comprehend syllogisms. *Reading Research Quarterly, 12,* 55–92.

Piaget, J., & Inhelder, B. (1960). *The early growth of logic in the child: Classification and seriation.* London: Routledge & Kegan Paul.

Piaget, J., Inhelder, B., & Szeminska, A. (1960). *The child's conception of geometry.* London: Routledge & Kegan Paul.

Pugh, A. K. (1978). *Silent reading.* London: Heinemann.

Redder, A. (1983). Kommunikation in der Schule—zum Forschungsstand seit Mitte der siebziger Jahre (Classroom communication—state of the art since the middle of the seventies). *OBST, 24,* 118–144.

Regan, J. (1983). Weltweite Entwicklungen der Analyse von Diskursen im Klassenzimmer (Worldwide developments in the analysis of classroom interaction). In K. Ehlich & J. Rehbein, (Eds.), *Kommunikation in Schule und Hochschule (Communication in school and higher education)* (pp. 261–274). Tübingen: Narr.

Stubbs, M. (1980). *Language and literacy: The sociolinguistics of reading and writing.* London: Routledge & Kegan Paul.

van Peer, W. (1984). *Three paradigms of reading research: A critique and an outlook.* Utrecht: mimeo.

CHAPTER 17

The Initial Reading Scheme
Is There an Alternative?

STEPHEN PARKER

1. INTRODUCTION

The context of education to which this chapter refers is monolingual, though this is not the overall situation in the United Kingdom. However, I believe that some of the principles to which I refer are significant in relation to reading development in any language, first or second. The approach which we adopt in the U.K. has been called "whole-language" by American commentators. By this term is meant an approach which integrates the four modes (reading, writing, speaking, and listening) and centers upon communication in "real" situations for a real purpose. "Children learn what language is by finding out what language does" is the working maxim. The practitioners with whom I work do not consider this to be anything so precise as a method but rather a natural, commonsense way of doing things. There is a strong tradition of curriculum development from the base upwards, that is, by practicing teachers working through teachers' centers or professional associations. Educationists and researchers in curriculum development interact with teachers at that level, with the effect that the United Kingdom, which does not have a centrally determined curriculum, has been rich ground for curriculum development in first-language learning.

However, it is difficult ground for research and has not been extensively explored in the literature for at least two reasons. Firstly, much of this development is at the local level and may not be widely known in the profession.

STEPHEN PARKER • School of Education, University of East Anglia, Norwich NR4 7TJ, England.

Secondly, the integration of the linguistic modes means it is difficult to isolate particular items out of the overall program without risk of omitting an essential component for that item's success. When integration and practical application are the two central principles of mother-tongue teaching, the number of variables in any teaching situation will be considerable. Therefore, it is with some caution that I have selected as my subject the content of initial reading, since I am aware that in a brief chapter I will raise a great many issues from a complex area and cannot do justice to either the material or to the questions that may be raised.

I would like to begin with two personal anecdotes. Some years ago now, my first attempt to teach a child to read using a standard reading scheme went like this. Sitting beside a 5-year-old boy, I pointed carefully with my finger at the following immortal lines, which the child attempted to decode, word by painful word. The first three pages of the primer read:

> This is Dick (picture of a boy)
> This is Dora (picture of a girl)
> Here is Nip (picture of a dog)

Now this is not gripping stuff, even for a 5-year-old, or, perhaps I should say, particularly for a 5-year-old. Since the boy expected page 3 to read *"This is Nip,"* on the pattern of the previous pages, and was caught out by the wiley writer of the scheme, we had to spend the next few minutes trying to see why "h-e-r-e" did not say "this." The boy then tried the three pages again, and fell into the trap again—several times. I tried not to throttle him. Neither of us had a good time of it, but there is no doubt that both of us were doing what the author of the reading scheme intended us to do. Learning to read from such a scheme gives the child very many chances to fail, and the slow learner may quickly build up a picture of himself or herself as the failed reader.

2. ALTERNATIVE SCHEMES FOR LEARNING TO READ

Some years later, on the Primary Committee of the National Association for the Teaching of English (NATE), I met a head teacher, a true enthusiast, who claimed that every child who entered her school went home within the first week able to read a book; not a three-word/twenty-picture book but a long, "real" book, and by "real" she meant one that had been independently published, was not part of a scheme, and was to be found in any bookshop with a good children's literature section. I was very interested—agog—to know the secret. Open sesame! She listed several titles of books which in her experience were so attractive to children that they were pulled into reading—which made them want to listen intently, look closely, and then recreate their own version of the story using graphic clues including text. Two of the books she mentioned have since become classics in the alternative approach to teaching reading known (rather vaguely) as individualized reading. Both books are now nearly 16 years old, but I doubt if you would know that without my telling you. The first one, *Rosie's Walk,* by Pat Hutchins (1968), reads for all the world like a primer if you look only at the words on the page:

> Rosie the hen went for a walk—across the yard—around the pond—over the haycock—past the mill—through the fence—under the beehives—and got back in time for dinner.

That is what the text says—but the pictures tell a different story, and the child can see that instantly. Rosie, completely unaware of it, is being pursued by a fox, who is sneaking up on her with evil intent but is always foiled by some accident or other. Rosie gets home safely, but her near misses and the humor of the fox's accidents are enthralling for children, who not only can later retell the text version (reading through remembering) but also add to it an account of what the fox does. Because the book is not color coded or numbered as a "first-stage" primer, children do not mind coming back to it months, even years, later, perhaps to write down the fox's version of the story. Children very quickly perceive that teachers, parents, and peers measure them by the level of reader they are on, and there is humiliation in going back to a lower grade of reader. With individualized reading there is no problem with such forwards–backwards movement. A good story can always be revisited without fear of being labeled as regression.

The second book, *The Very Hungry Caterpillar,* by Eric Carle (1969), is an attractive blend of fact and fiction. It also has an intriguing format—very unlike the usual primer—because the hungry caterpillar, in his search for new and interesting foods, eats neat holes in the page. On the first day he eats through one plum (one hole), on the second day through two apples (two holes), and so on. Finally, the hungry caterpillar has the stomachache and bursts, turning into a beautiful butterfly. The colors of the pictures are bright, the story line is strong, and the format is striking. Much of the appeal, though, lies in the listing of food. Writers of popular children's literature have long realized the appeal of food to young readers; consider the popularity of Roald Dahl's *Charlie and the Chocolate Factory* and *James and the Giant Peach,* both of which are set inside food, and this being surrounded by food fascinates children.

Such creativity is exceptional. The writer of a complete scheme cannot hope to be so creative over a whole range of books. But the teacher who knows what is available from the range of children's literature currently in print and is able to build it into a program of reading development can use the powerful motivating force of good literature to the child's advantage.

As to the content of these books, it is interesting to note that they both have animals as their protagonists. It is worth reflecting that animals are classless, timeless, and acultural (i.e., are not culturally charged), whereas almost any representation of the human form makes a culturally related statement in terms of age, sex, class, or ethnic origin. One of our reading schemes popular a while ago became famous in the debate on cultural focus because of its version of Dick and Dora helping daddy wash the car outside a suburban detached house. That may be an image of normality for one sector of our community, but not for children without such houses or cars—or even daddies. The criticism was that if the reader did not happen to belong to that subset of the culture focused on in the scheme, the educational system was highlighting that distinction, and that deprivation.

In the content of reading we can postulate four points of reference with regard to cultural focus:

1. Cultural identity: where the child recognizes his or her own culture represented in the text and finds this acceptable.
2. Cultural awareness: where a different culture from the child's own is represented in the text, but the child is sympathetic toward it.
3. Acultural: where the representation in the text makes no significant cultural statement (e.g., many animal stories).
4. Cultural dissonance: where the child recognizes the culture depicted in the text but is unsympathetic toward it, and even rejects it.

Now, cultural dissonance is most easily demonstrated in relation to minority groups, who see, for instance, only images of white, middle-class society in official classroom literature. But such dissonance is in fact only part of a much more pervasive phenomenon. Very many children, from all kinds of backgrounds and across the spectrum of social class, may become increasingly alienated by the subculture of the school system, seeing schoolbooks themselves as representing an alien culture. They feel that the content of education is not of their choosing and not relevant to their lives. In seeking to create a convergent society, we may be ignoring the reality that the whole is made up of unique individuals. Which one of us is truly typical of our own culture? Are we not all unique individuals, representing a subset of our respective cultures? If we accept that individuals may be permitted to diverge, within acceptable norms, from a culture's essential character, should we not accept that literacy may be shaped according to an individual's perceptions, abilities, and needs? Just as we have realized in linguistics that individuals speak an ideolect, so the same token would suggest that we should teach toward an "ideoliteracy"—by which I mean a personalized program of reading and writing.

This idea is the basis of the argument of that group of teachers in the United Kingdom called by Peter Doughty (1974) the "progressive consensus": those committed teachers in the forefront of ground-floor curriculum development. Because of this commitment to an ideoliteracy, a growing number of teachers, including my head-teacher colleague of the NATE Primary Committee, have abandoned a formal reading scheme in favor of a loosely structured resource base of reading materials. Some of these materials are from the supplementary readers of several schemes, but a large part of the resource is of the *Hungry Caterpillar* kind.

Since our system is not centralized, this change is administratively possible. It is also made more attractive by the current (and obviously cumulative) wealth of high-quality books now available, and more feasible by guidance published by the Reading Centre of the University of Reading (pronounced 'redding') in its *Individualized Reading* pamphlets, by Jill Bennett's (1979) *Learning To Read with Picture Books,* and by the work of one enterprising publisher who will make up packages of books suitable for any particular stage. Since the movement began in the late 1970s, reading schemes have moved forward, particularly expanding in range to include language development more broadly (writing and speaking integrated with reading). Those in the movement have also attempted to avoid a narrow cultural focus. *One, Two, Three and Away* (McCullagh, 1979) is built around the notion of a model village and the lives of its inhabitants, a setting which "can be, as far as is humanly possible, classless." The Ginn 360 scheme uses a different approach to the problem of drawing together a wide range of folktales from around the world, giving something of a multicultural substance to the reading program. It also includes informational texts, which clearly avoid the more obvious pitfalls of cultural specificity. However the criticisms of published reading schemes remain:

1. They contain a narrow range of reading functions and forms.
2. They limit the forwards–backwards–sideways progress of reading development and hence always need supplementation.
3. Their materials lack emotional depth and are bland at best.
4. Their aesthetic quality is unadventurous; no young reader would choose to read them in preference to ungraded literature.

At the present time, then, there are three possible approaches to the teaching of reading in our schools:

1. The traditional—using a monolithic reading scheme, representing a consistent theory of reading development across an extended range of ability and supplemented by other reading materials related to particular levels of attainment.

2. The progressive—where the teacher interacts with the children individually using a kaleidoscopic resource base culled from many sources, though with a large measure of literature, loosely structured to take account of broadly defined developmental stages.
3. The composite—drawing upon parts of several published schemes for the bulk of the material, with an enriched resource base and a range of teaching strategies beyond those determined by the schemes.

3. USING AN ALTERNATIVE READING SCHEME IN SCHOOL

In choosing one school as a descriptive reference point for this chapter, I decided to avoid the progressive approach, partly because the enthusiasm of such teachers typically affects powerfully the impact of the methods and materials used, making objective appraisal very difficult. Also, however, I have found in my work as a teacher–trainer that the progressive approach is a confusing model for the beginning teacher, who frequently fails to achieve the same results as the experienced progressive teacher and needs a far more explicit structure with which to work successfully. The Hawthorne effect, where participants in an experiment work beyond normal expectations because they know they are being watched, is misleading in both research and in teacher–training, and so I have chosen instead a school which offers a composite approach, involving parts of several reading schemes and a range of teaching strategies applied to texts taken from outside reading schemes.

The school to which I now refer is a primary school of 600 pupils aged 5–11 on the outskirts of a large town in East Anglia. The age range is divided up into three phases of 2 years, hence, 5–7, 7–9, and 9–11. The school is open-plan, and the staff of each phase tend to work in teams. The reading program in phase 1 begins with the use of the "Breakthrough to Literacy" scheme (Mackay *et al.*, 1970)—unfortunately marketed as a scheme when in fact it is a method which links speaking with reading and writing. It was devised in 1970 as part of the Schools Council "Program in Linguistics," with Michael Halliday as its director. To briefly describe the essential approach of the method, the child thinks of something he or she wants to write (e.g., "I went to the zoo"). From a folder containing cards printed with basic words, the child (helped by the teacher or ancillary helper, if necessary) compiles that sentence, mounting the individual words in order on a stand, then copies it down. New words have to be written out for the occasion, and so in this school the child builds up a sight vocabulary of around 80 words before moving on to preset primers associated with the scheme. There are many extension applications to that basic pattern. At the next stage, some of the supplementary readers were written and illustrated by one of the teachers. I did not find these impressive—simple line drawings (which did, though, allow for wide identification possibilities) and text related to simple everyday events of common experience. But such homemade efforts do allow teachers to contribute creatively to the reading material and help them consider it to be their own—an important motivating factor in the career of a professional.

At the next stage in phase 1, children move to a larger pool of readers graded into three bands of difficulty. Most are easy readers graded by a variety of publishers, that grading being standardized by the school. Throughout this phase the children are read to each day by the teachers, are allowed to browse through those books in reading time, and have access to library books. You can see how the variables begin to accumulate.

In phase 2, 7- to 9-year-olds have a greatly increased range of books from which to choose. Most are again from supplementary reading sets and parts of six reading schemes, selected for their high interest level. A recently published scheme becoming very popular has two monkeys as the central characters (the classless appeal of animals again) and has the strong emotional appeal of its humor. There are many more information books available at this phase. Teachers claim that children very much enjoy the social activity of reading in groups, particularly playlets in which they can all take a part. However, that is not to say that theirs is not a conditioned response. It is significant that at this stage teaching techniques known as DARTS (i.e., Directed Activities Related to Text) are used by the teachers. This range of strategies, such as cloze procedure, group prediction, and sequencing, has been developed outside the context of formal reading schemes and is seen as a bridge to mature reading. Whereas the library for the phase-1 children is a small class collection, the more able phase-2 children use the main school library independently. Less able children are given specific remedial help, using readers with a high interest level. As the gap between chronological age and reading age widens, interest level becomes more and more critical.

At phase 3 (9–11 years) the remedial program becomes more intense for the smaller number of children still involved. For children just above the remedial level (reading age 1 year below chronological age), there is a wide range of independent readers, not part of a scheme. All other children are selecting independently from class and school library both fiction and nonfiction, much of this choice being related to project work which integrates the four modes and extends across the curriculum subjects—the integrating aim of "whole language" now being fully realized.

Through the three phases, the most recent innovation has been the use of the microprocessor. In phase 1, teachers use a "concept keyboard" as an experimental adjunct to the "Breakthrough to Literacy" sentence maker. Using the keyboard, children can create sentences out of the preset lexical and structural items by simply touching the pressure sensitive pad in the right place. In phase 2, children write stories using a simple story generator program. In phase 3, children use a simple word-processing program for narrative and transactional writing across the curriculum.

The head teacher claims that over the years of development to the present complex structure there has been no noticeable decline in reading standards observable in school-administered tests. That is the only result available from data on performance. Teachers quite clearly know what they are doing in terms of selecting materials, managing resources, and directing pupil activity. Most importantly, they feel pride of ownership in the school's reading program. It is a demanding system, but they see it as a challenge with its own rewards. I asked each teacher if he or she would prefer a single reading scheme alone, and each said no; a single scheme would not do the job as they wanted it done.

4. CONCLUSIONS

1. Departure from a monolithic reading scheme creates great demands on a teacher. We can propose an equation; the weaker the base of the single scheme, the stronger the management skills, teaching techniques, and resource base need to be. Let's make an analogy with the circus performer who spins plates; a reading scheme is two plates, a composite approach is three plates, and an individualized approach is four plates—for the weak teacher that may be three plates too many to handle.

2. Big systems breed little systems. The curriculum is a system within education within the system of society. We must respect the fact that systems will expect convergent behavior from individuals contained within them. But curriculum systems run the risk of excluding knowledge which cannot be easily systematized (the domain of the affective is the largest case in point). For individuals, what is a helpful support to one person is a straitjacket to another. There is then an inbuilt dynamic tension between the tendency toward convergence of curriculum systems and the divergent need of individuals—child and teacher alike. We can only hope that in the U.K. the educational system will continue to tolerate the divergent behavior of professionals who depart from narrowly defined curriculum paths for justifiable educational reasons. In this chapter I have tried to give an example of one such justifiable departure.

3. The present pattern of teacher training in the U.K. is likely to be inadequate in the long term, given the current speed of change in relation to the size of the teaching force. Our only realistic solution is to harness the presently ad hoc in-house curriculum and staff development and enable it to expand. First-wave teachers can certainly train the second wave, and such democratic self-development does already go on to an extent. It does not need a man from

the ministry to direct it, but it would help if he would facilitate it and pay for it.

4. There is in the English language a link between the words *literacy* and *literature*. Most of the reading material I see in our schools is in the narrative mode. Although I admit that there are complex narrative structures, informational texts are generally more difficult than narrative for the young reader to understand. The logic of the chronological is powerful, and current U.K. thinking is that information books are most likely to be read successfully by children in primary school when they use narrative structures to carry the information. James Britton's (1975) model of language functions describes the increasing cognitive demands of informational writing, and although it is outside the age range of our considerations here, criticisms of the unintelligibility of secondary school subject textbooks have been well rehearsed. I believe that we need to know more about phasing the structures of transactional material in reading development, and this is one area of the content of reading development that is in need of research.

5. Finally, the selection of "books that work with children" to replace or to supplement a monolithic reading scheme is a client-driven approach (rather than author or authority driven) and, hence, likely to respect three basic principles which I would like to recommend:

a. The child's world picture is not patronized or belittled or circumvented.

b. Literacy has in significant part a real purpose of the child's own, not one which is externally imposed by the culture of schooling.

c. Content or meaning is recognized as more important to the child than the language which carries that meaning.

For the reader, content is almost certain to be of higher priority than linguistic structure, but the language structuring demanded by the schematization of reading is likely to obscure that fact. Linguistic simplicity of text too readily leads to paucity of meaning in text. I do not know what happened to the little boy to whom I tried to teach the Dick and Dora scheme—but I hope that in his next 11 compulsory years of schooling he met some of the fascinating material that we now have available, as an alternative to the stark unreality of "This is Dick," "This is Dora" where he began.

REFERENCES

Bennett, J. (1982). *Learning to read with picture books* (2nd ed.). London: Signal NBL.
Britton, J., Burges, T., Martin, N., Mcleod, A., & Rosen, H. (1975). *The development of writing abilities 11–18*. London: Macmillan.

Carle, E. (1969). *The very hungry caterpillar*. London: Hamish Hamilton.

Doughty, P. (1974). *Language, English and the curriculum*. London: Edward Arnold.

Hutchins, P. (1968). *Rosie's walk*. London: Bodley Head.

Mackay, D., Thompson, B., & Schaub, P. (1970). *Breakthrough to literacy*. London: Longman.

McCullagh, S. (1979). *One, two, three and away*. St. Albans: Hart-Davis.

CHAPTER 18

Learning to Read and Write
The Results of an Experiment

JEANNE MARTINET

1. INTRODUCTION

The experiment we are reporting on has been conducted in a number of French pre-elementary and elementary schools near Paris and Marseilles and has become normal pedagogical practice for most of the teachers involved in the matter. Although it can by no means be considered representative of prevalent trends in present-day French education, I do not intend to contrast it with the various reading methods most frequently employed or to engage in a discussion of their comparative merits, since my purpose is not to start any kind of controversy.

What makes the experiment a daring as well as an original undertaking is the fact that it is based on a linguistic theory—functional linguistic—and that its practice closely tallies with the theoretical principles underlying it.

The tool at the core of the experiment was devised in 1970 by André Martinet in answer to a request from a group of teachers who were distressed at the poor results when their pupils tried to express themselves in writing. They put the blame for this situation on the oddities of French orthography and asked whether one could do away with it or, in other words, whether French could be written just as it is spoken, using one letter per sound (phoneme) and resorting only to the Latin alphabet, so that standard typewriters and school printing equipment could be used to produce the teaching material, which could not be done with the IPA.

JEANNE MARTINET • Ecole Pratique des Hautes Etudes, Section IV, Sorbonne, 75005 Paris, France.

The phonematic alphabet developed by André Martinet, meeting all the requirements mentioned above, was called by the teachers G.P.M. (Graphie Phonologique Martinet) and, eventually, with minor modifications, became known as *alfonic,* a word coined by the late Charles Peignot, president of the International Typographic Association.

G.P.M. fully satisfied the teachers who used it: their pupils wrote with gusto, and the teachers were deluged with stories, poems, and lively accounts of the children's experiences. But having proved their point about the inhibiting effect of French orthography, these teachers lost any hope of replacing it with G.P.M. or any similar system in the near future: they gave up this experiment and passed on to others in body expression, music, or social relations within the class group.

The experiment we are concerned with here was begun more recently, in 1973, with children in the final year of pre-elementary school.

But, before dealing with alfonic as a tool for learning to write and read, in this order, let us make some remarks about the structure of language, the nature of writing, and the way children go about learning both.

2. THE DOUBLE ARTICULATION OF LANGUAGE

French allows us to distinguish between language (singular), a human faculty of communicating, by means of signs of all kinds, and more precisely linguistic signs, *le langage,* and languages (plural) as they are spoken in human communities, *les langues,* such as French, Italian, English, Chinese, Swahili, and the like.

A functionalist linguist will stress the fact that language cannot be approached except through the observation of individual languages, and understandably his or her first task will be to define what a language is. We find such a definition in Martinet's *Elements of General Linguistics* (Section 1.14):

> A language is an instrument of communication in virtue of which human experience
> is analysed differently in each given community into units, the monemes, each en-
> dowed with a semantic content, and a phonic expression. The phonic expression is
> articulated in its turn into distinctive and successive units. These are the phonemes,
> of limited number in each language, their nature and mutual relations varying from
> one language to another.

3. WRITING AS A SEMIOTIC SYSTEM

Although this point has been challenged, writing is to be considered as a substitute for speech, and this, without any doubt, is what concerns us here.

Studied in itself, without any reference to speech, it appears as a means of communicating information through signs, that is, units combining form and meaning. But straightaway we have to remark that the information carried by writing is precisely linguistic information, and we could hardly conceive of writing except in connection with a specific language. Surely enough, writing is a graphic system, but not all graphic systems are writing.

It is true that in the course of time and because they answer different communicative needs, in different types of situations and circumstances, speech and writing will undergo independent evolution and tend to diverge. Nevertheless, they keep influencing each other, and what really matters, synchronically speaking, is how they compare in the case of each individual language and, particularly, to what extent writing reproduces the double articulation of languages. Can one say that ideograms, the Chinese ones for instance, reflect the first articulation of that language, whereas alphabetical writing, that of Italian or Finnish, would display the second? Yet, the contrast between the ideographic and alphabetical systems constantly tends to be blurred. On the one hand, the phonic face of the significant units which should not affect the shape of the ideograms constantly intervenes in order to enable writers to distinguish between synonyms. On the other hand, the advantage of preserving the written forms throughout the ages unaffected by the changes occurring in the phonic forms results in spellings like the French *oiseau* /wazo/ for 'bird', where not a single letter has preserved its normal phonetic value: *oiseau* is normally perceived by readers as an ideogram.

In fact, alphabetical writing does exhibit a double articulation: the text is articulated into words with meaning, the *signifié,* and form, the *signifiant* (first articulation), and those forms, in turn, are articulated into distinctive units, say, the letters, deprived of meaning (second articulation). Only, this double articulation does not necessarily coincide with that of the spoken language: the French *nous chantions* is written in two words of, respectively, four and nine letters, while the corresponding spoken form is analyzed into three monemes— (1) "sing," (2) first person plural, (3) imperfect—and a total of only seven phonemes: /nuʃãtjõ/. Of course, the distance between speech and alphabetical writing varies considerably from one language to another. It may be minimal where the spelling system is comparatively recent and/or is periodically revised in order to make it conform with the spoken language. It is maximal where the inherited spelling is felt to be part and parcel of the people's cultural patrimony, or even god given, and when any change in it would be felt as a blow to its integrity. Nonetheless, a close conformity between speech and spelling would seem to be the ideal, as, after all, nothing prevents the reader from reacting just as globally, "ideographically," to the faithfully phonematic form *parasol* as he or she does to the aberrant *oiseau.* To achieve that ideal has been the aim of alfonic, as we see below.

4. MASTERING ONE'S LANGUAGE: THE FOUR SKILLS

The mastering of a language has been analyzed into the command of four skills; namely, *speaking, listening* (which means understanding the spoken language), *writing,* and *reading,* the last two constituting what is called literacy. Achieving literacy is the first aim in school education, and it provides access to scientific knowledge. In today's world, many communities do not have any writing system at their disposal, and their members have to resort to a second language in order to attain literacy first, and then make their way toward higher education or simply participate in the economy of our times.

Even in countries where a written language has been taught for generations, there still are illiterate people. In France, for instance, many secondary-school teachers, in all disciplines, complain that their pupils "cannot read." It would seem that, whereas acquisition of the oral skills of language seems to go without saying, it is not so as far as reading and writing abilities are concerned.

Among the four skills we find, on the one hand, two oral versus two written skills; on the other hand, we find two nonproductive processes, listening and reading, versus two productive ones, speaking and writing. I for one would rather say "receptive" than nonproductive, as I think listening and reading should not be merely passive. What is meant here is that they involve perceptive (i.e., sensory) and intellectual processes, whereas speaking and writing imply motor activity, either of the speech organs or of the hand.

An important point that needs to be raised is that of the balance among the four skills throughout a child's development. Are they acquired separately, that is, successively, or jointly? It would seem that the receptive skills are acquired before the productive ones, and speech before writing, so that the order of acquisition would be (1) receptive oral, (2) active oral, (3) receptive written, and (4) active written. But there are considerable overlappings, so much so that while children may still be learning receptive speech they have also begun to learn how to write their own productions. What should be stressed really are the interactions among the four skills in the course of learning: on the plane of phonology and on that of grammar and vocabulary, we observe that children hear the distinctions between phonemes better when they can produce them, and they understand words and syntactic structures better when they are able to make active use of them. In short, the active use of the language strengthens and improves whatever passive, receptive knowledge is already there.

5. A NATURAL ACQUISITION OF THE FOUR SKILLS

The oral skills are acquired naturally by children, that is, without any formal teaching, and some people have wondered whether it could be so for the writing skills as well, so that it would suffice to expose children to written material and let them learn all by themselves. In fact, it is the conditions of oral communication, be it the behavior of the speaker or the presence of objects and actions referred to, that ordinarily provide a considerable amount of non-linguistic information which helps the child to discover how sound and meaning are associated in language, whereas, generally speaking, written communication does not offer the clues that would help the reader to gather what meaning is associated with which graphic symbols. So, let us bear in mind that the function of written communication is precisely the transfer of information *out of situation* and see if "natural acquisition" of the writing skills can also take place.

Note first that the natural acquisition of speech takes a considerable length of time: on the average, French children are 5 to 6 years old before they may be considered to have mastered the phonological system of the language, its basic syntactic structures, and the amount of vocabulary needed for the un-impeded communication of their experience. French children are legally sup-posed to enter primary school at 6 years of age, when they are expected to start learning to read and write, among other things. From then on no more natural learning is expected on their part, because they are systematically taught all sorts of subjects. We may also start wondering whether, if natural learning were to be pursued in earnest, the acquisition of these new skills (i.e., reading and writing) might not take just as long as that of oral skills, namely, 5 or 6 years; if so, children could not reasonably be expected to master them before the age of 12. Besides, could natural learning really work in this case? We know that systematic teaching ought to speed matters up. So, let us examine the role played by natural learning.

Note that acquiring new skills is not learning a new language; children already know their language. This fact constitutes a solid basis for the acqui-sition of the new skills. Besides, they have already had contact with writing and have probably gathered that it associates graphic symbols and meaning just as speech associates sounds and meaning; they have seen adults read newspa-pers, books, magazines; their mothers have read aloud to them stories from picture books, letters with news and good wishes from far away relatives or friends; they have seen names written on stores, cars, wrappings, bottles, and cans, almost as early as they have heard language talked around them. Conse-quently, there is no reason why natural learning could not take place for writing just as it did for speech; in fact, it does work out for some children. But maybe they are particularly gifted or privileged, lucky enough to be taken care of by parents who are fond of reading, with books and a lot of written material avail-able. Of course, the environment of a child varies considerably, depending on the literacy or illiteracy of his or her parents, their general attitudes toward books, the interest they show in his or her achievements, and whether the child lives in a city or in the country, has access or not to TV and its commercials, and so on.

Observation has shown that a 2-year-old, playing with blocks, can learn to name letters just as easily as pictures of animals or objects. This is not reading, but it shows that very young children are able to recognize and operate with a great number of signs, whether they are conventional, motivated, or nonmotivated. In many pre-elementary schools, every child's belongings are identified by a specific picture—say, a butterfly for Robert, a cat for Alice—or maybe just a circle, a square, or a cross, in other words, an arbitrary symbol. Children will remember all sorts of signs and emblems, as soon as they have been told their meaning: police, firemen, supermarket, and so on. Japanese children learn a good many ideograms (Chinese characters) quite early, provided they come across them often enough in daily life and in motivating situations.

As regards alphabetical writing, we have to distinguish between languages like Hungarian or Finnish, whose spelling systems are comparatively recent, where the same letter or group of letters regularly corresponds to a given phoneme, and those such as French or English, which have kept the old graphic forms, disregarding the evolution of the spoken language, so that the original phonic value of letters has been in most instances completely lost. No wonder some people have expressed the view that in spite of being alphabetical, the orthography of those languages is really ideographic. This has led to the theory that written words, say, sentences, should be learned globally. We now have quite a number of reading methods totally bypassing the possible phonic equivalence of letters. But this is throwing the baby out with the bath water and hastily dismissing the serious advantages of alphabetical writing. What is really to blame is not the term-to-term correspondence between sounds and letters but the loss of that correspondence in the course of time and the preservation of a graphic tradition at loggerheads with the contemporary form of the language.

It is interesting to remark that the situation is not quite the same for French and for English. English is probably more ''ideographic'' than French, and it is not safe to guess the pronunciation of a word from its spelling, nor the spelling from the oral form. But once you have learned the spelling, you play safe, since the word undergoes no change in writing that does not appear in speech: when an *s* is added to *boy,* when we speak of several boys, or to *jump,* when we say *Tommy jumps,* that *s* appears both in speech and writing—no tricks.

In French, it is not too risky to pronounce a word which is known only through its spelling, but the form of most lexical items is subject to variations, depending upon their syntactic connections in the sentence. Those variations do not affect speech and writing in the same way. If we contrast the following sentence with its subject in the singular, *Le petit garçon joue* 'The little boy is playing', with the same sentence with a plural subject, *Les petits garçons jouent*

'The little boys are playing', we notice that in speech the only difference lies in the definite article: /lə/ versus /le/. In writing, the plural is indicated by three mute *s*'s added to the article, the adjective, and the noun, plus a mute *-nt* added to the verb. This is what is called agreement, or concord. A child cannot spell correctly before mastering the whole system of agreement, knowing which classes of words are affected by it, which are not, and how to recognize the one to which a word belongs. Is *danse* a noun or a verb? How should it be spelt in *les danses d'autrefois* 'the dances of the past' and in *Les jeunes filles dansent* 'The girls are dancing'? Not a few children, not to speak of adults, get mixed up in their unpronounced *-s*'s and *-nt*'s and distribute them more or less at random. Teaching grammar, as the unavoidable basis of correct spelling, weighs heavily on the French school curriculum.

To what extent can a French child learn the written language naturally, that is, out of school, at his or her own pace? Here is the answer.

A boy interested in cars, and driving with his parents, will know everything about refilling the tank at gas stations and recognize the emblems of each gasoline company, their particular shapes, colors, and letters. He will have heard their names and is able, to his parent's astonishment, to repeat them as if he were reading them: *Esso, Shell, Total.* He will, of course, do the same with the names of supermarkets, *Casino, Sodim, Codec,* and the designation of various stores such as *boucherie* 'butchery', *boulangerie* 'bakery', *epicerie* 'grocery', *pharmacie,* and the like. The identification of the words themselves is backed up by the accompanying features of color, style, the surroundings, and the displays in the window. At a further stage, the child will identify the names of the firms on wrappings or shopping bags. Some day, he will be heard rhyming *Esso* and *Casino,* thereby more or less identifying the letter *o* and the corresponding phoneme. He will soon start looking for partial similarity, such as *bou-* and *-erie* in *boucherie, boulangerie,* and for the relation between letters and sounds whatever their position is in the word. He will come across difficulties, such as different values for the same letter: *s* for /s/ in *Sodim* and /z/ in *Casino;* silent letters: the two *e*'s of *boucherie;* new roles for *p* and *c* when followed by *h,* as in *pharmacie, boucherie,* and so on. All those peculiarities will discourage many, but others will take them in their stride. Trying their skill on a story in a book, they will encounter and overcome quite a bundle of such difficulties: different values for the same letters, different ways of noting the same phonemes, silent letters in endings and elsewhere, and the same words written differently. So much for the natural learning of the receptive skill.

Turning to the productive skill, we hear many pre-elementary school teachers say that children are eager to write before being attracted by reading. True enough. We have watched children say "I am writing," when they were just scribbling. Scribbling is to writing what babbling was to speaking: just playing at producing sounds with the vocal organs or lines on paper when holding a pencil or a pen is a way of developing one's capacity to do things with one's body. Note that the child distinguishes drawing, when aiming at representing things, and what he or she calls writing, some mysterious black forms on the sheet of paper. We have heard children ask "Please, Mommy, read for me what I have written." Proper writing appears when the child endeavors to reproduce what he or she knows to be written material. Mani, a boy of 5½, in a Swiss pre-elementary school where early teaching of reading and writing is prohibited, is elated at receiving a game of cards with pictures of objects with their names. He asks for a pen and paper and struggles to reproduce the word *fraise* 'strawberry', knowing that what he writes is pronounced [frɛz] and means *fraise,* as shown by the picture. Such an urge to write, for one's own pleasure and, at the same time, for communicating with others, is rapidly blocked by all the traps orthography sets for the inexpert writer. Teachers in elementary schools note that children get discouraged in their attempt to write texts by the fear of making mistakes and meeting with either punishment or mockery.

6. ALFONIC

Alfonic is based on the hypothesis that the acquisition of writing and reading skills could be separated from that of orthography and precede it. Thus, at a first stage children can express themselves freely without being blocked by the fear of making mistakes. Alfonic gives them gradual access to texts written in traditional spelling and a means of gradually and systematically approaching the intricacies of orthography.

First of all, it must be clearly stated that alfonic has been devised for the benefit of French-speaking children who have a command of the spoken language, that is, the first two skills. This does not exclude the possibility of enlarging its scope, but we will not tackle this question now.

Alfonic is meant as a tool for written communication between people who cannot, for some reason or other, exchange spoken utterances. This point, as we see later on, is of importance when coming to pedagogical strategies.

Alfonic rests on the hypothesis that a semiotic system is the simplest and easiest if there is a term-to-term correspondence between *signifié* and *signifiant,* that is, between the information that is to be carried and the means offered to carry it, in our case the phonic units (the phonemes) and the graphic symbols (the letters).

7. PHONEMES

The first task was to determine precisely what phonic units had to be noted. French, as spoken from Lille to Perpignan or Strasbourg to Brest is far from being monolithic. Now, André Martinet's goal was to offer all French-speaking children the possibility of putting into writing what they say the way they say it, refraining from prescribing any orthophonic norm so that they would have to rely on themselves only to decide what they were going to write. Would that mean that alfonic was to split into a host of varieties? On the contrary, notwithstanding their differences, the French from Perpignan, Strasbourg, Lille, or Brest do communicate successfully, which means that they have been trained to disregard a number of minor differences and actually operate with an overall phonematic system. All this is well known through the numerous *enquêtes* carried out from 1941 onward (Walter, 1988, pp. 18–21). This overall system has been taken as the basis for alfonic. It is a common denominator of all the varieties inventoried, retaining only the phonematic distinctions really used by all speakers. It is simpler than the so-called Standard French commonly used in the teaching of French as a second language. It does not mean that alfonic does not enable children to express their own phonological varieties, but they do it in such a way as to distinguish between what is fundamental and what is marginal. The letter *e* covers both [e] and [ɛ], but those who distinguish between [e] and [ɛ] in word final position—*donné* 'given', *donnait* 'gave'— may use *è* for the latter.

8. LETTERS

Once we had delimited and itemized the information to be carried over, the second task was to decide on the means—the graphic symbols—best suited to meet our purpose, considering all the factors involved: the users (children, teachers, and why not parents?), the implements (French typewriters, printing equipment), the French situation, and the eventual necessity of shifting from alfonic to "normal," traditional spelling.

At this point a question will inevitably arise: Why not the I.P.A.? Firstly, it does not meet the requirements concerning French typewriters and printing equipment. Secondly, and this is more important, when shifting from alfonic to orthography, for the purpose of reading as well as writing, it will be easier for children to find in the traditional spelling the same phonic values for letters as the ones they had in alfonic. Why teach children to give the letter *y* the value it has in [kalkyl] *calcul* when they will have to use it with the value of [j] as in *yoga?* Lastly, in cases of neutralization, that is, the loss of a distinction under specific conditions, the I.P.A. does not offer any satisfactory solution. As suggested before, there is no need in French to distinguish between [e] and [ɛ], except in word final position, and consequently we need a symbol which will do for either where no distinction is called for.

9. A SUBPHONEMIC NOTATION OF FRENCH

At this point, we can present in a single table (Table 1) the phonemes together with the letters they are associated with in alfonic.

We say "notation" and not "transcription" because we do not shift from one type of writing to another, as when we transcribe into IPA what is written in English spelling, in order to indicate how to pronounce, say, *meadow*. Here we start from what is pronounced, referring either to our own articulation of the sounds or to what we hear, and we note sounds, just as we would reproduce music or dance, by means of adequate notations.

We call it subphonemic because, as we said before, it only retains the overall pattern of French, leaving out, at the start, whatever distinctions are not shared by all speakers. But additional conventions have been provided to give

Table 1. Letter Values in Alfonic

Each letter corresponds to a sound: jac *Jacques,* il z-em *ils aiment.*

Have their common value:

p	b	f	v	t	d	j	l	r	z	a	i	u
par	bar	fil	va	tic	dur	java	lac	roc	zoo	as	il	uni
											miel	lui

Have their most frequent value:

y	m	n	s	c	g
yoga	mal	nu	sel	calcul	gogo
	lam	fin	asiz	celc	gi
	lame	*fine*	*assise*	*quelque*	*gui*

Divergences:

h	ny	w		ğ	x (a simplified œ)	ẍ		ä	ë	ö
hoc	peny	wrs	wisci	parciğ	pxr	fx	brxbi	parfẍ	vä	vë	vö
choc	*peigne*	*ours*	*whisky*	*parking*	*peur*	*feu*	*brebis*	*parfum*	*vent*	*vin*	*vont*

e without accent:

ete perdu sel lese
été perdu sel laisser

è only at the end, for those who pronounce *était* and *été* in a different way:

etè   forè
était   forêt

o without accent:

mo   mo   hamo   roc   oral
mot   maux   chameau   roc   oral

ô not at the end:

pôl   bôte   hôd
pôle   beauté   chaude

â x̂ ê, for those who want to distinguish between pat *patte* and pât *pâte*, jxn *jeune* and jx̂n *jeûne*, fet *faite* and fêt *fête*.

each speaker a chance to explicate the whole range of his or her own phonematic system.

Provisions have been made to keep a sharp and clear distinction between alfonic and orthography: alfonic will be written in print type and red ink, while script and black or blue ink will be reserved for traditional spelling, so as to signal clearly which of the two systems is being used at a given moment.

The principle of one and the same letter for one and the same phoneme allows no exception. No capital letter is ever used, nor groups of two or three letters for a single phoneme, but it has been necessary to resort to some diacritics in order to provide a sufficient number of symbols to meet the needs of even the minimal system of French.

A "minimal" alfonic, limited to the archiphonemes of French, shows 30 units (as against the 36 of Standard French for foreign students). Table 1 offers 32, and we come up to 33 if we include the receding distinction between front *a* as in *patte* and back *a* as in *pâte*.

The traditional phonic values of French spelling are kept as much as possible: *a* stands for /a/, *p* for /p/, *r* for /r/ and also *j* for /3/, and *u* for /y/, so that when passing from alfonic to ordinary texts, children will identify many words at once because the letters are the same in both spellings *(avec, calcul, joli)* with just a few silent letters in the orthography *(pâle* [pal], *colle* [col], *ils cachent* [il cah]). Children will soon discover that the dieresis (as in [ä], [ö]) usually corresponds to some *n* or *m* after the vowel, as in *danse* [däs] or *pompe* [pöp], and with the help of context, they may all by themselves make the connection. This is one of the two fundamental reasons why the IPA was not resorted to. As the *I* of IPA indicates, it is an international alphabet, while alfonic is strictly meant for French people using their own language.

Writing is a means of communication people use when speech is not possible. Teachers should create situations in which there is real motivation for written communication: letter writing plays a great role, either from class to class in the same school or between distant schools or between individual children in each class.

10. LEARNING WITH ALFONIC

In the contemporary French educational system, pre-elementary and elementary schools are two different worlds. All children are supposed to enter elementary school at the age of 6—not before—and to learn reading and writing in the first year; writing implies the ability to hold a pen or pencil and trace words, and this can immediately create orthographical problems. In spelling matters there exist scales (Ters *et al.*, 1964) pointing to the levels to be reached from year to year. Teachers are painfully aware of the "program" and anxious to reach definite goals each year. In spite of the *Instructions officielles* allowing 2 years for attaining a satisfactory mastery of reading, teachers make it a point of honor to obtain it by the end of the first year, so as to match the parents' expectancies. This does not make it an easy ground for pedagogical innovations which might be the source of disturbances and delays.

Pre-elementary school, on the other hand, is not compulsory, but it is attended by a large majority of children, who can be admitted in any of the 3 years of the curriculum: *Petite* section, PS, age 2½; *Moyenne* section, MS, age 3½; *Grande* section, GS, age 4½. There is no rigid curriculum here, but attractive surroundings and equipment and a hearty pursuit of all the activities that can develop a child's faculties and personality, in accordance with the teacher's artistic gifts. In principle, no formal early (meaning ''premature'') teaching of reading or writing is allowed; only some awareness of the written materials is welcome. This leaves room for a wide range of pedagogical strategies. The child is offered a choice of ''activities'' (painting, cooking, card games, etc.) and can join one or the other according to his or her mood of the day, and the teacher is attentive to guide each one toward the activities where he or she will have a better chance to prove successful.

As soon as he or she is supposed to write, a French child is beset by the fear of making mistakes: each word can prove a trap. Therefore, the child writes as few of them as possible, and always the same safe ones: *rose* rather than *chrysanthème*. Nothing of the sort with alfonic, /crizätem/ being just as easy as /roz/. It is conceived of as a tool at the child's disposal from the moment he or she shows he or she wants it. The question was of course: when does the child want it? Quite naturally, the first year of elementary school, *cours préparatoire*, CP, or *Grande* section were felt to be the place and the moment. But average CP teachers were reluctant to engage in what they felt to be such a hazardous experience, although a few did so with great success. Nothing was to be forced upon the child and, in an experimental framework, teachers and researchers were just watching how things would mature, the child being offered whatever intellectual material seemed suitable to induce that ripening.

No prerequisites have been stated. To be sure, some have questioned the advisability of presenting the child with a phonematic alphabet before making sure he or she has attained a full mastery of his or her own phonematic system. Indeed, we know that some distinctions, /s/ ~/ʃ/, /z/ ~/ʒ/, for example, or the opposition of voiced/unvoiced may be acquired quite late by some children. But, in such cases, far from raising problems, alfonic, by offering distinct graphic representations, proved to be a help to the child attempting to get a better grasp of articulatory and acoustic distinctions.

The only instructions given to the teachers are to let children make use of alfonic in their own way, expressing all the phonemic distinctions they operate with and wish to show, without compelling them to record those they do not know or feel they can leave out. The following progression, consisting of four stages, was proposed to lead children from their oral practice to that of the written language, no definite age being set for each:

1. Writing alfonic ⎫
2. Réading alfonic ⎬ print type + red ink
3. Reading orthography ⎫
4. Writing orthography ⎬ script + black or blue ink

Note the reversal of the procedures between 1 and 2 (the alfonic stages), on the one hand, and 3 and 4 (the orthographic stages), on the other hand.

One should not forget that what is at stake from beginning to end is communication, and communication will be both the aim pursued and the means to achieve it. Through communication—that is, oral intercourse at first, exchange of written material later—children will learn how meaning is conveyed by means of distinct sounds or letters producing distinct meanings. From the age of 3 onward, songs, rhymes, puns, riddles, and speech games of all sorts train children to distinguish between the various things they understand and the various things they want to convey.

Alfonic is introduced in the class when the teacher feels her pupils are ready for it, when some occasion arises in which written communication is needed: sending a note to a sick schoolmate or corresponding with another class; cassette recordings of songs, stories, or riddles are exchanged at first, together with each other's pictures, presents, or paintings. "Now how would our friends know who's who, and who sends a present to whom, without resorting to writing?" Very soon each child wants to add his or her own message to his or her personal faraway friends. As the years go by, we notice that the *Grande section* teachers gain confidence about alfonic; they will not hesitate to present it to the children earlier than they did at the start, practically at the beginning of the year, so that most children will write and read alfonic fluently by February. At first the children are more interested in expression than communication. But when the desire to communicate appears, the children become aware that the text will have to be written clearly, and as soon as it exceeds a short sentence, the advantage of separating the words for easy reading will make itself felt.

In short, at this first stage, the child learns:

1. To analyze his or her own speech into a succession of phonemes without any need or use for syllables in that accentless language, Modern French.
2. To associate each phoneme with a given letter, only one and always the same one, using the children's first names, posted up in the class, as reference.

3. To associate letters in the same way that phonemes are associated in speech, in order to produce written "stories" (as the child calls whatever he or she writes), paying attention to the relevance of the presence or absence of phoneme/letter and the respective order of phonemes/letters (commutation, permutation, addition, or subtraction).
4. To isolate "words," that is, sequences of phonemes/letters that preserve their meaning when shifted from one context to another.

All this can be achieved by means of movable letters, easy to pick up and assemble, shift from one place to another, and space out until a satisfactory result is obtained. Holding a pencil or pen to trace letters is another problem which can be tackled at some other time or in decorative graphic activities. Many a child enjoys composing his or her story with the movable letters before transferring it to paper.

In stage 2, the child looks for the meaning of the "stories" by his or her fellows or teacher, using as a consumer what he or she had learned as a producer in stage 1. We have to reckon with some guessing, since the child probably knows beforehand what the text is about, but he or she will soon be induced to rely on the letters of the text.

As an incitement to understanding a written text, the child is given a sheet of paper with the date and an indication of what he or she should draw underneath. The complexity of what the child has to read increases as time goes on. Here is an illustration of the progression:

1x 16 jăvie. desin:	January 16th. Draw:
x̌ pwasó	a fish
1x 21 mars. desin:	March 21. Draw:
x̌ pomie; dă 1x pomie, ya si pom. sw	an appletree; on the appletree there are
1 pomie ya trwa pom.	six apples. Under the appletree there are three apples.
1x 13 mè. desin:	May 13th. Draw:
ë n-wazo ci a ë bec jôn, un cx blx, de	a bird with a yellow bill, a blue tail,
plum vert, e ci è poze sur lx twa d un	green feathers, perched on the roof of
mezó	a house

Since no texts in alfonic are available in print so far, clever teachers, with the help of parents and students from teachers' colleges, provide some by pasting alfonic texts over the "normal" orthographic texts of children's books, so that the children get plenty to read and can, if they wish, lift the alfonic leaf to look at the orthography underneath, thus becoming familiar with the similarities and discrepancies between the two codes.

This quite naturally leads to stage 3, when the child takes advantage of his or her alfonic reading capacity to pass on to orthographic texts. It probably starts with reading names on shop windows and packages, TV commercials, comic strips, and storybooks. The child keeps alfonic for writing, but he or she is taught script, *l'écriture liée,* and little by little the most frequent or striking orthographic forms encountered in reading will tend to force themselves upon him or her and take the place of alfonic, and the child will produce two-code texts, originally in two colors, as shown in Figure 1.

It will be time for the teacher to proceed to stage 4 (in a normal alfonic progression, in the middle of CP) and undertake a systematic study of spelling, still allowing the child to use alfonic for free expression and whenever he or she is not quite sure about the correct spelling of words. The child is welcome to admit his or her ignorance of the conventional forms, but no spelling mistakes are accepted. Some parents were afraid that, given alfonic, the child would yield to laziness and refuse ever to make the necessary effort to learn spelling. That was to ignore the child's yearning to imitate the grown-ups. Spelling not being forced upon the child, he or she asks for it and makes a game of discovering all its facets and oddities. Learning at his or her own pace, the child drops alfonic when he or she no longer needs it and ends up with a better command not only of spelling but of the general functioning of language.

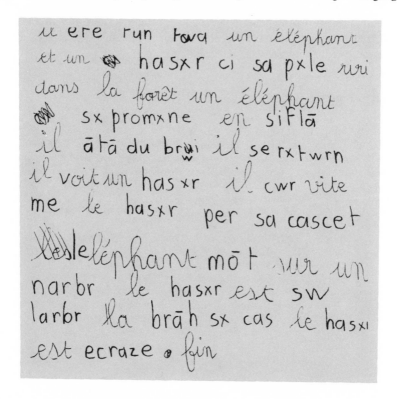

Figure 1. A two-code text written by a CP pupil (age 6½). In script are the words the child can spell. In print are the words reproduced according to the child's pronunciation.

Beyond reading, writing, and spelling, alfonic trains the child to analyze, detect relevant facts, and be precise. It also teaches the child to reckon with and accept others as different from him or her as they may be.

11. CONCLUSION

Alfonic has been devised for the benefit of French-speaking children. But there is hardly any classroom in France that does not include a number of children from other countries and speech communities. Experience has shown that alfonic has helped them overcome the problem of learning French. Cases are on record where migrant parents have derived great benefits from it.

Alfonic, as such, could not be used for writing any language other than French. But for other languages, similar systems could be devised, with due consideration of the different factors involved. Note that where bilingual education is at issue, no single system should be used for both languages. The specificity of each language should always be kept in mind. But experience has shown that when acquired for one language, reading capacity can easily be transferred to another, even if the phonic values of letters are as different as they are in French and English, for instance.

REFERENCES

Martinet, A. (1975). *Le français sans fard.* Paris: P.U.F.

Martinet, A. (1980). *Éléments de linguistique générale,* Paris: Armand Colin. English translation by E. Palmer, *Elements of general linguistics* (1969). London: Faber and Faber.

Martinet, A., & Martinet, J. (1980). *Dictionnaire de l'orthographe—alfonic.* Paris: SELAF.

Martinet, A., & Walter, H. (1973). *Dictionnaire de la prononciation du français dans son usage réel.* Paris: France-Expansion; Genève: Droz.

Ters, F., Mayer, G., & Reichenbach, D. (1964). *L'échelle Dubois Buyse d'orthographe usuelle française.* Neuchâtel: H. Messeitter.

Villard, J., Martinet, A., Martinet, J., Boyer, D., Dominici, A., & Dominici, G. (1983). *Vers l'écrit avec alfonic.* Paris: Hachette.

Walter, H. (1977). *Phonologie du français.* Paris: P.U.F.

Walter, H. (1988). *Le français dans tous les sens.* Paris: Robert Laffont.

In addition, Alfonic (Association pour la promotion de l'écriture et de la lecture en français,) created in 1983, publishes a bulletin, *Liaison-alfonic,* three times a year. Contact Madame Liliane Witkowski, Ecole maternelle des Peupliers, 24 Avenue du Maréchal Joffre, 78000 Versailles, France.

CHAPTER 19

Early Bilingual Reading
Retrospects and Prospects

RENZO TITONE

1. INTRODUCTION

The problem of the feasibility and advisability of teaching reading in two languages simultaneously at preschool age has recently become an important and
fascinating issue for psychologists and educators. The study of the aspects and
factors underlying the process of early bilingual reading has attracted the interest of students of child bilingualism and bilingual education, developmental
psychologists and psycholinguists, and educators of bilingual children and of
migrant workers' children. There is a growing conviction regarding the possible
positive effects of early reading and early bilingual literacy upon intellectual
growth and general education.

It is more and more commonly believed that the benefits found to be present in a score of cases recorded by a few attentive authors can be generalized
to larger populations of bilingual children at preschool and elementary school
age. However, anecdotal experience needs boosting by well-grounded experimental research.

It is the purpose of this chapter to outline both bygone experiences and
ongoing research in order to define new prospects and perspectives.

RENZO TITONE • Department of Developmental and Social Psychology, University of Rome
"La Sapienza," 00185 Rome, Italy.

2. THEORETICAL PERSPECTIVES: EARLY BILINGUAL READING (EBR) AND THE CHILD'S PSYCHOLOGICAL DEVELOPMENT

Bilingual reading is related, on the one hand, to intellectual growth and, on the other, to basic education. It is therefore necessary to define some basic concepts connected with the three areas of primary concern, namely, the mutual relationship between language and intelligence from a developmental point of view, the interdependence between bilingualism and reading, and the relationship between bilingual reading and basic education.

2.1. Early Bilingualism and Intelligence

Bilingualism is not a monolithic state of mind and behavior but a kind of linguistic competence having varying degrees. Usually one language is dominant, at least in one area or level of communication. True bilingualism, or fully fluent or balanced bilingualism, implies a functionally sufficient command of two language systems with regard to phonological, grammatical, lexical, and pragmatic abilities. Only with respect to balanced bilinguals is it possible to consider the effects of bilingualism on cognitive growth.

Contrary to earlier indications, more recent findings confirm that bilingual children appear to have a mental flexibility, a superiority in concept formation, and a more diversified set of mental abilities (Bain & Yu, 1978; Pearl & Lambert, 1962).

More particularly, it has been claimed that

> metalinguistic awareness is the primary variable mediating the positive effects of bilingualism on academic achievement. The argument, in summary form, is that fully fluent bilingualism results in increased metacognitive/metalinguistic abilities which, in turn, facilitate reading acquisition which, in turn, leads to higher levels of academic achievement. (Tunmer & Myhill, 1984, p. 176)

Metacognitive abilities imply the habitual capacity to reflect upon and manipulate thought processes, while metalinguistic consciousness implies the ability to reflect upon and manipulate language concepts and functions. The suggestion is that the process of conceptually separating two languages into functionally independent systems results both in an increase of metacognitive ability and in the strengthening of metalinguistic awareness. In support of this suggestion are several recent studies which seem to indicate that bilinguals do, in fact, enjoy superior metalinguistic, as well as metacognitive, functioning (e.g., studies by Ben-Zeev, 1977; Cummins, 1978; Feldman & Shen, 1971; Ianco-Worrall, 1972).

2.2. Early Bilingualism and Reading

There is sufficient evidence that reading acquisition depends to a very large extent on the development of both metacognitive and metalinguistic abilities. In other terms, the development of conscious control of perception and cognition, on the one hand, and of the formal aspects of language, on the other, play a central role in learning to read. More specifically, it can be stated that learning to read efficiently requires good phonological awareness (recognition and distinction of sounds of phonemes), distinct word awareness, sufficient form awareness (i.e., conscious control of grammatical forms and functions), and pragmatic awareness (or ability to use and appropriately select communication rules in pertinent situations).

Furthermore, "the view that metalinguistic awareness is a prerequisite skill is not inconsistent with the possibility that reading *instruction* increases metalinguistic awareness, which would explain the sharp increases in metalinguistic abilities often observed among beginning readers" (Tunmer & Bowey, 1984, p. 167).

On the other hand, it remains true that balanced bilingualism enhances, in turn, metacognitive and metalinguistic development in very young children (4–8 years of age). The argument then could be phrased as follows: both bilingualism and reading are stimulated and fostered by the gradual acquisition of metacognitive and metalinguistic abilities, whereas bilingual reading is expected to enhance both linguistic competence and cognitive development to a very high degree and at a very precocious age level. A great many findings support the conclusion that learning to read as early as at the age of 3 results in greater intellectual flexibility, conscious cognitive control, and richer linguistic competence as compared with illiterate peers (Cohen, 1977; Doman, 1964). It is therefore safe to infer that early *bilingual* reading ability should have a strong impact upon the child's cognitive and linguistic growth.

2.3. Early Bilingual Growth: An Objective of Basic Education

It is more and more widely granted today that interethnic communication and world-mindedness are basic needs of the cosmopolitan citizen of the future. A defence of this statement will seem superfluous. The progress of human civilization depends on producing a generation of peace-makers, peace-lovers, and peace-bearers. It is also unquestionable that democracy is built upon education for personal as well as international understanding and cooperation. . . . But it is essential, also, that the "New Man" of civilized society will have to be a creative learner, endowed with an ability to decode cultural and moral messages from all the experiences of humankind. Now these axioms imply a rejection of monoculturalism and of its allied state, monolingualism, taken in its narrowest sense. They also demand that we take a new look at basic education. Education, understood as the formation of the human personality in its fundamental dimensions, will have to step beyond the mere teaching of the "three R's"; it will have to reflect concern for the socialization of the human infant, and his ethical orientation in the world of values. It will demand a basic capacity for communication and will seek to promote a sensitivity to the diversity of cultures and languages. . . . I believe that . . . bilingual education must seek to ensure personality formation and mental health, broad-mindedness in solving human problems, flexibility in strengthening intellectual powers, and metalinguistic awareness. (Titone, 1984, pp. 7–8)

Reading is considered most rightly to be central in the instrumental system leading to general education. Therefore, no doubt bilingual reading can become the main source for all-round personality formation, intellectually, emotionally, and socially.

Among other authors, it is encouraging to find in Donaldson's (1978) book, *Children's Minds,* the suggestion that a better induction into formal activities such as reading will aid the child in grasping the formal or disembedded character of thinking which schooling demands. In Donaldson's view, *reading* in particular will contribute to language awareness. Much more so with *bilingual* reading, which, if carried out from very early childhood, will certainly lay the foundations of open-minded education at an age when prejudices are still unknown.

3. RETROSPECTS: CASE STUDIES OF EARLY BILINGUAL READERS

Theodore Andersson (1981), in his captivating booklet, *The Preschool Years,* on family reading in two languages, starts off by quoting Burton White, who expressed with emphasis his belief "that the educational developments that take place in the year or so that begins when a child is about eight months old are *the most important and most in need of attention of any that occur in human life"* (1975, pp. 129–130). What Benjamin Bloom (1964, p. 68) reports is particularly to the point, namely, that "put in terms of intelligence measured at age 17, from conception to age 4 the individual develops 50% of his mature intelligence. . . . This would suggest the very rapid growth of intelligence in the early years and the possible great influence of the early environment on this development." All this amounts to underscoring the unique importance of early reading carried on while the child's brain shows a high degree of plasticity and undifferentiation.

3.1. The Case for Early Reading

The movement in favor of learning to read early is becoming impressive, involving many different countries. The starting point was signaled by the marvellous experience reported by Glenn Doman (1964) in his book *How to Teach Your Baby to Read: The Gentle Revolution,* which recounted convincing principles and fascinating cases. According to Doman (1964, p. 9):

1. Tiny children *want* to learn to read.
2. Tiny children *can* learn to read.
3. Tiny children *are* learning to read.
4. Tiny children *should* learn to read.

The facts proving the truth of Doman's assumptions are numberless. Doman acquired valuable experience with early readers, which he set forth persuasively in his popular book, addressed to mothers. In it he declares: "Children can read words when they are one year old, sentences when they are two, and whole books when they are three, and they love it" (1964, p. 1).

Following Doman, many educators since the early 1960s have tried out his method or similar ones and have reached wonderful results. Andersson (1981, chap. II) quotes 23 instances of which at least 5 are not mere case studies but experimental investigations. Besides Doman, the names of Söderbergh, Torrey, Goodman, Fries, Durkin, Terman, Cohan, Fowler, Hughes, Lado, Callaway, Steinberg, Emery, Witte, Ledson, Smethurst, Perlish, and Watson have become widely known as marking significant milestones in the history of the movement.

Besides these cases related to home influence, some investigations can be quoted, like the one conducted by the Denver Public Schools (1961–1962), another reported on by Harvey Neil Perlish (1968) on the effectiveness of television reading programs, the CRAFT Project (Harris, Morrison, & Gold, 1968) on a comparison of academic achievement of early readers and nonearly readers, and, especially, Durkin's first study (1966) on the achievement of early readers from first grade to the end of sixth grade. Her main conclusion was that "over the years, the early readers in this research continued to show higher achievement in reading than non-early readers with whom they were matched" (1966, p. 110).

Andersson's accounts of early reading are far from exhaustive. In Europe the movement has found followers. A rather detailed account by Schmalohr (1973) reviews several home case studies (Kratzmeier, 1967; Walter, 1967) and also institutional investigations carried on in kindergartens. Of particular interest is the experiment on 2-year-old children organized by Lückert (1967, 1968) with the cooperation of 240 families. Specific studies (Brem-Graeser, 1969; Rüdiger & Knauer, 1971; Schmalohr, 1969; Schüttler-Janikulla, 1969; Wilke & Denig, 1972) are aimed at examining young children in school settings so as to ascertain the effects of early reading on intelligence, language development, socioemotional growth, and long-range reading ability. Results were by and large positive (Schmalohr, 1973).

One of the best experiments was carried out by Rachel Cohen (1977) in France and reported on in her book *L'apprentissage précoce de la lecture*. A total of 161 children between the ages of 3;8 and 4;11 were tested. The use of a multiple test battery evidenced that young children of preschool age can learn

to read and that reading can help them develop their ability to grasp and formulate basic concepts.

Finally, it can be added that since 1976, the Chair of Educational Psycholinguistics of the University of Rome (headed by R. Titone) has assigned
five experimental doctoral dissertations (partly published) dealing with early
reading projects carried out in different kindergartens throughout Italy. Three
conclusions have been drawn as a result of such investigations: (1) children can
learn to read starting at the age of 3; (2) their intellectual improvement can be
seen as a result of proper reading instruction (in comparison with control groups
of nonreaders); and (3) reading can be taught in kindergarten settings by well-
trained teachers (Annessi, 1979).

3.2. The Case for Early Reading in Two Languages or Early Bilingual Literacy (EBL)

What kind of relationship can there be between preschool reading and the
bilingual child? Andersson (1981, p. 31), rightly comments:

> If a monolingual child can get a headstart by learning to read before going to school,
> why can't a bilingual child get a double headstart by learning to read two languages
> before entering school? No one would deny the educational importance of skill in
> reading; nor would many deny the advantage of a knowledge of two spoken lan-
> guages. The theoretical advantage of knowing how to read and write in two lan-
> guages would seem to be self-evident, and yet biliteracy is rarely emphasized as an
> objective in our schools.

In order to examine more closely the psychological aspects and the educational outcomes of early bilingual reading, Andersson (1981, pp. 32–45)
presents three cases of preschool biliteracy.

Mariana and Elena Past have learned to read in both English and Spanish,
the former beginning at age 1;5, the latter at about the same age. Word games
with word cards were used following approximately what Doman suggests in
his method. During her third and fourth month of reading, Mariana was already
skilled in reading sentences, and she was frequently reading independently. At
age 3;8 she was reading English at the level of the average first grader in the
second half of first grade. The same stage was revealed with regard to Spanish.
At age 4;11 her entering a bilingual kindergarten completed her achievement.

Raquel and Aurelio Christian also learned to read English and Spanish
very early. At 18 months Raquel had already asked her parents the names of
the letters, as they bought her an alphabet book in Spanish. Aurelio took no
interest in the alphabet until much later but absorbed words by mere association. Neither child had much interest in reading books of any length until about
the age of 5. Reading Spanish at home transferred to reading English when

they entered school. Later progress in grade school was excellent for both children.

Yuha and Chinha Ok Ro Lee are Korean–English bilinguals and biliterates. Since Yuha's development in Korean was far in advance of her development in English, her father decided, in order to prepare her for kindergarten, to initiate her into reading in English, her weaker language. Yuha liked to watch TV, especially "Sesame Street," and learned all of the letters of the English alphabet. Then her parents taught her reading systematically. She learned how to read first in English, while the language of instruction and explanation was Korean. But later on, in one month, thanks to a special program, Yuha learned to read and write Korean just before she became a first grader. Lee observes that at the end of one month's instruction, Yuha's skills in reading and writing the Korean language were better than her corresponding English skills. Biliteracy is more than just knowledge of two languages; it implies behaving properly in two cultures. In fact, Lee writes about his daughter: "She speaks and behaves like an American among Americans; she speaks and behaves like a Korean among Koreans. Early bilingual reading seems to have aided her for her bilingual and bicultural adjustment in the United States" (Lee, 1977, pp. 143–144).

Andersson (1981, pp. 44–45) submits the following correct conclusions:

> The experience of the children in the three bilingual families . . . suggests that, far from being a double burden, learning to read in two languages is a double joy, leading to a positive self-image.
>
> The term "early" in the expressions "early reading" or "early reader" is seen to vary all the way from age six months, as with Kimio Steinberg, to nearly five years, as in the case of Yuha Lee, suggesting that this concept is, or at least can be, quite flexible.
>
> One notes significant uniformities among the parent–teachers involved in the cases I have cited. They exert no pressure on the child; rather they try to sense what will interest the child. The parent–teacher's task seems to consist in reading the child's wishes and in inventing games to stimulate this interest. Successful parents seem to include their young child in their conversations and activities. Above all, early reading appears, as in the case of Yuha Lee, to be related to establishing a sense of personal and social values. Parents who read, study, and discuss interesting or important subjects in the presence of their children and who answer their children's questions create a close relationship with their children, a relationship which older children are quick to adopt with their younger siblings.

Experiences and investigations on early bilingual reading are taking impetus now, as is documented by research reports and the launching of the new *IPRA* (International Preschool Reading Association) *Newsletter*. Among more recent reports it is worth considering what Els Oksaar (1984), University of Hamburg, has tried to check, with her investigation of a group of bilingual children. Of the 20 bilingual children (from middle and working classes) who grew up hearing and speaking German and Swedish, German and English, or Swedish and Estonian, 13 (65%) could read and write both languages more or less fluently by the age of 4 to 5 years. In the control group of six monolingual German- or Swedish-speaking children, four (67%) demonstrated the ability to read.

Oksaar adds that of the 13 children in her project who learned to read two languages before they were 5 years old, 10 children were not exposed to any one particular method but rather to a sort of methodological pluralism, in which the interaction between the child and the mother or other reference person played a dominant role. The children were to read aloud in both languages very early, following the well-known rule "one language—one person"; they knew much of this by heart and, finally, wanted to read themselves.

Furthermore the author notes that in bilingual marriages the children usually learn to read first in the language of the mother or in the family language. The fact that in learning to read the second language they had no difficulties, and progressed even more quickly than in the first language, would seem to support the generally accepted statement that children actually only have to learn to read once because this skill can be transferred from one language to another.

The transfer effect from one language to the other is also confirmed by Hélène Businger (1984, p. 8), writing about her bilingual child:

> His ability to visualize and memorize words was transferred to the second language and he succeeded in reading with a short book in English entitled *Teddy Bears 1 to 10*. So the experiment has had a very positive effect on his bilingualism. It has also encouraged him to become biliterate.

With regard to method, it is worth recalling what Nguyên Ngoc Bìch (1984, p. 8) writes in concluding her report on the progress in reading of her Vietnamese-speaking child, Victor Quang:

> The element of play is an integral part of the learning process of young children; one needs to start with vocabulary that is not only simple from the linguistic point of view but also is immediately recognized in the child's environment; comprehension and miscue analysis are all very important parts of teaching as one tries to structure the child's learning environment. And, of course, it is of primary importance that the child be allowed to test and use his creative power to develop new sentences and gain a sense of power, of ownership. Thus, far from being a passive process of decoding and understanding only what is there, the reading process should be seen and allowed to be the creative process it has always been.

Now the question is: can bilingual reading be taught in pre-elementary schools by teachers? And why not use early bilingual reading instruction as a means to aid disadvantaged children such as migrants' children? The answer to such questions can be given only by institutional experiments carried on with larger samples of young subjects. It is this perspective that is now illustrated.

4. PROSPECTS: RESEARCH PROJECT ON EARLY BILINGUAL LITERACY

I will try to summarize the main lines of a research project designed by the writer aimed at developing the experimental conditions for teaching early bilingual reading in institutional settings. The essential traits of this project have already been outlined in a previous essay (Titone, 1983).

4.1. The Early Bilingual Reading Experimental Project

Stepping from mere experience to scientific experimentation means defining more accurately objectives, materials, instruments, and evaluation measures.

It is advisable (1) to clarify the basic issues connected with early bilingual reading (during the preschool years), its psychoeducational aspects, and its advantages and possible drawbacks; (2) to prepare a transition from mere occasional experience in family circles to true scientific experimentation in kindergarten and/or nursery schools; and (3) to design and build appropriate teaching materials linked with child motivation and language abilities.

The present author has built special materials (a reading kit and guidebook for parents and teachers) for teaching children to read through play in two languages simultaneously (viz., Italian/English; Italian/French; Italian/German; Italian/Spanish is being prepared; Castilian-Spanish/Basque is being tried out).

A discussion of the experimental paradigm follows.

4.2. Aims of the Research

This research intends to check: (1) the possibility and effectiveness of learning to read simultaneously in two languages from the age of 4 years (in any case, before 6); (2) the correlation between early literacy and bilingual development; (3) the correlation between early biliteracy and cognitive development; and (4) the correlation between early bilingual literacy and the overcoming of cognitive and linguistic disadvantages of lower-class or immigrants' children.

4.3. Research Methodology

The experimental control of the above variables will consist of the following procedures:

1. Pretesting verbal intelligence and ascertaining the nonexistence of reading ability at the start.
2. The systematic use of appropriate reading materials (Titone, 1977): the materials should be applied for at least one school year.
3. Posttesting bilingual reading competence on the basis of the above material.

Special scoring scales are being produced in order to compare individual results. Subjects will be assessed with respect to age, sex, socioeconomic level, learning motivation, IQ, and rate of oral language development. Raw scores will be processed by Titone's research team. Teaching can be carried on also by parents if they are competent; but as a rule kindergarten teachers will do the teaching under supervision.

4.4. Evaluation Instruments

The following data and measures will be collected:

1. Intelligence pretest: the Wechsler Intelligence Scale for Children at preschool age or another equivalent verbal intelligence test can be used. It is to be administered before starting the experiment.

2. Bilingualism pretest: for checking linguistic competence in L1 and L2 on the basis of visual or motor stimuli (picture test). Verbal responses in terms of short narratives will be evaluated as to:

a. Phonological correctness.
b. Grammatical correctness and completeness.
c. Lexical richness (quantity and appropriate use of words).
d. Verbal fluency.

Practically, one should check for:

a. Number of pronunciation errors on the total of words.
b. Number of errors on the total of sentences.
c. Number of words and number of errors of meaning on the total of words.
d. Rhythm (fast, middle, slow) of utterances.

3. Prereading test: reading of one's own first and last names printed on the blackboard or on cardboard (in capital letters).

4. Reading posttest: based on the reading material of the last booklet presented in the kit: check speed, correctness, comprehension (total number of errors).

5. Bilingualism posttest: the same initial picture test: check number of words, sentences, and descriptive details and compare with initial results (pretest).

6. Intelligence posttest: by means of the same initial test in an alternate form.

7. Questionnaire: to be submitted to both parents and teachers (see below).

4.5. Questionnaire on Early Bilingual Reading Experience

The questionnaire can be administered orally or in writing.

1. At what age did your child begin to speak?
2. When did he/she begin to find amusement in scribbling?
3. When did he/she show interest in writing or in writing things, like: neon signs? advertising in TV? posters? comics? words connected with pictures? (Please indicate age in general, if remembered, for each type of object.)
4. At what age did the first reading take place: in one language? in the other language?
5. What did he/she learn to read: in one language? in the other language?
6. Did he/she show fast or slow progress?
7. How often does he/she show the desire to read: during the day? (number of times), during the week? (number of times).
8. How long does his/her application to reading last: less than 10 minutes? more than 30 minutes?
9. Has he/she been undergoing an ebb and flow process in his/her reading interests? In what period of age (and for how long) did he/she keep his/her reading interest alive? In what period of age (and for how long) did he/she neglect or reject reading?
10. What is his/her *present* degree of interest in reading: high? middle? low?
11. Are you in favor (or against) reading at preschool age? Why?

4.6. Teaching Method

The general hints given here refer to Titone's Bilingual Reading Method as materialized in the already mentioned reading kit. However, keeping these indications in mind, other types of materials can be designed, especially if the two languages do not include Italian. The present hints concern the general teaching approach, some basic suggestions, and the use of the material.

One preliminary question is: is reading in two languages really easy? In order to answer this question we must first point out the activities which facilitate the child's learning to read in a single language:

1. Search-and-naming games for objects, animals, loved persons; games dealing with the inexhaustible curiosity toward an environment, where surprise is continuous and where the unknown is a potential for personal conquest.
2. Global attainment of some realities and later tentative analyses: in the kitchen—utensils; in the garden—plants; in the train—wheels; in dolls—legs, arms, head, and so on.

It is not different in the handling of bilingual reading: some basic activities come into play in enjoyable games which solicit spontaneous curiosity toward:

1. The oral and written knowledge of words or sounds having to do with objects, animals, or people of particular interest.
2. The global perception of easy sentences dealing with the child's experience, that is, well-defined, known objects of certain interest: one's own body, a boy, family members, and the like.

Objects which are not familiar or words which are not yet possessed in the oral form should be avoided, as should single letters totally isolated from the context of a phrase or sentence. The spoken and known must always precede the written.

Our method implies some preliminary suggestions such as the following:

1. Begin with a game or pleasant conversation.
2. Focus upon a word or a sentence in one of the two languages, writing it on a card or indicating it on the appropriate chart or in a booklet (see Titone's material); read it aloud and have the child repeat it.

   In the first phase one should not worry about having the child distinguish between the single letters. These will be discovered spontaneously by the child, and one can, in any case, point them out later in the written or spoken word.
3. The main method of teaching a child a language is through play. Everything should appear like a game of discovery and invention in which words, and later letters, serve to construct sentences, as if it were a question of placing one block upon the other, brick upon brick. Many spontaneous games can come about through the child's initiative, others may be invented by the educator.

The games may be numerous and varied. Some may be of the following types: matching the cards with words and then later with sentences; rapid reading contests; finding the fight card, as in a game of cards; action cards, such as those in Montessori's "command game"; construction of sentences. In construction of sentences, cards with words or parts of sentences should be used. The child is asked to read, understand, and link up the single cards in such a way as to make up a sentence and, when finished, to read the constructed sentence aloud.

The material included in the box prepared by Titone (1977) is divided as follows:

1. The words *mommy* and *daddy* on two separate cards, which have the word written in L1 on one side, and the word written on L2 on the opposite side.
2. Twenty words dealing with the child himself or herself, each on a separate card, in both languages.
3. Basic vocabulary relative to the immediate world of the child.
4. Essential vocabulary for the formation of sentences.
5. Vocabulary to be inserted in structured sentences.
6. Four booklets for progressively difficult reading, having a series of pictures, each of which is coupled with a sentence in both languages.
7. The alphabet in both languages, with references to words of immediate use.

The subdivision of the material corresponds to an exact grading of difficulty to be met with by the child.

As educators (parents and teachers) have found out, the child does not find it strange that objects and actions are not only said in two different languages but are also written and read in two different languages. If, in fact, the child lives in a bilingual environment, he or she will be ready not only for hearing sounds, words, and sentences in two languages but also for seeing books, magazines, comics, and printed matter of all sorts in two languages as well.

Detailed instructions on how to teach each phase are given in the guide accompanying the material (Titone, 1977). Basically, the instructional method is grounded on the assumption that optimal learning takes place when there is harmony between:

- Visual sensations (V)
- Auditory sensations (A)
- Tactile sensations (T)

The VAT language learning system emphasizes the fundamental aspects and factors of an easy means of learning bilingual reading based on the use of (1) the visual (recognition of the forms of words), (2) the auditory (association of sound and written word), and (3) the tactile (touching the cards on which the words are written), as a pattern of meaning integrated by the direct and joyful experience of the child interacting with the adult.

One step at a time, one word at a time, one sentence at a time, one page at a time! The material is never shown all at once to the child, nor are successive parts shown before the preceding step has been conquered.

5. CONCLUDING REMARKS

Who are the targets of this early reading method?

At the moment the use of the Early Bilingual Reading Kit by R. Titone is recommended and being used with children from the age of 4 years living:

- In bilingual families.
- In bilingual or multilingual areas (in Italy—especially the French–Italian-speaking area of Valle d'Aosta and the German-Italian area of Alto Adige/Bozen—and in the Basque Country).
- In immigrants' children's homes or schools.

However, a few attempts are being made in bilingual or international kindergartens (Turin, Milan, Rome). Results are not yet available due to the short time that has elapsed since the beginning of the experiment, although impressions gathered from parents and educators are so far favorable.

It is noteworthy that Titone's method and material has been adapted to an experimental project which is being carried on in the Basque Country with Basque-Castilian bilingual children (ages 4 to 6). The coordinator, Dr. Antton Kaifer Arana, has translated and adapted the Early Bilingual Reading Kit into Castilian and Euskara and is using it to teach a large number of children to read in both languages at the same time. The project will achieve the result of strengthening command of L1, namely, the Basque language, which has lost ground in recent times. The project is stimulating wide popular interest.

No doubt many problems are still open to discussion and research. But the writer believes that there is sufficient warrant for positive confirmation of the main hypotheses outlined at the beginning of this chapter. In particular, it is believed that great advantages will be achieved on behalf of the maintenance of bilingual competence in immigrant children in many countries. This expectation seems to have been fulfilled by an attempt to apply the method to Italian immigrant children in some German-speaking areas of Switzerland. Promises are substantial. This opportunity cannot be missed.

REFERENCES

Andersson, T. (1981). *The preschool years. A guide to family reading in two languages.* Rosslyn, VA: National Clearinghouse for Bilingual Education.

Annessi, A. F. (1979). La lettura precoce, fattore positivo dello sviluppo cognitivo. *Rassegna Italiana di Linguistica Applicata, 11,* 1–2, 327–334.

Bain, B. C., & Yu, A. (1978). Toward an integration of Piaget and Vygotsky: A cross-cultural replication (France, Germany, Canada) concerning cognitive consequences of binguality. In M. Paradis (Ed.), *Aspects of bilingualism* (pp. 113–126). Columbia, SC: Hornbeam Press.

Ben-Zeev, S. (1977). The influence of bilingualism on cognitive strategy and cognitive development. *Child Development, 48,* 1009–1018.

Bich, N. N. (1984, Winter). Learning to read in a bilingual setting. *IPRA Newsletter,* pp. 1–8.

Bloom, B. S. (1964). *Stability and change in human characteristics.* New York, London, Sidney: Wiley and Sons.

Brem-Graeser, L. (1969). Bericht über die Ergebnisse der Frühforderung in Münchner Kindergärten. *Schule und Psychologie, 16,* 334.

Businger, H. (1984, Summer/Fall). A case study in early reading. *IPRA Newsletter,* p. 1.

Cohen, R. (1977). *L'apprentissage précoce de la lecture.* Paris: Presses Universitaires de France.

Cummins, J. (1978). Bilingualism and the development of metalinguistic awareness. *Journal of Cross-cultural Psychology, 9,* 131–149.

Doman, G. (1964). *How to teach your baby to read.* New York: Random House.

Donaldson, M. (1978). *Children's minds.* Glasgow: Collins.

Durkin, D. (1966). *Children who read early. Two longitudinal studies.* New York: Teachers College Press.

Feldman, C., & Shen, M. (1971). Some language-related cognitive advantages of bilingual five-year-olds. *The Journal of Genetic Psychology, 118,* 235–244.

Harris, A. J., Morrison, B. L., & Gold, L. (1968). *A continuation of the CRAFT Project comparing reading approaches with disadvantaged urban negro children in primary grades.* New York: Division of Teachers Educators, City University of New York.

Ianco-Worrall, A. D. (1972). Bilingualism and cognitive development. *Child Development, 43,* 1390–1400.

Kratzmeier, N. (1967). Kleinkindlesen. *Schule und Psychologie, 14,* 215.

Lee, O. R. (1977). Early bilingual reading as an aid to bilingual and bicultural adjustment for a second generation Korean child in the U.S. Ph.D. dissertation. Washington, DC, Georgetown University.

Lückert, H. R. (1967). Lesenlernen im Vorschulalter als Aktion der basalen Bildungsförderung. *Schule und Psychologie, 14,* 297.

Lückert, H. R. (1968). *Lesen—ein Spiel mit Bildern und Wötern.* Ravensburg: Quelle und Meyer.

Oksaar, E. (1984, July). Bilingual reading and writing in the early years. Paper presented at the Third International Congress for the Study of Child Language, Austin, Texas.

Pearl, E., & Lambert, W. E. (1962). The relation of bilingualism to intelligence. *Psychological Monograph: General Applied.* (Vol. 76), 1–23.

Perlish, H. N. (1968). In W. Smethurst (Ed.), *Teaching young children to read at home* (pp. 20–35). New York: McGraw Hill.

Rüdiger, D., & Knauer, K. (1971). *Beiträge zum Problem des Frühlesens.* München. (In Schmalohr, 1973).

Schmalohr, E. (1969). Psychologische Untersuchung zum Duisburger Frühlesenversuch. *Schule und Psychologie, 16,* 145.

Schmalohr, E. (1973). *Frühes Lesenlernen.* Heildelberg: Quelle & Meyer.

Schüttler-Janikulla, K. (1969). Vorschulisches Lesenlernen und intellektuelle Leistungssteigerung. *Schule und Psychologie, 16,* 169.

Titone, R. (1977). *A guide to bilingual reading.* Rome: Armando.

Titone, R. (1983). Early bilingual reading: From experience to experiment. *Rassegna Italiana di Linguistica Applicata, 15,* 79–83.

Titone, R. (1984). Early bilingual growth: An objective of basic education. *The International Schools Journal, 7,* 7–16.

Tunmer, W. E., & Bowey, J. A. (1984). Metalinguistic awareness and reading acquisition. In W. E. Tunmer, C. Pratt, M. L. Herriman (Eds.), *Metalinguistic awareness in children* (pp. 144–168). Berlin: Springer-Verlag.

Tunmer, W. E., & Myhill, M. E. (1984). Metalinguistic awareness and bilingualism. In W. E. Tunmer, C. Pratt, M. L. Herriman (Eds.), *Metalinguistic awareness in children* (pp. 169–187). Berlin: Springer-Verlag.

Walter, K. H. (1967). *Sollen kleine Kinder lesen lernen? Kleine Kinder lesen, schreiben, rechnen.* Duisburg: Goldmann.

White, B. L. (1975). *The first three years of life.* Englewood Cliffs, NJ: Prentice Hall.

Wilke, J., & Denig, F. (1972). Vorschulerziehung und Steigerung der Intelligenzleistung. *Schule und Psychologie, 19,* 37.

CHAPTER 20

Problems of Language Growth and the Preparation of Schoolbooks in Africa

ALBERTO M. MIONI

1. INTRODUCTION

Some cases of the successful growth of African languages are examined here. We do this from the peculiar (but, we think, highly representative) point of view of the history of book production (mainly schoolbooks), and an attempt is made to show some of the objective reasons for this growth.

The present overview covers languages for which we have more or less complete bibliographies: Swahili (van Spaandonck, 1965, supplemented by Mioni, 1967b); Hausa (Baldi, 1977); Rundi[1] (Mioni, 1970; Rodegem & Bakara, 1978); with some hints at the situation of Somali (since the most recent bibliography, Carboni, 1983, contains only a few items written in Somali, our data are taken from Agostini, Puglielli, & Moxamed Siyaad, 1985).

2. HISTORY OF BOOKS IN THE SCHOOLS

To a certain extent the history of the teaching of those languages is also a history of some different paths to bilingual and multilingual education. In some of the countries where those languages are spoken, their introduction into school curricula coincided with the very beginning of the school system, as happened with Hausa and Swahili, at least in their original regions. Indeed, English (or

---

[1] With class prefix, kiSwahili and kiRundi, respectively.

ALBERTO M. MIONI • Department of Linguistics, University of Padua, 35137 Padua, Italy.

German, in the case of *Deutsche Ostafrika,* now continental Tanzania) was reserved for the pupils going beyond the first few school years.

After this start, Hausa and, even more so, Swahili became curricular subjects and, later, media also in higher grades, invading teaching domains which had been previously covered by the exolanguage. Rundi, on the contrary, probably took the place of previous teaching in Swahili and is now creeping into the predominantly French-medium curriculum of upper grades. Somali has become, in the few years after the adoption of the official Latin orthography (1972), the all-pervading medium for teaching at all school grades: we see later some consequences of such a lack of gradualness.

In some regions of East Africa (Kenya, Uganda) and of Nigeria, Swahili and Hausa, respectively, are gradually introduced as a school subject and, in some cases, also as a teaching medium after some school years in a minor vernacular (such as Kikuyu or Luhya in Kenya and Fulani or Kanuri in Nigeria). In such schools English is also present, either as a subject or as a teaching medium for some subjects. We can, therefore, say that these languages are part of a bilingual or multilingual education system.

In sketching this historical overview, we have been compelled to stick to the data available in bibliographies. It is quite likely, however, that some of the first schoolbooks escaped the attention of the bibliographers, because schoolbooks do not usually enjoy the favors of librarians and therefore are not always carefully classified in libraries, and some makeshift locally produced material is not extant.

The history of school traditions for each of these languages is summarized in Table 1. It lasts 100 years for Swahili, 75 for Hausa, 60 for Rundi, and 15 for Somali. There are, of course, other African languages that can claim a history of school use comparable with that of Swahili or Hausa.[2] However, we have been compelled to limit our survey to well-documented cases, especially since we had direct contact with the environment of all these languages except Hausa. Table 1 displays some important achievements in the scientific study of each language, showing the basic requirements for the development of school use, that is, first dictionaries (we did not limit ourselves to short word lists) and grammars. In fact, they presuppose stable orthographic habits and a certain body of metalinguistic reflection. On the contrary, the existence of a monolin-

---

[2] The following are probably the African languages which have enjoyed an earlier standardization (Bantu languages are quoted with their class prefix in parentheses): Mende (Sierra Leone); Twi, Fante, Gan (Ghana); Ewe (Ghana, Togo); Yoruba, I(g)bo (Nigeria); (li)Ngala, (ki)Kongo (Congo, Zaire); (ci)Luba (Zaire); (kinya)Rwanda (Rwanda); (lu)Ganda (Uganda); (isi)Xhosa, (isi)Zulu, (se)Sotho, (se)Tswana (Southern Africa); Malagasy (Madagascar). Standardization was more recent in the case of Fulfulde (various West African countries); Efik (Nigeria); Luo (Uganda, Kenya); (ci)Bemba (Zambia); (ci)Nyanja-(ci)Cewa (Zambia, Malawi); (ci)Shona (Zimbabwe); Dinka (South Sudan). Many other languages have been standardized even more recently (see, e.g., UNESCO, 1985).

Table 1. The Most Relevant Steps in Linguistic Descriptive Studies and in Scripture Translation[a]

Subject matter	Swahili	Hausa	Rundi	Somali
First grammars	1850 (Krapf) 1870 (Steere)	1862 (Schön) 1897 (Robinson)	1903 (v.d. Burgt) 1908 (Ménard)	1892 (Schleicher) 1902 (Reinisch)
Dictionaries	1882 (Krapf) 1894 (Madan)	1843 (Schön)	1903 (v.d. Burgt) 1970 (Rodegem)	1902 (Reinisch) 1985 (Agostini *et al.*)
Monolingual dictionaries	1981 (Institute of Swahili Research)	1965 (Skinner)	—	1976 (Keenadiid)
Scripture translations[b]	1883 NT 1891 OT + NT 1953 Qur'an	1880 NT 1932 OT + NT 1953 Qur'an (?)	1951 NT 1967 OT + NT	1972 NT 1985 OT + NT ? Parts of Qur'an

[a]We put in parentheses the names of the authors and/or editing agencies; full data are to be sought in the bibliographies of those sources given in the Reference list.
[b]NT = New Testament; OT = Old Testament.

gual dictionary (or at least of a dictionary in which the glosses are more or less predominantly written in the African language) is the symbol of an already attained maturity. Furthermore, the availability of a translation of the entire Bible or of a substantial part of it, or even of the Qur'an, is a token that the language has been developed as a tool for long *written* texts belonging to different literary genres, some of them not already present in the indigenous oral literature (Mioni, 1967a). The importance of this has increased in recent years, as such translations are more and more the work of native speakers (and not of foreign scholars and missionaries).

A few remarks on Table 1. The earlier dates for Swahili and Hausa show us that their actual and potential role of lingua franca had been correctly identified at an early stage. For Swahili this role had been attained by means of the Arab trade (ivory and slaves) with inland Africa (Whiteley, 1969) and for Hausa because of important state formations in the past. The interest in major vernaculars that do not play the role of a lingua franca, for example Rundi and Somali, dates to some 40–50 years later.

In Table 2, we show a list of school subjects with their respective first schoolbooks. As might be expected, the production started with primers and reading books and also with books of elementary arithmetic. The fact that the first schoolbook attested for Swahili is an arithmetic book is probably due to incomplete documentation for primers.

The date given are the ones of the earliest attested books for each subject. Of course, a few years after this first appearance, whole sets of primers and arithmetic books were already available. This offered enough material for some years of primary school. The books were small (less than 100 pages), and the

Table 2. The Publishing of Schoolbooks[a]

Subject matter	Swahili	Hausa	Rundi	Somali
Primers and readings	1894	1857(?); 1909	1923(?)	1966–67; 1971
Arithmetic	1887	1914	ca. 1930	1972(?)
Sciences	1929	1949; 1956	ca. 1945	1976(?)
History	1894	1932	ca. 1945	1976(?)
Geography	1903	1918	ca. 1945	1975(?)
Hygiene	1924	1914	ca. 1945	1975(?)
Teachers' guides	191–(?)	1932	ca. 1945	+ (journal)

[a] As our bibliographical sources are sometimes imprecise, or even contradictory, in giving the data of publishing of some works, we appended a question mark wherever there was some doubt. In one case we have only been able to give the decade 191–(?).

rest was left to oral teaching (teachers' books were made available some years after). However, we know that in many developing countries rural teachers have always been able to do their best even with poor equipment. In conclusion, the minimal needs for a few school years had already been met for Swahili some years before 1900 and for Hausa, circa 1916–1917. For Rundi we have to wait until about 1930–1932, but we must not forget that, as Burundi had been previously part of *Deutsche Ostafrika,* Swahili was probably in use for school purposes before that date.

In subsequent years the curriculum is enriched by books for geography, history, hygiene, and science (the first Swahili book of history, 1894, is an isolated case dealing with local history). It is probably at this point in our history that some linguistic complications have come to the fore. Apart from the orthographical and other linguistic questions, which worry more the author of the book than its users, both primers and books of readings did not require special interventions for enriching the language ("language expansion"), with the possible exception of the few grammatical terms needed in advanced primers. Probably no major difficulty arose with elementary maths, especially with experienced traders, such as the Swahili and Hausa speakers.

With the beginning of formal teaching in geography, history, hygiene, and science, even if these subjects were predominantly limited to local situations, the language began to be improved by a simple stock of scientific terms. This is an important step because it involves the production of neologisms. Think, for example, of the very delicate transition from folk botanical and zoological taxonomies to the scientific ones! It was probably at that moment that in Swahili, for example, it was decided that the indigenous word for *name (jina)* could also be extended to the grammatical meaning of *noun;* that the term for *verb (kitenzi)* was obtained by changing the prefix of *u-tenzi, action,* while the words for *world (dunia)* or for *insect (mdudu)* were taken from Arabic, and the ones for *geography (jiografia)* and *history (historia)* from English. Thus far the needs of primary school curricula. It is worth mentioning that each set of such schoolbooks was usually supplemented by a teacher's guide.

The real growth of a language, however, cannot be judged strictly on the basis of books for the minimal needs of a curriculum. There must be a substantial amount of other material to be read in school and at home. Here the differences between Swahili, Hausa, and Rundi (we discuss the Somali situation later on) are quite remarkable, and not only in terms of time gap. A pupil with a Swahili medium has now at his or her disposal a large amount of books, especially of fiction: short and long novels, both original and translated. Among the translations of Western books, one might quote Aesop's *Fables,* Lamb's *Tales from Shakespeare, Robinson Crusoe, Pinocchio, Animal Farm,* Voltaire's *Zadig,* and *King Solomon's Mines.* Moreover, Swahili transcriptions of traditional chronicles and oral histories of single ethnic groups are also available as a reinforcement for the teaching of history, in a locally oriented perspective. Hausa does not have such a rich choice; as for Rundi, this kind of book is hardly represented at all. Another important point is the availability of books, booklets, and periodicals as tools for maintaining literacy among adults. The most representative topics covered by such materials have also been summarized in Table 3. Swahili comes up tops here, too, both in variety and in quantity of production.

As for teaching in postelementary school, for mother-tongue teaching there is need for both classic and modern literature. Swahili has a large body of old epics already prepared and annotated for school usage. Hausa has substantially

Table 3. Relevance of Works for General Reading, Original and/or Translated[a]

Subject matter	Swahili	Hausa	Rundi	Somali
Local classics	+ +	±	+	+
Modern literature	+	+	±	±
Literary translations	+ +	±	−	±
Other subjects	Agriculture, politics, midwifery, family planning	Agriculture, dietetics, driving	Politics, dietetics, child care, housekeeping	Politics, traditions, agriculture

[a] In this table, we use a four-value scale for giving an idea of the relative amount of book production in different fields: + + = important production; + = some production; ± = a few titles; − = no production.

less, while Rundi is just beginning: practically no modern literature, and the rich traditional literature has been only partially incorporated into school texts.

For formal language study at an advanced level, the lack of wide reference grammars written in the local language represents a major desideratum.

3. CURRENT LANGUAGE GROWTH AND CHANGE

Now we dedicate some attention to the recent history of the use of Somali in schools. Before the adoption of an official Latin orthography (1972), the material for teaching in Somali was limited to a couple of simple primers. This can be easily understood, since the school languages at that time were Arabic (the language of Islam) and Italian or English (a legacy from colonial times). In 1972 it was decided to adopt, after a short transition period, the Somali language not only as a subject but also as a teaching medium for the whole school system. The last 15 years have seen a desperate struggle against time in order to prepare some materials, no matter how or what. But local resources— both human and financial—have hardly kept pace with such a sudden and diversified demand. It would have been impossible, of course, to achieve in 15 years what Swahili had achieved in a century. A more gradual approach might have given better results, but the previous situation, with a multilingual system based on three exolanguages, was both politically and practically untenable. As a result, in the present situation most of the teaching is based on a more or less explicit use of foreign books by teachers as a supplement to official handbooks. This can be considered a sort of hidden bilingual education.

As for the present situation of the other three languages, we would like to add some further remarks. Swahili, standardized in the period 1920–1930, is now official in Tanzania (literacy rate: 25%), Kenya (45%), Uganda (25%), and eastern and south-eastern provinces of Zaire (35%). Only in Tanzania is it the teaching medium for the whole curriculum, while its situation in Kenya (where it is, at any rate, an overall subject in the curriculum) is not improving; its position in Uganda and Zaire has oscillated quite a lot in the past 20 years, following the vicissitudes of politics. Deliberate policies for its growth and development have been both elaborated and implemented by officially supported language committees (now in Tanzania: Institute of Swahili Research, attached to the National University). Centuries of bilingualism with Arabic on the coast had already given an impulse to an intellectual–scientific enrichment of the lexicon, so that language growth has only been fostered and accelerated during the colonial administration and after independence. The efforts of the language committees were not limited to promoting standardization, but they also prepared full and consistent terminologies for new sciences and technologies. The first monolingual Swahili dictionary of a certain relevance, however, is that of 1981 (containing about 20,000 words).

Hausa is spoken especially in Northern Nigeria (25% of literacy for the whole of Nigeria) and the Niger Republic (5%); it lags behind Swahili, as there is no fully "hausanized" curriculum for upper grades. In the various northern states of the Federation of Nigeria, different language policies are implemented (first teaching medium, then subject). The standardization dates back to the 1930s, but it was slightly revised in 1966. Though Hausa shares with Swahili a history of contact with Arabic (thus producing many loanwords), the modernization of this language is not much advanced.

Rundi is spoken in Burundi (literacy rate: 18%) and is almost coincident with Rwanda, the language of neighboring Rwanda (where the literacy rate is slightly higher: 25%). This is, however, a case of the same language shared by two countries divided by centuries of separate history and traditions. There is, therefore, a careful *Ausbau* (elaboration) policy in order to compensate for an *Abstand* (linguistic distance) that is minimal. Rundi is a teaching medium at the elementary level, then only a subject (medium: French). As in many other parts of Africa, the knowledge of the exolanguage (French) can be used as a tool for discriminating against possible new emergent elites. Indeed, only lip service has been paid so far by the authorities to a further development of Rundi and toward a possible increase of its use in school. Though no Rundi monolingual dictionary is available, the *Dictionnaire Rundi–Français* by Fr. F. Rodegem (1970) is to be considered as the best dictionary of a Bantu language. As far as the renewal of Rundi is concerned, 780 neologisms are listed by Rodegem, three-fourths of them being loanwords, mainly from Swahili (but also from French and, to a limited extent, from English and German), and only one-fourth being indigenous formations (Reh, 1981, p. 550). The work of terminology committees has so far produced no relevant results.[3]

The right of a person to become literate in his or her mother tongue (UNESCO, 1953) is, among human rights, the one that has the most difficult implementation. In its extreme interpretation, the "mother-tongue principle" would lead to absurd conclusions. Grimes (1984) gives a list of all the languages of the world in order to decide in which there is a possible need for Bible translation. Her proposals can be considered, to some extent, the religious counterpart of mother-tongue literacy: the goal of offering the Bible translated in every possible mother tongue. According to the author, there would be a (more or less definite) need of Scripture translation into 3,427 different languages out of the 5,445 languages that, in her account, are presently spoken throughout the world. Let us suppose for the moment that the goal of Bible translation into 3,427 languages were a reasonable and attainable one. What will be the result if we apply the same figure to languages to be used for literacy purposes?

---

[3] Mioni (1988) offers a discussion and typification of the linguistic repertoires of African countries, and also shows some linguistic data for a better understanding of the standardization processes of the languages dealt with here.

Luckily, multilingualism is, at least in the Third World, widespread to such an extent that, in our opinion, a maximum of about 1,000 languages to be used in some (even incipient and rudimentary) degree of literacy seems to be a more acceptable estimate. This would involve, for Africa, a maximum of about 250 languages. However, it is reasonable to think that only about 100 of them are likely to be extended and are worth extending beyond the first 2 or 3 school years.

Another relevant factor is the importance of European languages in African communication networks. The prevalence in school curricula of an exoglossic policy, mainly based on the language of the former colonial power, or of an endoglossic one, based on local languages, are the extreme options of colonial times. They depended very much on the option of the colonial power toward assimilation, on the one hand, or toward indirect rule, on the other. However, the linguistic situation of single territories (e.g., presence vs. absence of a local lingua franca) also played a role. The minor departures from this policy which took place after independence are in the direction of an increased stress on exolanguages in former endoglossic states rather than, vice versa, of an introduction of local languages into former exoglossic countries. If in countries like Uganda, Zaire, and Ghana one sees, indeed, an increased use of the exolanguage, on the other hand the instances of development of the local languages in former exoglossic countries are very limited both in quantity and scope. In the former French dependencies in Africa we are faced with the important trend toward education in Arabic only in Maghreb countries and with a wide use of Malagasy in Madagascar, while the use of African languages for education in other countries has only had a rather timid start, mainly limited to adult literacy campaigns. This is the case of some local languages in former French West Africa: Hausa, Fulfulde, Bambara-Mandingo, Songhai, Kanuri, Tamasheq, Moore, and Wolof (UNESCO, 1985). For comparative purposes it is important to remark that some of these languages have, on the contrary, a tradition of school use in neighboring English-speaking countries. It is rather astonishing that after more than 20 years of independence the situation shows only minor departures from trends already established in preindependence times (exceptions are represented by Togo, Guinea, and Burkina, on the exoglossic side and by Ghana, Uganda, and Zaire, on the endoglossic one). The most notable instance of radical change in trend is that of Somalia, with its sudden transition to a Somali-medium school system. The many important achievements obtained in Nigerian languages (especially in the minor ones) are also particularly worth noting (Reh, 1981; UNESCO, 1985).

The present situation, in conclusion, does not show the developments one might have reasonably expected as a possible consequence of the new cultural awareness brought about by independence. We might advance two possible reasons for such an unexpected result. First, the lack of resources. A major change in language policy, in fact, would have required important investments of money. On the contrary, the increased funds allotted to education have been spent for expanding the school system as it was or to foster technical education. Second, there is more stress on "vertical" linguistic media than on "horizontal" ones, to use Heine's (1977) words. This is the privilege given to elite formation by means of European languages rather than to overall education through African languages. By the way, this choice may also be instrumental in preserving the existing elites, defending them from the dangers of possible emergent new ones. Many conferences, surveys, and expert missions for language planning and development, widely supported by the international organizations (UNESCO, 1985, p. 11; Ohannessian, Ferguson, & Polomé, 1975), did not have all the practical consequences one might have expected.

4. CONCLUSION

The examples discussed show that the path toward a fully fledged linguistic status is long and difficult. Only a few African languages have reached it so far; among them are Swahili and Hausa. It is quite unlikely that many minor languages will follow the same path. For them an intermediate degree of development is both possible and desirable. In this way they might find their rightful position as teaching media in the first school years, giving way, in later years, either to local lingua francas or to an exolanguage. It is also to be noted that the production of strictly local linguistic material (obtained with some of the modern and cheap techniques of multicopying) does not necessarily demand the longstanding and expensive procedures of full standardization. It only needs the presence of goodwill teachers able to apply to their local vernacular the orthographical rules of a major indigenous lingua franca.

Also, exolanguages cannot be dispensed with. The postindependence age has shown an increased demand for them, even if their standard runs the risk of being locally somewhat lowered, because the expansion of education cannot be implemented by using only expatriate metropolitan native speakers. In fact, it is often left to local teachers whose knowledge of the exolanguage is sometimes heavily interfered with by their mother tongues.[4]

In conclusion, for most African states a possible future trend might be that of multilingual education: local vernacular (no matter if it is formally used or

---

[4]The existence and legitimacy of local standards of English (and, sometimes, also of French and Portuguese) is now generally admitted, provided that they do not impair communication with speakers using it as L1 or L2 in other parts of the world. Also, the opinion on pidgin and creole varieties of the same languages is now changing, and their usefulness as lingua francas and/or vernaculars is widely accepted (see, e.g., UNESCO, 1985, where sociolinguistic information on many such varieties is offered).

not: it will at any rate creep out at least in the teacher's oral explanations) + lingua franca + exolanguage. Which and how many lingua francas and exolanguages will be part of this future is a matter of political decisions.

REFERENCES

Agostini, F., Puglielli, A., & Moxamed Siyaad, C. (Eds.). (1985). *Dizionario Somalo-Italiano.* Roma: Cooperazione Italiana allo Sviluppo.

Baldi, S. (1977). *Systematic Hausa bibliography.* Roma: Istituto Italo-Africano.

Carboni, F. (1983). *bibliografia somala.* "Studi Somali" 4. Roma: Ministero degli Afferi Esteri, Dipartimento per la Cooperazione allo Sviluppo.

Grimes, G. F. (Ed.). (1984). *Ethnologue. The languages of the world.* Dallas: Wycliffe Bible Translators.

Heine, B. (1977). Vertical and horizontal communication in Africa. *Afrika Spectrum, 77,* 213–218.

Heine, B., Schadeberg, T., & Wolff, E. (Eds.). (1981). *Die Sprachen Afrikas.* Hamburg: Buske.

Mioni, A. M. (1967a). Quindici anni di editoria in lingua africana: un bilancio. *Africa* (Rome), *22,* 210–213.

Mioni, A. M. (1967b). La bibliographie de la langue swahili. *Cahiers d'Études Africaines, 7,* 485–532.

Mioni, A. M. (1970). *Problèmes de linguistique, d'orthographe et de coordination culturelle au Burundi.* Napoli: Istituto Universitario Orientale.

Mioni, A. M. (1988). Standardization processes and linguistic repertoires in Africa and Europe. In P. Auer & A. di Luzio (Eds.), *Variation and convergence* (pp. 294–320). Berlin: de Gruyter.

Ohannessian, S., Ferguson, C., & Polomé, E. (Eds.). (1975). *Language surveys in developing nations: Papers and reports on sociolinguistic survey.* Arlington, VA: Center of Applied Linguistics.

Reh, M. (1981). Sprache und Gesellschaft. In B. Heine, T. Schadeberg, & E. Wolff (Eds.), *Die Sprachen Afrikas* (pp. 513–557). Hamburg: Buske.

Rodegem, F. M. (1970). *Dictionnaire Rundi-Français.* Tervuren: Musée Royal de l'Afrique Centrale.

Rodegem, F. M., & Bakara C. (1978). *Documentation bibliographique sur le Burundi.* Bologna: EMI.

UNESCO. (1953). *The use of vernaculars in education.* Paris: UNESCO.

UNESCO. (1985). *Les langues communautaires et leur utilisation dans l'enseignement et l'alphabétisation.* Dakar: UNESCO-BREDA.

van Spaandonck, M. (1965). *Practical and systematical Swahili bibliography.* Leiden: Brill.

Whiteley, W. (1969). *Swahili. The rise of a national language.* London: Methuen.

Index

On the brighter side there has been some development of inter-disciplinary studies. Areas such as social psychology, biochemistry, astrophysics, social anthropology, economic psychology, and economic sociology have been developed in order to emphasize the interrelationships of previously isolated disciplines. More recently, areas of study and research have been developed which call on numerous subfields. For example, cybernetics, the science of communication and control, calls on electrical engineering, neurophysiology, physics, biology, and other fields. Operations research is often pointed to as a multidisciplinary approach to problem solving. Information theory is another discipline which calls on numerous subfields. Organization theory embraces economics, sociology, engineering, psychology, physiology, and anthropology. Problem solving and decision making are becoming focal points for study and research, drawing on numerous disciplines.

With all these examples of interdisciplinary approaches, it is easy to recognize a surge of interest in larger-scale, systematic bodies of knowledge. However, this trend calls for the development of an over-all framework within which the various subparts can be integrated. In order that the *inter-disciplinary* movement may not degenerate into *undisciplined* approaches, it is important that some structure be developed to integrate the various separate disciplines while retaining the type of discipline which distinguishes them. One approach to providing an over-all framework (general systems theory) would be to pick out phenomena common to many different disciplines and to develop general models which would include such phenomena. A second approach would include the structuring of a hierarchy of levels of complexity for the basic units of behavior in the various empirical fields. It would also involve development of a level of abstraction to represent each stage.

We shall explore the second approach, a hierarchy of levels, in more detail since it can lead toward a system of systems which has application in most businesses and other organizations. The reader can undoubtedly call to mind examples of familiar systems at each level of the following model.

1. The first level is that of static structure. It might be called the level of *frameworks*. This is the geography and anatomy of the universe. . . . The accurate description of these frameworks is the beginning of organized theoretical knowledge in almost any field, for without accuracy in this description of static relationships no accurate functional or dynamic theory is possible.

2. The next level of systematic analysis is that of the simple dynamic system with predetermined, necessary motions. This might be called the level of *clockworks*. The solar system itself is of course the great clock of

the universe from man's point of view, and the deliciously exact predictions of the astronomers are a testimony to the excellence of the clock which they study. . . . The greater part of the theoretical structure of physics, chemistry, and even of economics falls into this category.

3. The next level is that of the control mechanism or cybernetic system, which might be nicknamed the level of the *thermostat*. This differs from the simple stable equilibrium system mainly in the fact that the transmission and interpretation of information is an essential part of the system. . . . The homeostasis model, which is of such importance in physiology, is an example of a cybernetic mechanism, and such mechanisms exist through the whole empirical world of the biologist and the social scientist.

4. The fourth level is that of the "open system," or self-maintaining structure. This is the level at which life begins to differentiate itself from not-life: it might be called the level of the *cell*.

5. The fifth level might be called the genetic-societal level; it is typified by the *plant,* and it dominates the empirical world of the botanist.

6. As we move upward from the plant world towards the animal kingdom we gradually pass over into a new level, the "animal" level, characterized by increased mobility, teleological behavior, and self-awareness. Here we have the development of specialized information-receptors (eyes, ears, etc.) leading to an enormous increase in intake of information; we also have a great development of nervous systems, leading ultimately to the brain, as an organizer of the information intake into a knowledge structure or "image." Increasingly as we ascend the scale of animal life, behavior is response not to a specific stimulus but to an "image" or knowledge structure or view of the environment as a whole. . . . The difficulties in the prediction of the behavior of these systems arises largely because of this intervention of the image between the stimulus and the response.

7. The next level is the "human" level, that is, of the individual human being considered as a system. In addition to all, or nearly all, of the characteristics of animal systems man possesses self-consciousness, which is something different from mere awareness. His image, besides being much more complex than that even of the higher animals, has a self-reflective quality—he not only knows, but knows that he knows. This property is probably bound up with the phenomenon of language and symbolism. It is the capacity for speech—the ability to produce, absorb, and interpret *symbols,* as opposed to mere signs like the warning cry of an animal— which most clearly marks man off from his humbler brethren.

8. Because of the vital importance for the individual man of symbolic images in behavior based on them it is not easy to separate clearly the level of the individual human organism from the next level, that of social organizations. . . . Nevertheless it is convenient for some purposes to distinguish the individual human as a system from the social systems which surround him, and in this sense social organizations may be said to constitute another level of organization. . . . At this level we must concern ourselves with the content and meaning of messages, the nature

and dimensions of value systems, the transcription of images into historical record, the subtle symbolizations of art, music, and poetry, and the complex gamut of human emotion.

9. To complete the structure of systems we should add a final turret for transcendental systems, even if we may be accused at this point of having built Babel to the clouds. There are however the ultimates and absolutes and the inescapables and unknowables, and they also exhibit systematic structure and relationship. It will be a sad day for man when nobody is allowed to ask questions that do not have any answers.[4]

Obviously, the first level is most pervasive. Descriptions of static structures are widespread. However, this descriptive cataloguing is helpful in providing a framework for additional analysis and synthesis. Dynamic "clockwork" systems, where prediction is a strong element, are evident in the classical natural sciences such as physics and astronomy; yet even here there are important gaps. Adequate theoretical models are not apparent at higher levels. However, in recent years closed-loop cybernetic, or "thermostat," systems have received increasing attention. At the same time, work is progressing on open-loop systems with self-maintaining structures and reproduction facilities. Beyond the fourth level we hardly have a beginning of theory, and yet even here system description via computer models may foster progress at these levels in the complex of general systems theory.

Regardless of the degree of progress at any particular level in the above scheme, the important point is the concept of a general systems theory. Clearly, the spectrum, or hierarchy, of systems varies over a considerable range. However, since the systems concept is primarily a point of view and a desirable goal, rather than a particular method or content area, progress can be made as research proceeds in various specialized areas but within a total system context. The important aspect of such a hierarchy of system concepts revolves around the critical element of communication. McGrath, Nordlie, and Vaughn express it as follows:

Consequently, while scientists from many fields contribute to the area, and bring with them a wide range of scientific tools, the steps necessary to provide *all* applicable methods have not as yet been accomplished. This lack leads to less than optimal application of scientific tools, and to relatively ineffective communication among scientists from different fields working on similar problems, which in turn retards the rate of development of the system research field.

The impetus for the present research program comes from recognition of the need for a more systematic catalogue of methods applicable to system research problems, in order to provide a basis for a common language of method by means of which system research scientists can inter-communicate more adequately.[5]

Clearly, general systems theory provides for scientists at large a useful framework within which to carry out specialized activity. It allows researchers to relate findings and compare concepts with similar findings and concepts in other disciplines. With the general theory and its objectives as background, we direct our attention to a more specific theory for business, a systems theory which can serve as a guide for management scientists and ultimately provide the framework for integrated decision making on the part of practicing managers.

SYSTEMS THEORY FOR BUSINESS

The biologist Ludwig von Bertalanffy has set forth a new concept of general systems theory which he calls open systems.[6] The basis of his concept is that a living organism is not a conglomeration of separate elements but a definite system, possessing organization and wholeness. An organism is an open system which maintains a constant state while matter and energy which enter it keep changing (so-called dynamic equilibrium). The organism is influenced by, and influences, its environment and reaches a state of dynamic equilibrium in this environment. Such a description of a system adequately fits the typical business organization. The business organization is a man-made system which has a dynamic interplay with its environment—customers, competitors, labor organizations, suppliers, government, and many other agencies. Furthermore, the business organization is a system of interrelated parts working in conjunction with each other in order to accomplish a number of goals, both those of the organization and those of individual participants.

At times scholars in the field of management have depicted organizations as smoothly running machines. This would coincide with Boulding's second level in the general systems theory, that of "clockwork" systems. Organizations were described as highly mechanistic and predictable, and the various resources available—men, material, and machines—were manipulated in just that way.

Another common analogy was the comparison of the organization to the human body, with the skeletal and muscle systems representing the operating line elements and the circulatory system as a necessary staff function. The nervous system stood for the communication system. The

[5] Joseph D. McGrath, Peter G. Nordlie, W. S. Vaughn, Jr., *A Systematic Framework for Comparison of System Research Methods,* Human Sciences Research, Inc., Arlington, Va., November, 1959, p. 2.

[6] Bertalanffy, *op. cit.*